North Country Troopers

The Banner Collection

Case Histories and Personal Stories of the Alaska State Troopers

These are the personal stories of those who enforce the law on the Last Frontier and are reprinted from the pages of **The Banner**, quarterly magazine of the Fraternal Order of Alaska State Troopers.

North Country Troopers

Hard cover ISBN: 978-1-57833-610-4
Soft cover ISBN: 978-1-57833-611-1

Library of Congress Control Number: 2015935900

Printed in the United States
through Alaska Print Brokers, Anchorage, Alaska.

Editor: Col. Tom Anderson (Ret.)
Assistant Editor: Tom Brennan
Design: Vered R. Mares, Todd Communications
Cover art from an original painting by Laura Caperton, executive director of the Fraternal Order of Alaska State Troopers.

Published by:
FRATERNAL ORDER OF
ALASKA STATE TROOPERS
Alaska Law Enforcement Museum
245 W. 5th Ave. Ste 113
Anchorage, Alaska 99501
foast@gci.net

Distributed by:
Todd Communications
611 E. 12th Ave.
Anchorage, Alaska 99501-4603
Phone: **(907) 274-TODD (8633)** • Fax: (907) 929-5550
with other offices in Juneau and Fairbanks, Alaska.
e-mail: sales@toddcom.com • **WWW.ALASKABOOKSANDCALENDARS.COM**

FOREWORD

1991 was the 50th anniversary of the Alaska State Troopers. A Golden Anniversary Committee formed to organize the celebration and I was elected President of the committee. We all agreed a newsletter was necessary to communicate with both active and retired Troopers and I agreed to take on this responsibility. The newsletter was called "The Banner." The anniversary celebration was a huge success and resulted in the establishment of the Alaska Law Enforcement Museum located in downtown Anchorage, Alaska.

The Golden Anniversary Committee's assets were merged into the Fraternal Order of Alaska State Troopers whose board agreed to take on the responsibility for the operation of the Museum. I continued as Editor of The Banner with the understanding someone else would take on the responsibility at a later time. 24 years later I remain Editor.

During these 24 years I've worked hard to include historical information on Alaska Law Enforcement as well as humorous incidents that highlight the unusual character of an Alaska State Trooper's work in the Far North. The contributors to this book are all former Alaska State Troopers or closely associated with the organization.

I think it's safe to say that only the Royal Canadian Mounted Police in Canada have experienced the unique and one-of-a-kind police challenges that have occurred in Alaska. The Alaska State Troopers are one of a kind in duties and responsibility that makes this collection of stories priceless.

A special thanks to all the Troopers and friends who have contributed to The Banner. It is their contribution and dedication that makes this collection of stories special. Also thanks to old friend Tom Brennan for his work in writing and help in preparing this work for publication.

I started my Trooper career in 1961 serving in Fairbanks, Point Barrow and Anchorage. On retiring in 1983 I continued my involvement with the Fraternal Order of Alaska State Troopers, serving as President several times and winning a Life Time Achievement Award in 2012. I'm as excited to be involved today as I was as a rookie in 1961.

Tom Anderson

Colonel Tom Anderson
AST Director, retired

All proceeds for the sale of this book will go to the
ALASKA LAW ENFORCEMENT MUSEUM
Managed by
Fraternal Order of Alaska State Troopers
245 W 5th Ave, Suite 113
Anchorage, Alaska 99501
www.alaskatroopermuseum.com
foast@gci.net

CONTENTS

AUTHORS

(In Order of Appearance)

Trooper Joe Rychetnik

Lieutenant Bill Bellingar

Trooper Wallace E. Hill

Colonel Tom Anderson

Colonel Gordon R. Nelson

Trooper Dan Decker

Captain Bob Penman

Agent Ray Tremblay

Lieutenant Gerald O. "Jerry" Williams

Sergeant Mac McKinley

Major Mike Korhonen

Trooper R.M. 'Ron' Costlow

Trooper Marc Stella

Lieutenant Eugene (E.L.) O'Brien

Sergeant George B. Cole

Lieutenant John Elmore

Trooper Geoff Engleman

Chief Deputy US Marshal
James "Jim" Chenoweth

Senior Special Agent
Robert "Bob" Olson

First Sergeant Mike Metrokin

Deputy Commissioner
Harold "Syd" Sydnam

Tom Brennan

Investigator William "Bill" Roche

Trooper George Glenn Rodgers

Radio Dispatcher John Eberth

Captain Steve Reynolds

Sergeant Bob Robertson

First Sergeant Gene Kallus

Clerk Flo Janning

Trooper Bertram C. Kellogg

D.S. "Skip" Braden

Trooper Barry Pegram

Lieutenant Chuck Lamica

Trooper Lew Rieth

First Sergeant Drew Rotermund

Lieutenant Howard Luther

Agent Dick St. John

Trooper John Broderson

Death in the Tall Grass

Trooper Joe Rychetnik

It was one of those typically quiet afternoons in Palmer, with just a few tourists coming into the detachment office to find their way. But August 8, 1978 will be a day 1st Sergeant Charles Grutzmacher will never forget. A man named Maurice Abel had just driven the 40 miles from Anchorage, had picked up and dropped off a "strange" hitchhiker, and wanted the police to know.

The hitchhiker was strange because he never removed his hand from the flap of his duffle bag, which he insisted on keeping in his lap. He asked questions regarding the local police and gave the impression he was trying to avoid them. The time was 2 p.m. and within five minutes the First Sergeant would be as close to death as he would ever come during his 19 years as a Trooper

After filling out a field interrogation card on the transient report, Grutzmacher, who was reviewing some data with Investigator Mark Stewart, up from Anchorage checking on a burglary ring, asked the plainclothes Trooper to join him and they could talk on the way. The state patrol car was in the shop, so the pair took the unmarked investigator's car, with Grutzmacher driving, as he knew the local territory better.

Grutzmacher was not one of the old line "Billy Club" cops who delighted in sending hitchhikers and other "hippies" on their way in short order. He was an honor graduate from Washington State University who had majored in Police Science, played well enough as a star linebacker for the Cougars to be sought after by the Dallas Cowboys, but passed up this chance at gridiron glory to complete his degree and serve in the Army. After two years playing "Europe" in the 7th Army Band as lead trumpeter, he returned to civilian life and a position with the elite Montgomery Ward Plant Protection Dept. One assignment brought him to

Anchorage, where he quickly succumbed to the Last Frontier, and joined the Troopers.

The pair of state policemen quickly patrolled the perimeter of Palmer and located what appeared to be the suspect hitchhiker at the corner of Glenn Highway and Arctic Avenue. A Tesoro gasoline station was just in from the intersection. A family of tourists was filling up their car.

Noting two men hitchhiking, Grutzmacher pointed the car between them and parked beside the ditched edge of the intersection. It was apparent the two were not related and that one fit the description exactly. Grutzmacher, in uniform, got out of the car and approached him as Investigator Stewart made the usual radio call. Stewart departed the car from the other door and followed.

At the sight of the uniformed officer, the suspect fled the top of the road berm and dragged his duffle down into the high weeds of the drainage ditch. Once partially obscured by the weeds, he dropped the duffle, drew a large revolver from a belt holster and fired a shot at the officers above him. The bullet zipped between the policemen and clipped the top off the car antenna. Grutzmacher drew his .357 Model 19 Highway Patrolman revolver, knocked the second hitchhiker out of harm's way and yelled to Stewart to take cover. He dove for the ditch, rolled to his knees for a perfect two-hand hold on a target just a dozen feet away and fired. He knew he hit him and was very disappointed to find that the highly touted .357, 125-grain police bullet did not put the suspect down the first time.

The suspect lunged through the grass to get a clear shot at Grutzmacher and fired. His bullet (exactly the same weight and make of the police bullet and from exactly the same gun and barrel length) pierced Grutzmacher's chest just below the left pocket seam. Grutzmacher felt the blood spurt out and knew he could not last long bleeding that way. He poked his left index finger in the hole and fired back twice with his right hand.

Again, he had a good sight and knew he hit the suspect at least once "in the K-5 zone." Again frustration upset his concentration. In the meantime, Investigator Stewart put in an officer-down gunfight call and yelled at Grutzmacher, trying to locate the suspect in the tall grass. Spotting the suspect's head briefly, Stewart let fly with a double-handed burst from his Browning 9 mm.

The suspect went down but got up yet again. Grutzmacher could see the suspect then and, working like an artillery spotter, directed the 9 mm fire from above until it was on target and Stewart emptied his 14-shot magazine. The suspect, later identified as Roger Earl Williams, 29, lay still. (The identification check revealed he was wanted for multiple felonies.)

Grutzmacher lunged out of the ditch and collapsed on the roadside, dropping his revolver as he folded. Stewart reloaded the Browning and jacked a cartridge into the chamber before going down to check on the suspect. Grutzmacher was still complaining about the lack of killing power in his "Magnum" pistol. That thought crossed Grutmacher's mind several more times as he was loaded into the back of a volunteered pickup truck and rushed to the Palmer Emergency Room.

Autopsy would reveal that Williams had been hit so repeatedly that his body was crisscrossed with bullet holes completely piercing his body. Nine holes from the 9 mm bullets went from side to side and out. Riddled would be the proper term for his condition. Stewart had not been hit nor had any of the bystanders at the Tesoro Station, one of whom had the presence of mind to make photos of the shooting.

Grutzmacher had one .357 bullet in his chest, which is lodged against his back to this day, a permanent souvenir. The other magnum hollow-point wrecked his right shoulder after tearing the right tricep muscle. Never losing sight of his condition, the wounded officer kept his finger plugged into his spurting chest wound. His thoughts ran from cursing the .357 Magnum revolver he had used to wondering why the people had tossed his body into the back of a pickup which had just been loaded with horse manure and hay. He knew that tetanus lurked in such places.

The ride to the Palmer Emergency Room was bouncy, and his already bad mood took another drop when he heard two young doctors there say that he was dying and that they didn't have the equipment to save him. Their words were unsettling and did nothing to improve his mood while they waited for the Anchorage ambulance to arrive.

Fearing that the Trooper Sergeant was dying, the ambulance attendant spared no efforts to get him over the 40 miles. Halfway to Anchorage the ambulance blew two tires but he kept racing on the rims to meet another ambulance heading down the Glenn Highway to meet them. The transfer was made and again that ambulance blew a tire on the way to the emergency room entrance. Grutzmacher, being tossed from side to side and knowing what speeds the vehicle was making, wondered if he might not die in a flaming highway wreck. But the final jolt was the emergency ramp.

Grutzmacher could see the bright lights and chrome fixtures as he was rushed in. Like the TV show counterpart, nurses and medics hovered over him as they ran the gurney into the operating room. Again he heard the fatal diagnosis - "He's got a thousand to one chance of making it; he's lost a lot of blood." And, "It's a wonder he isn't dead already, look at those holes."

Taking this all in, Grutzmacher began to lose confidence in the system that had placed him there. He was completely out of patience with the emergency room staff when a nurse approached him with a big pair of shears to cut through his uniform trousers waist band.

"Hey, can't you just unbutton my pants and slide them down my legs," he growled. These things cost $75 and I just got 'em!"

The staff said that was his last complaint for several days as the anesthetic and drugs took over his life and sent him on a long road to recovery.

Twelve years later, First Sergeant Grutzmacher received the first Purple Heart medal from the Alaska State Troopers. He retired after 19 years and looks back with a great deal of pleasure on his years in investigation and as head of the Anchorage White Collar Crime unit.

He bought his service revolver when he retired. At his retirement they presented him with another in stainless steel. He told me it had always served him well— he had killed many moose with it although he was tending to rely more heavily on the 12 gauge shotgun for his highway clearance work.

"I guess I should have taken the shotgun into that ditch with me, but I had such faith in the .357 Magnum! Now, when I have a moose down on the highway I always borrow a shotgun from one of the Trooper's cars. It's very deadly at close range, and being a Sergeant, I can hand it back to the man and not have to worry about getting it clean and shiny for the next shift."

Today, Charles Grutzmacher lives the good life on his Matanuska Valley homesite, running his four-wheeler to the mailbox and building radio-controlled airplanes for sale to hobbyists. His wife Barbara still teaches kindergarten in the Palmer school district. With a summer cabin on a privately owned lake within an hour's drive, and a boat tied up in Homer, he lives the Alaska dream. But the big cop, who just recently survived a serious hip operation, feels he still has some deductive skills left and has accepted a position as applicant investigator for the State Troopers. He may even get a badge and big blue car. You can't keep this good man down on the farm.

February 1992

Joe Rychetnik was born in 1927 and passed away in Richmond, California March 5, 2003. Joe started his service as an Alaska State Policeman in the 1959 Academy Class 4-A. He served in Anchorage, Fairbanks, and Nome and left the department in 1963. Joe was a raconteur, authored three books including "Bush Cop" in 1991, was a staff writer for two magazines, and a well-regarded photojournalist who worked with National Geographic, Time Life, and many other publications. He was a Marine, co-founder of the San Francisco Explorers Club and a member of the Tailhook Society, an organization of former naval aviators. Joe was a member and enthusiastic supporter of the Fraternal Order of Alaska State Troopers.

Trooper Brewer Busts a Bunch

Trooper Joe Rychetnik

Following statehood in 1959, the Alaska State Police had its Anchorage Detachment under Lieutenant "Turk" Mayfield at a surplus military building located at 1111 East Fifth Avenue. There was a locker-filled squad room, a desk where radio clerk Robert Garlow worked his dispatching, and offices for the commander, the investigators and a supply room. It was where we all ended up writing our reports at the end of the day on a funky old typewriter or dictated into a Gray Autograph record, which often failed to make any impression on the disk.

At shift change one afternoon I was alone for a swing shift, a typical situation. Normand Brewer was checking off duty. I left the place in one of the new '59 Fords we were issued and was well toward Knik River Bridge when a call came to return to the station. No reason was given so I made speed returning, hoping another of my tickets written was not bouncing back. The first ticket I ever wrote was for speeding and was given to Gov. Bill Egan's next-door neighbor in Valdez. Lieutenant Mayfield said it was not a good sign for my career.

I arrived to find the station full of people, adults and a few children, all the adults under arrest and waiting in line to be cited by Normand Brewer. There were 14 I think. I helped him awhile, but was soon called out on a traffic accident.

Brewer had been going down the station stairs when an altercation broke out across the street in some housing behind a liquor store. He was the kind of cop who did not shirk this dismal duty. He broke up the fight, which was flowing out of a ground floor apartment. Inside the apartment he found drunken men, half-clad women, and several children.

He arrested the adults for "contributing" and "D&D" and held the children, who all proved to be hungry, for the child welfare people. Brewer was still writing reports when I came into the station for my lunch, hours later. I had given my sandwich to the kids but still had some fruit to enjoy.

Brewer was a well-liked cop, often found off duty with his gigantic Belgian sheep dog. He and his family lived on Government Hill in a tiny apartment. I think the dog had the best part of the space. Brewer soon earned enough money to leave the State Police to attend to his primary career plans, which involved finishing college in Washington State and becoming a dentist.

He did very well, I heard. And the Troopers lost a good man. By the way, all the charges stuck and some new tenants were added to the State Jail.

The Alaska State Police then consisted of 66 guys, a large family of good cops trying to keep the lid on things.

July 1998

It Was So Cold...

Trooper Joe Rychetnik, Retired

Back in the mid-60s, Fairbanks had cold spells two and three weeks long, where the mercury went down to 60 below and stayed there. The patrol cars in the Quonset garage at the Illinois Street Trooper office were seldom, if ever, turned off. After a week or so of continuous running and all the driving being done on roads infested with ice fog, we found that 25 mph was about the top speed any of them could do.

Sergeant John Bradshaw, my supervisor, suggested we take the cars, one at a time, to the Fairbanks Airport, and get the tower to give us a few minutes to run them on the runway, trying for a higher speed and hoping the carbon build-up would "blow out." It did, but was back a few days later. If we parked anywhere long, the tires were square and steering was almost impossible because lubricants were solid with frost.

The colder it got, the safer the snow-covered roads were and when we could get the car to speed there was no risk as the snowy surface was like concrete. The big problem was the ice fog that covered the major roads and streets of Fairbanks and elsewhere. There was no visibility and rear-enders and other minor accidents could be heard but not seen. A red highway flare every 25 feet was needed to alert drivers behind. After a lot of research by the university and the FAA, the ice fog problem was analyzed to be from vehicle exhaust and the food service operation at the Fairbanks Airport. The airport ice fog often closed the airport to traffic. They had to re-engineer the exhaust system.

The deepest cold encountered was at Delta Post's Isabel Pass, where Trooper Tom Sweeney ran a one-man operation. High winds closed the pass with drifted snow, so Sweeney called on the Army at the nearby Arctic Test Station, had them send out a tracked vehicle and had it drag Sweeney's patrol car over the drifts and onto the highway on the other side.

He found people freezing in their cabins, their fuel oil turned to "Jello." He had to take a highway department helper with him to help steer the patrol car. It took both of them to move the steering wheel a little way. Sweeney was able to rescue many people from their cabins along the way and I believe received a commendation for his efforts. It was minus 72°. Nome Post was never that cold as it was located on the edge of the Norton Sound-Bering Sea, where minus 20° was the deepest cold we had. But there was wind often and the chill factor made dog sled patrol somewhat uncomfortable. Most of the Northern Bush patrolmen bought surplus Air Force flying suits— sheepskin lined jackets and best of all, heavy woolen-type pants.

Sergeant Bradshaw had a fit when I arrived in Fairbanks by Wien with two prisoners and dressed like a survivor of the ill-fated Scott Expedition. I wore Air Force or Army bunny boots for a while but preferred the Air Force mukluks with the felt liners. I still have them and am ready when the next ice age descends on California.

I had to spend the night on the trail when the mercury dropped to minus 36° and found the Eddie Bauer heavy duty sleeping bag I carried just barely livable. When I wrote Bauer, they reported that you were not supposed to be snug warm, but just a few degrees above freezing. It was!

In Nome the Alaska State Police patrol car froze solid in the winter in the unheated garage. The mechanics from the local garage would tow it over to their shops and put a blow torch on the engine blocks— for hours. This was a $100 service item and I was not allowed to thaw the Chevy Impala station wagon very often. It was cheaper to use the taxicabs (all Mercedes) to get to the airport or make joint patrols with the Nome City Police. Nome had four miles of opened roads.

On a patrol to Little Diomede the strait was frozen solid, so I walked over the ice more than halfway to Big Diomede, crossing the International Date Line and, according to the Eskimo Scouts that watched my progress with a 60X scope, got the Siberian troops alerted to an invasion. John Iyapanna fired a rifle when he saw them coming down on skis, so I made a U- turn on the ice and headed back. Lieutenant Bill Trafton didn't need to explain how Nome Post almost started WWIII. But I still think that too cold is better than too hot.

April 2000

Fearsome 'OB' leads A Gambling Raid

Trooper Joe Rychetnik

It must have been late 1959 in Anchorage when I was asked to join a group of raiders that were being assembled to crash a gambling parlor in Fairview, the low-income neighborhood running east from Gambell Street. It was a favorite hunting ground for state cops as it was not incorporated into the City of Anchorage at that time and was infested with liquor stores, bars, and low dives that offered fair game to us.

In charge of the raid was Investigator Gene "OB" O'Brien, and I guess I was pulled off patrol that evening to get some practical experience in fighting a higher level of crime than broken taillights. "OB" was a big man and with his half-going half-out cigar, was a picture of the tough, street-wise, and courageous cop that most of us would never be. "OB" always led with his jaw, and he seldom failed to make his case or screw up the evidence. The felons feared him.

Two of us uniformed state policemen joined "OB" and off-duty officer Normand Brewer, who volunteered. "OB" put Brewer in the alley behind the small house with orders to stop flight from the rear door and also to stop anyone coming into the tiny casino. Brewer took up position in a dark spot near the rear door and was told not to come in until after he heard that "OB" had secured the gambling scene.

We three went into the hall on tip toes and when "OB" was certain the noise he heard through the door was gambling noise, he waved us back, took a short run, and hit the door with his shoulder. We all had our Model 10 .38's out and we swept into the tiny apartment like gangbusters. "OB" hit the door so hard, I swear it took a good minute for the wood splinters, plaster dust and poker chips to settle to the floor. I was asked to bring in the camera for some overall photos.

Just before I left to get the camera from my patrol car, we heard a crash in the rear of the house. There was no easy way to the alley other than driving around the block, so "OB" said to let it go until we had our gamblers into cuffs and in the cars. It turned out that Brewer had a visitor sneaking down the dark alley heading for the back door.

It was very dark and not wanting to make a target of himself, he walked up behind the suspect and sapped him across the head. Brewer let the inert body fall into the doorway. He then realized that there was more than one door between him and the gambling room.

I came back with the camera and was making my evidence snapshots while the other police officer was taking names from the ID's and "OB" was talking to the dealer, who he knew. "OB" knew every shady character in Alaska, and it came as no surprise they had a lot to talk about. We rookies were all told to fill out field investigation cards when we patrolled and this was one chance to write one.

After I finished my photography and the paperwork was finished, the dealer asked if he could get a Coke from the fridge, and he made a step or so to open the fridge door. "OB" was on him like a flash, grabbing his hand off the door-handle and shoving him down into a chair. "OB" opened the fridge and inside, ready to go bang, was a cocked and loaded .45 ACP. He lifted it out by the grips and asked me to photograph the refrigerator's interior and the pistol. "OB" then picked it up by the grips and wrapped it in a hanky. We didn't carry plastic bags like the TV cops do today.

We were a bit undone by being so close to a shootout at close quarters where the .45 ACP does its best work. "OB" saved our lives and for sure, mine, as I was closest to the dealer. We learned there was no Coke in the fridge but several cans of Olympia beer. "OB" ordered us to cuff the lot we had captured and load up the patrol cars.

With the cars loaded and us anxious to deposit our captives in the State Jail, we started to drive off when "OB" thought about Brewer in the alley. So we all drove around the block and into the alley. Brewer was combing the shadows with his flashlight. He had lost the back door suspect! The fellow had survived the rap on the head and apparently crawled through the mud and darkness until he was clear, and then ran like hell.

"OB" put in a call to Providence Hospital, warning them that a man with a head wound might show up for medical treatment, but it never happened that way. "OB" found out the fellow was just another poker player late for the game. Brewer may have taught the poker player to always knock on the front door. Memories of "OB" crashing in will always be with me.

May 2002

Bad Bar Owner

Trooper Joe Rychetnik

Editors Note: To forego possible litigation, the names of the main subject and the bar in question are fictitious.

In keeping with the continuing education of the Troopers, it's only fair to offer the true story of Vicious Gus in Fairbanks. In 1963, I worked the night shift from the Illinois Street State Police Detachment. I think we had just became Troopers after being State Police. In those days of very slim budgets, there was only one patrolman on duty from 11 p.m. to 7 a.m. and it was a busy time when the final bar checks had to be made along South Cushman Street at 5:15 a.m.

Most of the bars there would be closed by 5 a.m. the proper closure time, but not the strip club owned and operated by Gus. He always stayed open until confrontation time with the patrolling Trooper. Some Troopers had been beaten up by him on bar checks.

One morning I pulled up into the parking area in front of the club and found lights on. I was just about to leave the patrol car to warn the bartender (which was usually Gus) about the hours he kept. He never had anything nice to say, and he knew he had protection from the big man in Juneau, as Governor Bill Egan would hang out at the club when he was in town, and I was told by Gus on many occasions that Egan didn't want to be disturbed when I made my bar check at 5 a.m.

I had just called in my location stop to the dispatcher when a man emerged from the shadows and shoved an automatic pistol in my ear and told me he was going to kill me. It was Gus. We all knew him well and could recognize him, even on dark winter nights. I instinctively picked up the mike and called in "Car 10 at Sunset Strip - Gus has a gun poked in my ear and says he'll kill me." The dispatcher answered "10- 4."

There was no one else on duty at that hour and only one Fairbanks city cop, a new man who had his hands full with his bar closures. I was bundled up in my parka and strapped in with my safety belt and could not make a fast move to save my life. I told Gus that I would get out as I didn't want the car soiled with my blood. We had a few cars then, and no spares.

I stepped out onto the snow and he backed off a few steps. I had the chance to draw my revolver from the clamshell holster and told him to drop his gun. He refused, screaming that he was going to get me once and for all. I could have killed him with one shot to the head with my .357 Magnum, but since no one had ever been shot by a State Police officer up to that time, I hesitated.

I edged up to him to take his pistol, and he backed away and ran up the stairs to his apartment. I chased him with my gun out and he fought with both guns as clubs, in his bedroom. He was trying to reach his top drawer, and I finally got a cuff on his wrist and dragged him out and down the stairs. There was another gun in the drawer.

My clamshell holster, a terrible device to equip policemen with—it took two hands to replace the pistol and I didn't have two hands available—flapped at my side as I tried to fight him down. We ended up rolling in the parking lot with both hands out—a wild scene! I clung to the open cuff for my life. I was just about ready to shoot him as I was exhausted and he was striking my head with his gun barrel when the lone city cop roared up and helped me cuff Gus. The cop was putting his job on the line as they were not allowed to work outside the city limits.

I charged Gus with assault with a deadly weapon and put him in the State Jail. He was out on bail before I had the paperwork completed. My supervisor, Sergeant John Bradshaw, showed up as I was writing and looked distressed; he had dressed hastily and knew he could not come to my aid in time. When I explained what happened, he said, "You dumb bastard. You should have killed the son of a bitch," and walked out.

I was not told when Gus was coming to trial but chanced being at the courthouse when another cop told me that Gus was, at that moment, before Judge Jay Rabinowitz being told not do it again, and was fined $200 for disorderly conduct. I stood up in court and objected loudly. Rabinowitz yelled at me to sit down. I had no duty or standing in the court. I resigned my commission two weeks later and we moved away from town.

September 1997

The Scuba Diver and the Daredevil

Lieutenant Bill Bellingar

I should have known things were about to become interesting. The big man in the wet suit carrying an underwater spear and all his gear, made his way down to the water's edge where three men were fishing with rods and reels.

It was a drizzly summer day on the Salcha River south of Fairbanks in 1964. I was working undercover attempting to locate possible king salmon snaggers. As I casually strolled out on the Richardson Highway Bridge (as many tourists often did at that time of year), I observed three fishermen casting good-sized lures into a deep pool. The lures appeared to be legal, with proper hooks, and the men were not using the "snagging/jerk" motion commonly seen when one attempts to foul hook a fish.

After these fellows made a few casts without hooking anything, the big guy appeared. He ambled down to the water's edge, close to where the three surprised anglers stood. Without a word that I could hear, he checked his gear (as divers do), slipped into his tank and fins, eased into the clear water, and disappeared beneath the surface.

As it was legal to take or attempt to take salmon in fresh water with underwater spear (if completely submerged), I wasn't really concerned. The three surprised fishermen, however, didn't seem to look at it quite that way! From gestures and the bits of conversation I could make out from my vantage point, it was obvious the three felt that they were there first. They weren't about to let some strange scuba diver ruin their day.

Well, after seeing only air bubbles and a large shadow in the fishing hole for a few minutes, a big king salmon broke the surface. After thrashing around a bit, everything was quiet again. There could be no question; the diver had struck the fish with his spear, but the salmon had escaped. This really seemed to agitate the three observers, and they began pointing and casting vigorously into the hole. It wasn't long before one of them set into something, reared back on the fishing rod, and the fight was on! While trying to figure out just what was going on, I saw the diver loom up from the bottom of the pool; and as he reached the surface, I knew he'd been firmly hooked in the back of his wet suit. As he lumbered out of the river toward the startled men, he appeared to grow larger and larger, even from where I stood!

Now as you might expect, I thought things were going to deteriorate rapidly at this point, but as it turned out it could have been worse. After a few rather loud words (mostly one-sided) the conversation centered around who would pay for the damage to the suit. Things calmed down, and the three disgruntled anglers and the scuba man parted company.

As I took a photograph I realized I had witnessed a most unusual occurrence. To this day, I'll bet those three lucky fishermen don't realize how close they came to total disaster that day on the Salcha. That was the day they snagged Trooper Walt Zahn, AST Fairbanks, with a big Daredevil, and miraculously survived unscathed.

June 1993

Bill Bellingar retired from the Department of Public Safety in 1982 after 20 years as a Fish and Wildlife Officer, investigator, and pilot. During those years he was stationed in Anchorage, Fairbanks, Delta, Tok, and Kodiak; with extensive time in and out of Bethel and Dutch Harbor. Since retirement he's written outdoor columns for several newspapers from coast to coast in the lower 48, and his wife and he present programs on Alaska to schools, civic groups, and other organizations. He self-published his book on Alaska, "A Little Further Up the Creek." Several schools in the Anchorage area have accepted it for extra credit for students from 5th grade up. He now resides in the foothills of the Brushy Mountains of North Carolina with his wife, Burma, and three cats.

A Little Further Up the Creek

Lieutenant Bill Bellingar, Retired

Although no more than 50 yards away, he not only didn't respond to my call but he wouldn't look at me, either. So I tried again. "Hello there, I'm with Fish and Game," I yelled. "I'd like to check your fishing license." Standing alone on this small island in the Susitna River with his Super Cub on floats beached by him, the well-dressed fellow was fishing away and choosing to ignore me.

It was June, 1962, and I had only been with the department a month or so. I was making a weekend foot patrol along the river. The road north from Anchorage and Palmer toward Mt. McKinley ended at Willow in those days, but the Alaska Railroad went all the way to Fairbanks. Hunters, anglers, miners, and trappers as well as residents living along the route rode the train a lot. It would stop and let you off or pick you up anywhere except on a curve or trestle. Scheduled stops included such places as Houston, Sunshine, Talkeetna, Gold Creek and Usibelli.

On this particular day I had boarded in Anchorage in the early morning hours, and left the train at Montana Creek, some 75 miles to the north, with my backpack, sleeping bag, small mountain tent and a few overnight provisions. This stretch made a nice two-day patrol over several small streams with mouths that were excellent holding areas for salmon. And it was here that I found this distinguished-looking man and his airplane.

Unable to get a response from him, I began to wonder what he had to hide. So I crawled out of my pack, propped it against a tree nearby, and looked until I located a limb about five feet long that the beavers had chewed off and peeled. After putting my wallet in my jacket pocket, I began wading toward the small island, probing the depths ahead of me as I went. I had to be careful as the Susitna is always glacial cold and murky whenever there are fish available, and its multi-channels often have sudden drop-offs. Any exposed clothing immediately begins to gather sand and grit particles, and soon feels heavy as lead. Combined with the frigid water, that's the reason clothed bodies of drowning victims seldom resurface in streams such as this.

As I made my way toward the man and the water reached my boot tops, he glanced over his shoulder as if to see what would happen next. He seemed a little surprised when I kept moving, and with my boots full and soaked to the waist I finally reached the small sand bar. And as I slogged his way with teeth chattering, he reeled in his line and rested his fish rod against the float of his Cub. He showed me his fishing license and answered the few questions I had for him, but would not be drawn into any idle conversation. It appeared he simply didn't wish to be bothered.

Finding everything in order, I was preparing to brave the icy waters and head for shore when he had a question for me: "Young man," he said sternly, "Before you leave, I'd like your name and badge number." It caught me a little by surprise as I thought I had identified myself. "Officer Bellingar, Badge No. 5," I replied. "Would you like to see it?" And with the same somber tone, he answered, "I don't believe that will be necessary." With that, he went back to fishing. I retraced my steps, emptied my boots when I reached solid ground, and headed on down the river.

The following Monday while reporting to my supervisor, I found out who the man with the Super Cub was. It was the Honorable Buell Nesbitt, Chief Justice of the Alaska Supreme Court. "He told me you got a little wet making contact with him," the boss chuckled. "Said in 30 years of hunting and fishing it was the first time he had ever been checked and he couldn't believe you'd go over your boots to do it." The Chief Justice went on to say he was glad to see that we were doing our job.

Well, about two months later I was moved from seasonal to permanent status, and given my very own district to work out of Delta Junction. And I often wonder if I was promoted because I was a pilot at the right place at the right time, or because I was persistent in that chance meeting with the top jurist of Alaska. Boy, am I ever glad he was legal.

September 1996

A Difficult Call Under Tough Conditions

Trooper Wallace E. Hill, Retired

In the early days of statehood, Troopers in remote locations were sometimes called on to make tough decisions.

The results might be considered insensitive by today's standards —and risked the wrath of offended superior officers even then—but the alternatives were usually worse. And with no way to call for assistance, you sometimes just did what it took to get the job done.

In the fall of 1962, I was assigned to the Glennallen Post and was notified of a missing person from Chitina, an elderly Native trapper who hadn't been seen for a while but was believed to have three or four trapping camps within 10 miles of Chitina and on the East side of the Copper River.

I kept an eye out for the man while on patrol between Glennallen and Paxson, and the road to Cantwell, checking on accidents and hunting violations. When the man still hadn't shown up by late September, I hired an aircraft and did a more intensive search on the east side of the river, but I still could find no sign of him.

After the New Year, the Glennallen magistrate told me that somebody was trying to cross-file on the missing man's claims. She gave me their locations and asked me to make one more try, and if he was deceased, bring his remains back to determine the cause of death and provide a proper burial.

I had checked three of the cabins earlier, but the claims indicated there was a fourth, further downriver and to the east, which had not been checked. I hired Jack Wilson of Jack Wilson's Air Service in Gulkana. He and I flew out with a local man on a cold February day.

Jack landed on the river, and I headed off with the volunteer, towing an ahkio sled and a body bag. The cabin was icy cold, and inside lay the trapper, frozen stiff. He had apparently died in his sleep with his arms and legs wide apart.

There was nothing to indicate anything but a natural death, so the problem then became how to get the body back to Chitina. With the trapper's arms and legs spread wide, we couldn't even get him in the body bag, let alone the ahkio.

There was no assistance to be had — and getting the man's remains back seemed better than leaving him to the animals — so we used the trapper's ax to remove an arm and a leg from one side.

After we got the body bagged, we headed back to the river and the plane, then loaded the body in the rear of the plane and tied the ahkio to a wing. I climbed in on top of the body while Jack and his friend got into the front seats. Back in Gulkana I drove to Glennallen Hospital and delivered the trapper's slightly modified remains to the magistrate and the local doctor.

Everything went fine until my report hit Anchorage and the desk of Lieutenant Turk Mayfield, who hit the roof. He was very unhappy with the decision I made in the field. It was one of those tough calls, but I'm still glad I didn't leave the man out there.

September 2010

Trooper Wallace "Ed" Hill joined the Alaska State Police in 1960 and attended the Alaska Public Safety Academy in Sitka in 1961. He was assigned to the Fairbanks Detachment before his transfer to Chitina and his involvement in the case he describes above. Ed transferred to the Highway Department soon after his report of the "modified" trapper reached Captain Mayfield's desk. When Mel Personett became Alaska's Commissioner of Public Safety, Ed was invited to return and join what had by then become the Alaska State Troopers. He was once again trained as a recruit and then assigned to Patrol. He returned to Anchorage and later left the department rather than accept a transfer to Juneau. He intended to become a veterinarian but instead began a 24-year career as a Fireman – Assistant Chief on the North Slope. He retired in 1998 and moved to Hayden, Idaho.

Power of the Spotlight-Organized Crime in the Pipeline Era

Colonel Tom Anderson, Retired

The recent death of prominent Valdez businessman John Kelsey brought back memories of Alaska State Trooper involvement in heading off organized crime activities in the Seventies. Kelsey, who was born in Valdez, was a WWII combat veteran, a very active member of the Valdez community and also served on many state commissions and boards. He was a good friend of Governor Bill Egan and a solid friend of law enforcement.

The huge oil discovery at Prudhoe bay in 1968 brought a flurry of activity to Alaska. Discussions began immediately on building a pipeline to tidewater. Colonel Ed Dankworth, head of the Troopers, was born and raised in Texas and predicted a Gold Rush type influx of people to Alaska to support pipeline construction. As a new Captain, I was directed to build a statewide Criminal Investigation Bureau composed of a Major Crime Unit, Fraud Unit, Narcotics Unit, Crime Lab Unit including EOD and an Intelligence Unit.

The Intelligence Unit (IU) in Anchorage was headed by Dean Bivins a polygraph operator and outstanding investigator; Bob Jent, a retired Agent from the U.S. Air Force Office of Special Investigations and also a great investigator; and in Fairbanks Hal Hume, a seasoned Trooper with a military intelligence background. To round out the team AST created a new Trooper position in Seattle to liaison with SPD and airport police and monitor the SeaTac Airport. This position was filled by Loren Thomas a fraud investigator with great networking capability.

The mission of the IU was to identify criminal activity with an emphasis on organized crime. Dankworth also directed me to develop a plan to educate the business community on organized crime. Under Bivins' direction, the IU immediately began networking with

Lower 48 police department IU's. The Los Angeles Police department was very helpful. LA had a reputation in the Sixties and Seventies in keeping Organized Crime (OC) out of that city. LAPD would meet organized crime figures at the airport, welcome them to the city and follow them everywhere they went. LA would expose any OC activity, including notifying the media. It seemed to work.

To educate the business community I contacted Ralph Salerno a highly decorated New York City retired police Sergeant who was considered to be the most knowledgeable expert on the Mafia in America. Salerno had sat on various Presidential Crime Commissions, was a consultant to the U.S. Dept. of Justice in Washington D.C. and was author of "The Crime Confederation," an authoritative book on organized crime — and best of all was a dynamic speaker. He agreed to come to Alaska. Salerno spoke to the Chambers of Commerce in Anchorage, Fairbanks and Juneau, several Rotary Clubs and capped his speaking tour at Anchorage's Sydney Laurence Theater.

In Salerno's presentations his main theme was that OC is involved whenever there is a market for goods and services. Among those he listed were drugs, gambling, prostitution, unions, labor relations, construction, transportation, real estate, loan sharking, securities and the list could go on. At the Sydney Laurence Theater when former Attorney General John Havelock commented "we have a Blackmail Statute but no Extortion Statute" Salerno answered "I hope the boys in Chicago don't hear about that." Salerno also met with Alaska Law Enforcement offering recommendations on legislation and police operations.

Our networking paid off. It came to the IU attention that a recognized Organized Crime figure, "PJM," was purchasing land and buildings in Valdez. Contact was made with John Kelsey who worked with us in monitoring PJM. All his activities were legal.

As time passed, PJM was ingratiating himself in the community by generous acts like financing the transportation of the local Little League team to Nome. Then we learned PJM was negotiating for a large piece of land that could have a significant impact on the pipeline. We met with Kelsey and learned a City Council decision was imminent.

We were stymied; then Kelsey picked up the phone and called Governor Bill Egan, who invited us to Juneau. Colonel Dankworth, Kelsey and I went to Juneau. The three of us and Commissioner of Public Safety Emery Chapple were invited to the Governor's Mansion for dinner.

The dinner conversation was light chitchat. After dessert, the Governor said "What's going on in Valdez?" I then briefed him on PJM's connection to organized crime and his activities in Valdez. The Governor said "I'll take care of it" and the meeting was over.

The following Tuesday the Valdez City Council was to make a decision on PJM's request to purchase the city land. The council unanimously voted "No" without discussion. From that day forth, PJM contacts in Valdez gave him the cold shoulder. He soon liquidated and left Valdez.

Alaska Teamster Union Local #959 came to the IU attention with complaints from Valdez to Fairbanks and beyond. We conducted an extensive investigation and took it before our state District Attorney in Anchorage. After a thorough review he concluded there wasn't enough evidence for the state to prosecute but encouraged us to review the case with the U.S. Attorney's Office. The same response came from the U.S. Attorney with a request to continue investigating.

We felt time was of the essence so "mysteriously" the report fell into the hands of two investigative reporters from the Anchorage Daily News. The May 1976 series resulted in a Pulitzer Prize for the paper. The series was entitled "Empire: The Alaska Teamster Story" and the lead reporters were Bob Porterfield and Howard Weaver. Weaver went on to be a senior executive with the McClatchy Newspaper Company and later wrote a book "Write Hard, Die Free" on his Alaskan experiences.

In the mid-Seventies, as the pipeline construction was peaking, the Colacurcio crime family of Seattle appeared under the auspices of its employment agency "Talents West." Frank Colacurcio was the head of the Seattle crime family; its primary business was running strip clubs and all the assorted activity that goes with it. Colacurcio was never charged with any crimes in Alaska but was indicted numerous times in the Seattle area for racketeering, money laundering, prostitution and other charges. He died while under indictment in 2010.

It is very hard to quantify but I believe the aggressive action of the Criminal Investigation Bureau and the Intelligence Unit kept organized crime from gaining a foothold during the Pipeline construction period.

October 2013

Tom Anderson was born in Marshall, Minnesota in 1938, the descendant of a Midwestern pioneer family. He first came to Alaska in 1957 with the U.S. Army. After completion of military service in 1959, he joined the Seattle Fire Department. In 1961 he was recruited by the Alaska State Police and remained with Alaska's statewide police force through its several name changes until retirement in 1983. His service with the Alaska State Troopers included five years as Director. He went to the FBI Academy in 1970 and earned an Associate Degree in Law-enforcement from Sheldon Jackson College in 1980. He has been active with the Fraternal Order of Alaska State Troopers since its inception. He was awarded FOAST's Life Time Achievement Award in 2012.

Lorry Schuerch Assists Troopers

Colonel Tom Anderson, Retired

A real-life action event just took place at Kiana, Alaska mid-September 2012. Kiana is a village of 360 people located 30 miles north of the Arctic Circle, northeast of Kotzebue and home to Lorry Schuerch.

Lorry spent five years with the Alaska State Troopers from 1968 to 1973. In recent years Lorry and his wife Nellie have owned and operated Kiana Lodge. Lorry guides for sheefish during the summer and is a commercial truck driver for the Red Dog Mine in the winter.

The action began on September 7th when Kiana resident Teddy Smith's mother died under suspicious circumstances. When members of the community arrived to assist, Smith fired random shots. Smith fled the home thereafter.

Fortunately no one was injured, but this activated State Trooper involvement and an extensive search ensued. Smith, a former United States Marine and, ironically, an actor in the recently produced television film "On the Ice," disappeared. The incident left Kiana residents in a state of fear and apprehension.

Fast-forward to September 18th, on the Squirrel River, approximately 50 miles north of Kiana. The Buckel brothers, one from Kotzebue and one from Michigan, were hunting caribou in the region. As they floated through the confluence of the Omar River and the Squirrel, they stopped at a cabin of a friend.

Unbeknownst to the brothers, Teddy Smith had been hiding in the heated cabin. As the brothers neared the cabin, rather than alert them to his identity and circumstance, he greeted them, invited them inside and was cordial. Following some conversation, one of the brothers indicated he was going to use his satellite phone to contact the cabin owner. Seconds later Smith allegedly turned on the brothers, shooting one in the chest and the other in the arm. The brothers, both seriously injured, were able to retreat into the woods.

Smith took the Buckel brothers' canoe, two rifles, 40 rounds of ammunition and the satellite phone and pushed off down the Squirrel River. The injured brothers returned to the cabin, contacted Troopers with the cabin radio, and were later medevaced to Kotzebue. Troopers responded in force with the SERT Team and other backup personnel. Trooper aircraft spotted Smith approximately 35 miles upriver from Kiana on Wednesday September 19th.

On the afternoon of September 19th, Troopers conferred with Kiana Mayor Brad Rich who summoned Lorry Schuerch. Lorry is known for his extensive lifelong knowledge of the Kobuk/Squirrel River country. Utilizing Lorry's knowledge of the river, the Troopers developed a strategy to intercept Smith approximately 22 miles upriver from Kiana. Lorry and Mayor Rich piloted Lorry's boats, delivering Troopers to the ambush location and Smith was apprehended without incident. Lorry would later comment on how the Troopers were very professional and he was proud to assist.

This isn't the first time Lorry Schuerch's knowledge of the Kobuk country has assisted the Alaska State Troopers. In 1970 three Native hunters were murdered during a 50-degree below zero cold snap on the Kobuk River near Kiana. The suspect and ultimately the convicted murderer was Butch Johnson, a 20-year old Caucasian whose father was a carpenter building houses in Kiana.

The evidence from the initial investigation immediately connected to Johnson. Residents of Kiana were in shock, which resulted in threats against white people in the village. It became so volatile that the school superintendent requested permission to remove his white teachers from the village.

Lorry, who was then a Trooper and working traffic in Fairbanks, was called in to assist in calming the local residents and prevent any further law violations. The Trooper administration had experience calling on the guidance of AST's Native Troopers in Southcentral and Southeast Alaska because of their local knowledge and rapport in Native communities, which afforded an advantage in handling delicate issues in local villages.

Lorry's first order of business was to calm the village down. His second priority was to deal with individuals who had threatened violence - many of whom were friends and relatives. Lorry balanced his role as a State Trooper with that of his concern and respect for Kiana friends and neighbors. He did a remarkable job in preventing violence and any lasting issues resulting from the murderer's actions. Additionally, Lorry assisted at the site and using his extensive outdoor knowledge helped reconstruct the crime scene.

The bottom line is that former Alaska State Trooper Lorry Schuerch, in both instances referenced, used ingenuity while embracing his Alaskan roots and ethnicity, coupled with intelligence and prudence, to get the job done. He helped solve and prosecute horrific crimes while averting mayhem and further injury and problems in Kiana.

In my experience, it was during the 1960s and 1970s that Troopers were more aware and cognizant of the location of former law enforcement officers in their assigned area. These former officers served as an unofficial reserve to assist active Troopers in investigations and other public safety support. I remain surprised this knowledgeable support system is seldom utilized in modern Alaskan law enforcement. Hopefully successful stories like Lorry Schuerch's will prompt a new networking effort to locate former Troopers residing in Alaska so that their experience and regional acumen can be volunteered if necessary, and public safety preserved.

(Tom Anderson served in the Alaska State Troopers from 1961 to 1983. On September 18, 2012, his birthday, he flew out of Kiana after a successful caribou hunt at Lorry Schuerch's Lodge. Tom just missed the action.)

Iron Lady 2000

Colonel Tom Anderson, Retired

No, I didn't race in the world-famous Iron Dog Snow Machine Race from Wasilla to Nome and on to Fairbanks. In a short bout of braggadocio, I have to report that I did participate in the trail-ride portion of the race. The trail-ride is a 900-mile segment of the Iron Dog, going from Nome to Fairbanks, in a non-racing mode.

The trail-riders take advantage of the logistics support of the Iron Dog Race, which includes trail marking and gas and oil support. There were approximately 20 people in the trail-ride portion of the ride, including my three-person team. Also included in the Nome team was Jessica Litera, then 29 and daughter of Sergeant Tim Litera, who retired from the State Troopers in 1995 and lives in Haines.

The odyssey started in Nome on Wednesday, February 23, and after a 270-mile run influenced by wind, water and cold, our team arrived in Unalakleet on the east coast of Norton Sound at about 7:30pm. We moved on the next day to Kaltag on the Yukon River, moving upriver north and east, reaching Ruby, Alaska for our second night on the trail. The third day we continued east to the Tanana River and spent the night at Bob Lee's Manley Hot Springs Roadhouse.

Old-timers will remember Bob Lee as a Trooper from 1967 — 1970. Bob has an advanced accounting degree and had a bright future with the Troopers as a member of the white-collar crime unit. He decided instead to venture into private enterprise and bought the Roadhouse at Manley Hot Springs in 1971. In visiting with Bob and reviewing his operation, it would appear that he pretty well runs Manley Hot Springs. Bob's the Postmaster, owns a store and has his own power plant. His lodge is the focal point for the community.

We left Manley Hot Springs Saturday morning, arriving in Nenana several hours later to stand by for the final segment to

Fairbanks. During the entire ride, Jessica Litera was an inspiration for all of the trail-riders. Her personality and enthusiasm, as well as her outstanding ability to keep pace with many older and experienced riders endeared her to the whole group.

Upon entering Nenana, disaster struck. Jessica hit an obstruction, knocking her off her sled and sending her to the hospital in Fairbanks. The trail-riders were devastated because she'd done such a good job and with only 50 miles to go, it seemed a shame she could not finish the ride. The rest of us all continued into Fairbanks, arriving late afternoon on Saturday, beginning the celebration party.

Shortly after arriving in Fairbanks, we got the word that Jessica had suffered a minor concussion. She located her snowmachine in Fairbanks, commandeered a ride back to Nenana, borrowed a helmet and necessary clothing, and was enroute to Fairbanks on her own in an effort to complete the race. Everyone was thrilled, and about an hour and half later, Jessica came through the finish line with the majority of the race committee and racers cheering her on. Jessica completed the race, concussion and all, and received accolades from all of us on her gutsy finish.

April 2000

The AST/RCMP Pistol Shoot History

Colonel Tom Anderson, Retired

Shortly after Alaska became a state in 1959, Inspector Joe Vachon, commanding officer of M Division of the Royal Canadian Mounted Police (RCMP), wanted to find some way for the RCMP and the Alaska State Troopers (AST) to get to know each other better on a personal, as well as professional basis, to strengthen their working partnership.

Inspector Vachon said, "You know that when you get a request for something from a stranger, you will do it— when you get everything else done that you have to do. But, when you get a request from a friend—that you will do immediately."

A pistol competition was among the ideas suggested to bring the two organizations together. This kind of competition would encourage marksmanship, which is considered a necessary professional skill, as well as help to develop that skill.

During a trip to Whitehorse, Alaska's Commissioner of Public Safety, Martin "Marty" Underwood, met with Inspector Vashon and agreed with the idea and philosophy of the pistol competition.

Since each agency was already working under limited finances, it was thought implementation of the competition idea might have to wait. When Calvin "Cal" Miller, owner of a hotel in Whitehorse and friend of the RCMP was contacted, he agreed to become the first sponsor for the pistol competition which would become known as "The Shoot."

The competition began in October of 1960. The first four-man team from AST traveled to Whitehorse not knowing what to expect. They wanted to make a good impression on their neighbors, but they weren't sure what kind of reception they would get. Their first encounter with the RCMP made quite an impression on them.

When they arrived at the border, their guns were sealed. (RCMP would later loan the Troopers .22 caliber weapons for the competition.) But, when they arrived in Whitehorse, they were warmly welcomed. The Alaskan team was invited to a nightlong social gathering, an early morning breakfast in their honor, a daylong tour of the RCMP headquarters and of Whitehorse, a formal dinner in their honor, and another evening of socializing.

The team was not in its best form the morning of the competition, especially when they were introduced to the four fresh young constables who had been missing from all of the other entertainment activities.

From that first AST/RCMP pistol competition, the friendship is what was remembered more than the competition itself. Of the competition, it is only remembered that the Royal Canadian Mounted Police won. High jinx set the pattern for a tradition that would be associated with the competition throughout the coming years.

In 1980 Inspector Vashon, by then retired, was invited to attend the competition and celebration. After 20 years of "The Shoot," Vashon was pleased to learn the very intent and purpose of the competition had been realized. The ties of friendship which began on the pistol range, continue the professional bonds between AST and RCMP in the Yukon Territory; bonds that have strengthened and enhanced the role of each organization in serving their separate jurisdictions. "The Shoot" has accomplished what it was intended to do.

Today, five-man teams represent each department, and each year the visiting team is accompanied by fellow officers. They meet with their counterparts in other units and discuss mutual problems and solutions, and compare notes on patrol, criminal investigation, narcotics, white collar crime and administration.

It became apparent in the early days that the RCMP and the AST would prove their professional cooperation and friendship on many occasions. In one case, a fugitive was reported fleeing from Alaska. Even as the description was being broadcast in Whitehorse, a constable saw the suspect's car at a local gas station. While the Trooper initiating the broadcast was still on the telephone, 700 miles away, the suspect was arrested.

In another case, following a brutal slaying in Anchorage in 1970, one of the suspects attempted to flee through Canada. An alert was given to the RCMP in Whitehorse. They knew a U.S. Army National Guard unit was moving up the highway for maneuvers in Alaska. When asked to be on the lookout for the suspect vehicle, the National Guard established a full roadblock with tanks, heavy weapons, and .50 caliber machine guns. When the suspect rounded a corner and saw the roadblock, he surrendered quietly and was soon turned over to the Troopers. He and a companion were subsequently tried, convicted, and sentenced.

The AST introduced the polygraph or lie detector to Canada and helped the RCMP in Whitehorse solve homicide investigations. One case involved a French student who disappeared in August of 1962. He had been hitchhiking across Canada after visiting near Dawson.

The student's disappearance was not reported until months later, and ultimately a suspect was arrested in Montreal in November. The RCMP had very little evidence, not even a body. During the investigation, the Mounties learned of the Troopers' work with a polygraph.

They contacted the Commissioner of Public Safety and asked for assistance. At the time, there was only one Trooper in the Pacific Northwest, Ed Dankworth, qualified to utilize a polygraph. He was called in and was able to learn the suspect knew more than he was admitting. Dankworth determined the hitchhiker had been killed and his body hidden somewhere near Mile 710 of the Alaska Highway.

The RCMP conducted the longest dog-team search in history, covering 125 miles of the Alaska Highway. The victim's body was found near Mile 693. During a preliminary hearing held in Whitehorse in January 1964, the suspect was held for trial. He committed suicide while in jail before the trial. Ultimately, the RCMP adopted the polygraph as an investigative instrument.

The Alaska State Troopers' 60th Anniversary in 2001 marked the 42nd year of the annual pistol competition between AST and RCMP, and it continues to fulfill its original purpose of strengthening the bonds of professional cooperation and friendship between the Alaska State Troopers and Royal Canadian Mounted Police.

60th Anniversary

The Demise of Old Yeller

Colonel Tom Anderson, Retired

In 1963 and 1964, I was assigned to Barrow, Alaska as the first permanent Trooper since Statehood in 1959. After Barrow's incorporation in 1958, the city had attempted to police the village with village policemen, without much success. Beginning in the mid-50s, Territorial policemen had been assigned to Barrow, primarily in support of the security requirements relating to construction of the Distant Early Warning Line (known as the DEW Line).

The Barrow assignment was one of the early contract positions wherein the Alaska State Policemen had a certain amount of required duties within the village of Barrow. We had responsibility as well for all villages north of the Brooks Range, including Barter Island, which is now called Kaktovik; Umiat, a staging point for oil exploration; Anaktuvuk Pass, a small Inupiat community in the North Central Brooks Range; Wainwright, a small village on the Arctic Coast southwest of Barrow; and Point Lay, also southwest of Barrow on the Arctic Coast.

Locations such as Prudhoe Bay and Nuiqsut, presently major oil development locations, were only remote points on the map at that time. Support for the contract included the village of Barrow supplying a trooper residence. The Naval Arctic Research Laboratory (NARL), located approximately three miles north of the village, supplied a '50s vintage military ambulance with DC3 tires, as well as a limited amount of air support throughout the Arctic. NARL had a small fleet of aircraft that regularly traveled throughout Northern Alaska, including significant long-range trips out on the polar ice cap to support various experimental stations.

The village of Barrow in the early '60s was composed of approximately 1,800 Inupiats (Eskimos). The few non-Natives in Barrow at the time were mostly employees of the National Weather Bureau,

Public Health Service Hospital, BIA school, and a few non- Natives who had married local residents. I distinctly remember the number of people at Barrow at the time because there was a rabies scare, and we had to vaccinate the entire dog population, which coincidentally happened to be about the same population as the local residents.

One of my first requests by the City Council of Barrow was to deal with the loose dog problem. The early to mid-'60s was the start of the snowmachine era, with a de-emphasis on the dog care practiced during the dog team years. The result was a significant number of large huskies running loose in the village, causing numerous complaints, serious injuries, and, from time to time, a death.

I was somewhat hesitant about taking on this responsibility but finally agreed to do it with the understanding that one day a month I would shoot loose dogs contingent upon the village of Barrow supplying a crew with a small track vehicle and sled to pick up the carcasses and dispose of them. Following that decision, each month I would pick a day and line up the carcass removal crew and shoot loose dogs.

I tried several firearms, including rifle and shotgun, and came to the conclusion that a shotgun with double-aught buck was the safest and best bet for getting the job done. It was somewhat of an unnerving experience because the nine pellets in double-aught buck are round and if all the pellets did not hit the dog, the pellets would roll down the frozen ground, rattling against houses and whatever else was in the way.

Early on, I became aware of a local dog dubbed "Old Yeller" who was famous for causing mischief throughout the village and had a sixth sense of when the monthly dog day came around. Locals were constantly pressuring me to take care of Old Yeller, but the minute the first shot rang out, Old Yeller headed for the tundra and wasn't seen until the day was over. Finally, I decided to play it smart and planned the first shot of the day on this particular month to be Mr. Old Yeller.

On the big day, I drove all over Barrow with my swamp buggy, finally locating the culprit in Browerville, which is a small section of Barrow, north of the main part of the village. Old Yeller was lying down right in the middle of a long series of staked dogs. As I slowly made my sneak to get within shooting range I was positive that Old Yeller could sense I was there, but he didn't move. Trying to get into range, I let fly, ending the saga of Old Yeller.

The pickup crew walked over to dispose of the carcass. I heard one of them say, "Oh no, Trooper Tom, Old Yeller is tied up." To everyone's surprise, it appeared that the original owner of Old Yeller had finally collared him and tied him up.

"Trooper Tom, what do we do?" I told the crew to unfasten the dog, put him on the sled and we went about our business. For a week I expected the phone to ring from the owner complaining about the situation, but fortunately, it never happened. I always thought the owner probably figured sneaky Old Yeller had somehow slipped away.

I disposed of 87 dogs during the winter of 63/64. The dogs were disposed of on the Arctic ice in front of the village, along with honey-bucket barrels, garbage, and every other type of refuse needing disposal. In the spring, when the ice moved away, it took care of Barrow's winter garbage.

Barrow today has a population of over 4,400 people, with three schools and approximately 1,200 students and a large Public Safety Department. It is part of the North Slope Borough, which employs hundreds of people, and it is home to numerous businesses that provide support services to the oilfield operations at Prudhoe Bay and the North Slope.

May 2004

Princess Margaret Visits Anchorage

Colonel Tom Anderson, Retired

A June 15, 2006 article in the Anchorage Daily News reporting the sale of the late Princess Margaret's personal possessions reminded me of her visit to Anchorage.

In the late '6Os, the Princess and her husband Lord Snowden made a short stop in Anchorage on an over-the-pole flight from the Orient to Europe. They requested a short tour of Anchorage. I was then a Sergeant and was selected to handle the tour, with the assistance of Troopers Jim Shook and Gene Rudolf for transportation and security.

Specific instructions were given to make no personal contact with the royal party, but simply drive them to selected locations; a tour guide would do the commentary.

At Earthquake Park, I was on one side of the entourage, Trooper Rudolf on the other, and Trooper Shook was standing near the middle a few feet from the Princess. Then I heard, "Princess, move over a little to your left," then some other directions, to assist in setting up a personal photograph.

Unfortunately the photographer was Trooper Jim Shook, who was ignoring previous instructions and decided upon his own to take a snapshot of the Princess and Lord Snowden. Due to the good nature of the Princess, an international incident was avoided. Trooper Shook was appropriately chewed out for his lack of discretion.

In recent years, Jim Shook has accused me of faulty recollection of the event, but the editor goes by the adage, he who writes the history makes it.

August 2006

A Famous Bloodhound

Colonel Tom Anderson, Retired

Although we have become accustomed to the presence of police dogs as an integral part of law enforcement in Alaska, there was a time when their presence was not commonplace. There was a time when only one dog was known to all... one who assisted Law Enforcement officers on many occasions. That dog was named 'Delilah,' a registered bloodhound.

Delilah was brought to the Territory of Alaska in the early fifties by Pattie and Bob Thiel. In the mid-fifties Delilah chased down criminals but became best known for her effective tracking of lost hunters and children. She did not become really famous until the Thiels turned Delilah over to C.W. 'Shorty" Bradley, a colorful ex-cowpuncher from Montana.

When Bradley received Delilah he also got Samson, another full-blooded bloodhound acquired by the Thiels in Michigan after a nationwide search. Together Samson and Delilah provided Bradley with a good team of dogs to assist law enforcement.

During their heyday, Delilah was considered the 'heroine' in searches that included tracking a rapist in Wasilla, locating a lost four-year-old boy near Nome, uncovering the trail of a runaway juvenile suspected of rape in the Anchorage area, and many others. Delilah was often called upon by people all over the state of Alaska to track suspects and lost people.

The case that made the front page of the newspaper and put her on the map involved a lost trapper from Dillingham. Billy Gurtler left Dillingham in late March on a snowmachine heading to his cabin 30 miles north of town. After several days and no sign of Gurtler at his cabin, a search was initiated. Local pilots combed the area and finally located his snowmachine, which had a broken belt. There was, however, no sign of Gurtler. The locals looked for a week, and having had no luck, they finally called in 'Shorty' Bradley and Delilah. By this time the trail was over a week old. Blowing snow and wind had made tracking difficult to impossible. After many hours on the trail, Delilah and Bradley found Gurtler's frozen body.

This find resulted in an award from the Division of Civil Defense, at the time part of the Department of Public Safety, for Bradley and Delilah's heroic efforts.

Bradley came to Alaska in 1922 from Montana where he worked as a cowpuncher. On arrival in Alaska he served as the Wrangell Chief of Police and later worked all over Alaska. He homesteaded on Cache Creek Road near Talkeetna and passed away in 1966 at the age of 65.

On his many searches he always said "give all the credit to Delilah." He never would accept any money for all of his time and effort in assisting law enforcement. It seemed second nature to him as much as it was first nature to that famous bloodhound, 'Delilah.'

December 2009

Cy (Boom Boom) Cederborg

Colonel Tom Anderson, Retired

In the early 70s it was almost a requirement that progressive police departments throughout the U.S. have an Explosive Ordinance Disposal (EOD) Expert on staff. The natural place to find an EOD Expert was the military and that's how the Alaska State Troopers hired retired Army Master Sergeant Cy Cederborg. Cy was hired in 1972 and did a great job for the AST.

In his nine years with the state, Cy left a trail of humorous and hair-raising incidents. The first one I'm acquainted with occurred around 1973. Cy had recently been hired and Patrol Sergeant Bill Nix was lamenting in the squad room that his sewer drain field wasn't draining.

Bill lived in Nunaka Valley, a very congested development in East Anchorage. Small two-bedroom houses were close together, and each had its own sewer drain field.

Cy heard the exchange and said he could fix that. It would involve dropping a small charge down the stand pipe to open up the drainage.

Several of us had to see this, and we all headed for Nunaka Valley.

Cy placed the charge in the standpipe in Bill's backyard and set off the charge. Unfortunately, it was around 4 p.m., and school had just let out. The streets were packed with children. After the charge went off, the standpipe blasted into the air, seemingly 500-feet up in the sky. It hung there momentarily and started coming down. We were all certain some kids were going to be killed.

Fortunately or unfortunately, depending on how you look at it, the standpipe blasted through the neighbor's roof. It drove through the ceiling and slammed into the floor of the kitchen 18-inches from the neighbor's wife, who was washing dishes.

Three observers, including myself, left in a hurry, leaving Cy and Bill to smooth over the incident and deal with a very unhappy housewife. We never heard another word about it.

Another incident occurred in April of 1974 in Juneau.

Cy was sent there to dispose of some old dynamite in a mine in the Mendenhall Valley. With age, dynamite starts losing its nitroglycerin, which helps keep it stable, and can become quite dangerous. The recommended disposal method is burning, but that's tedious and slow. Cy could never be called slow. He exploded the two cases.

The cloud cover at the time was heavy and low in the Mendenhall Valley. The concussion from the explosion bounced off the low-hanging clouds and sent a shock wave into the valley blowing out windows, cracking fireplaces, and causing other miscellaneous damage.

When the blast went off, Governor Bill Egan was on the Juneau radio station program "Problem Corner," and calls poured in.

Commissioner Pat Wellington got an urgent call from the Governor asking what the hell was going on. Pat quickly found out Cy was in town and deduced what happened. Pat spent the next afternoon and evening going around to homeowners explaining what occurred and assuring them that they would be compensated.

As Cy's supervisor, I met him at the airplane coming in from Juneau. I asked him why he didn't burn the dynamite, and he replied he wanted to catch the plane home to Anchorage.

One day Cy came to my office with a long face. "What's up?" I asked. He replied, "We have a little problem." He'd been in Fairbanks disposing of some dynamite and coming back his luggage containing dynamite caps was lost.

I hadn't thought to ask how he ordinarily disposed of ordinance, so it hit me like a bomb that Cy had been traveling around the state with caps and small amounts of dynamite on commercial airliners. Even in 1974 it was a serious federal offense to carry explosives on a passenger plane. I agonized on what to do and finally decided to call a friend who was Security Chief for Wien Airlines. He said, "No problem. We will find the bag." Fortunately he did and delivered it to our office. Needless to say, that practice was stopped.

Captain Steve Reynolds, Retired, told me he'd left the Department in 1975 to work on the pipeline and make some big bucks. Fortunately, the Department hired him back in 1977, but suggested Steve attend the 30th Recruit Academy to "pay his dues".

At age 40, Steve was an old guy compared to the rest of the recruits, but he wasn't the only old-timer at the academy. There were three others: Sergeant Bob Brown, Weldon Martin, and Cy Cederborg.

Steve, thought to be the oldest, was harassed and called "Grandfather." Retired Army master sergeant Cy Cederborg never said a word. He was 48.

At the academy graduation, Governor Jay Hammond came by to say hello. He looked out over the room of 40 shining faces, and recognized only Cy. "Hi Boom Boom," he said, "What are you doing here?"

Steve made one last comment to me about Cy. He remembered that the entire class wore tennis shoes during the rigors of academia except for one person. Cy Cederborg wore combat boots.

God rest his soul.

June 2010

Body Recovery

Colonel Tom Anderson, Retired

After Ed Hill's difficult body recovery in 1982 (see "A Difficult Call Under Tough Conditions) Commissioner of Public Safety Martin B. Underwood published a "Deceased Remains Handling Policy" that made it clear that during any body recovery, mutilation of the deceased remains would be grounds for immediate termination.

In the winter of 1983/84 I was on roving patrol visiting villages on the central Yukon River. At Ruby I was advised that an old prospector, who lived at Long Creek, approximately 30 miles from Ruby, had not come in for his normal Christmas visit. I chartered a Wien Cessna 180 and proceeded to Long Creek. We located the cabin and, while flying over, found no fresh tracks in the snow or smoke from the chimney.

The 180 was equipped with wheel skis so we landed in deep soft snow. I proceeded to the cabin and found the old prospector dead in his bunk. He was lying on his back with his left arm hanging straight down beside the bunk at a 90-degree angle and frozen solid. Earlier I had been authorized by the local magistrate to remove any body. I took a few quick pictures, did a short examination of the scene, and then the pilot and I removed the body to the plane.

There was no way we could get the body into the Cessna through the passenger doors. The new policy from the Commissioner's office was in my mind and we were at a loss on what to do. As I walked around the plane, I noticed that Wien had modified the freight door of the plane.

The freight door on a Cessna 180 is behind the pilot on the left side and in this case had been expanded to approximately 18" by 2'. I decided to load the body in feet first through the freight door. By pushing the frozen feet up over the passenger seat and leaving the frozen arm hanging out of the plane, I felt the problem was solved.

The only problem was the Cessna was a tail dragger, and the arm was hanging in the snow. The pilot assured me he could get off without any damage to the arm. We took off and proceeded directly to Galena. At that time, during the Cold War, the U.S. Air Force controlled the airfield. On our downwind landing an excited voice came on the air from the tower and advised that it appeared an arm was hanging out of the plane. We acknowledged and said don't worry about it.

At Galena the remains were loaded on to a Wien C-47 and transported to Fairbanks.

September 2010

First Working Police Dog in Alaska

Colonel Tom Anderson, Retired

Trooper Ernest "Ernie" Beauchamp and retired Captain Lowell Parker were the first state enforcement officers in Alaska to utilize professionally trained police dogs. Ernie Beauchamp was born in California in 1939, spent time in the United States Marine Corps, and started with the Alaska State Troopers in 1963. During his service with the Troopers, he served at Delta Junction, Kotzebue, and Anchorage.

While serving in Delta Junction, he was instrumental in starting the local fire department and through his efforts, fire equipment was obtained from nearby Ft. Greeley.

In 1965, Beauchamp and fellow Trooper Joe Holler tested studded tires in the Fairbanks/Delta Junction area and, as a result, recommended acceptance by the Troopers. From that point on, studded tires became a reality for the Trooper organization and Beauchamp also suggested yellow fog lights be installed in the rear window of patrol cars to deal with the heavy ice fog in the Fairbanks/Delta area.

While stationed in Anchorage in late 1967/early '68 Beauchamp and Parker, primarily through their own initiative, secured two German Shepherd police dogs. Due to budget limitations both Troopers initially fed the dogs out of their own pockets until the department could furnish funding for food and upkeep.

In the early 70s, Beauchamp transferred to the Department of Law as Chief Investigator, and ultimately retired from that position. Beauchamp passed away from a heart attack in April, 1990.

Anchorage 1968

A Promise Kept

Colonel Gordon R. Nelson

Looking back over a career in law enforcement in one's mind is in effect like watching a tape on a VCR and television. Some events and scenes stand out from the everyday events of a Trooper's life.

In 1953, one such scene found me in a deep ditch kneeling beside and facing a father lying across his dead 12-year-old son, the victim of a hit-and-run driver. At that moment I made a promise to myself and to the father: I would find and take the killer to justice.

The first break in the case was a sharp-eyed elderly man who didn't see the accident, but did see a car veer off the road momentarily and then go on down the highway. He commented it looked like one belonging to a man who usually spent his weekends at Big Lake.

An hour later I found the car parked in front of a cabin. The description fit.

A careful check of the car indicated it could have been the killing tool. The small dent in the hood and the evident smear of saliva toward the windshield made it possible that a small head had smashed down there. The driver likely would have seen the child at that moment. The car was impounded and taken to Palmer for a complete examination.

The owner was awakened and found to be very drunk. The worst part was it proved to be a man I knew and had liked. He admitted driving the car, but claimed no memory of the incident. He did admit running off the road near the scene but was able to return to the road and continue.

On the basis of the information available he was arrested and taken to Palmer. The charge was DWI.

The close examination of the car brought discovery of hair and blood samples. We also found a broken head light. A search at the accident scene turned up glass fragments which matched the headlight glass. I must note that in collecting the blood samples for testing, I removed only half the blood on the car. The defense appreciated the fact, so they could also have tests made.

Next I started a back-trail on the driver's time before the accident. We were able to establish where and how often the man had stopped for drinks prior to the accident. There was little doubt the man was intoxicated when last seen before the accident. One man was found who had offered to drive the man to Big Lake because he was much too drunk to be driving.

Then a few days later a motorist flagged me down. He reported that he and his family had met a car at the accident on the day of the boy's death. They had seen the car go off the road down into the ditch and then struggle back up on the roadway. He described the car as being down in the ditch where we had found the body. He further mentioned that they had stopped and picked up a boy's baseball cap where the other car had left the roadway. He handed me the cap. They had not connected the two incidents until recent newspaper reports.

The cap was identified by initials and the father. He had wondered what could have happened to his son's cap. He had been wearing it when he left home.

Now we could reconstruct the scene. The boy was hit on the side of the road and carried down into the ditch where we had found him. The driver, no doubt in panic, had floor-boarded the throttle and powered his way back up onto the road.

To me it was evident the man had seen and known about the crime. He had to have looked the boy right in the face before the child went down and under the car.

It was a month later when we placed our evidence before the District Attorney. He felt we had a good case, and the man was charged with hit-and-run homicide.

The trial was interesting as the defense was active. The evidence collected at the scene and the witnesses found who testified resulted in a guilty verdict.

I suspect this was the first successful vehicle homicide case in the territory's history. At least I don't know of one before this one.

September 1992

Gordon Nelson passed away August 19, 2004 in Palmer from complications of Alzheimer's disease. Gordy was born in Tacoma, Washington and moved to Alaska in 1923. He was raised in Wrangell, Petersburg, Ketchikan, Cordova, and Anchorage. Gordy served in the U.S. Army from 1943 to 1946 and joined the Alaska Highway Patrol in 1951. He served 21 years in the Highway Patrol, the Alaska Territorial Police, Alaska State Police and Alaska State Troopers. He was stationed in Anchorage, Glennallen, Fairbanks, Palmer and Juneau and was one of the few who served in all four eras of the organization. He was the first Colonel who formerly served as Director of Technical Services. He retired in 1971 and lived in Wasilla until his death. In retirement, Gordy wrote entertaining cookbooks that included "Lowbush Moose," "Smokehouse Bear," "Tired Wolf" and "Hibrow Cow."

Bush Guardians: A Tribute to all VPSOs

Trooper Dan Decker

Wait, take time and listen,
I have a story to share.
Of brave men and women.
"Bush Guardians," people who care.

We call them "VPSOs,"
a strange name to some.
For people of Rural Alaska,
a name most people welcome.

They serve and protect,
their people, their land.
In spirit and body,
alone often they stand.

Against all the odds,
they struggle to fight.
The wrongs and injustice,
during day, during night.

A job often thankless,
without praise or reward.
They march into battle,
without shield, without sword.

Understand now these letters,
"VPSO," proud letters indeed.
Our brave men and women,
"Bush Guardians," that we need.

AST 60th Anniversary Issue 2001

Dan Decker spent three years in the U S. Army Special Forces before beginning his career with the Alaska State Troopers in 1975. He was assigned to duty in Fairbanks, Prudhoe Bay, Cantwell, Ninilchik, Juneau, Anchorage Post, Criminal Investigation Bureau-Major Crimes Unit, Palmer Patrol/General Investigation Unit/Drug Unit and in Bethel as Supervisor of VPSO's. He received two medals for Valor and two medals for Meritorious Service. Trooper Decker was a member of the Special Emergency Response Team and participated in the SOME Run (Special Olympics Mileage Event) for several years. He retired in 1997.

Early Days of the Alaska State Police: Part I

Captain Bob Penman

More than 30 years have passed since I fulfilled a childhood dream to come to Alaska, not to live by hunting and trapping in a log cabin on the Yukon River, as I had planned as a youth, but as an officer of the Alaska State Police.

I was a Sheriff's Officer in Michigan when I encountered an article concerning Alaska's new police organization in the FBI Bulletin. A letter to Juneau asking about the qualifications brought a promising reply, and in February of 1960, I was notified the examinations were scheduled for March in Juneau.

The two-day trip was exciting, but the hotel was a little pricey for a Deputy making $65 a week. However, I was fortunate in making the acquaintance of J. Sherman Tanner, inventor of the Alaska Chainsaw Mill, and he invited me to sleep in a cot over his Glacier Avenue shop while the tests were in progress.

Turk Mayfield was one of the members of my oral board and his piercing blue eyes twinkled as he plied me with penetrating questions, which I answered as truthfully as I could. At the end of May, back in Michigan, I received a short telegram that said: "Sorry short notice. Tending your appointment in State Police Effective June 1st. Please Advise." It was signed M. Underwood, Commissioner.

I only had four days to get things together and was forced to leave my wife and new daughter in order to report for the Recruit Class in Anchorage on June 1st. Classes were conducted at East High School and lasted for two weeks. All the notes taken during the day's class had to be typed that night for inspection the next morning, and that made for some long evenings.

Frank Johnson, Bill Nix and I shared a motel room together. After completing the course, I received my first assignment – Fairbanks.

Gil Hagen and I drove up in his 1953 Chevrolet, along with several dogs. When we arrived I was issued used uniforms and equipment which had been turned in by officers who were no longer with the department. My uniform formerly belonged to Norman Andresen. It wasn't a perfect fit, but I was proud of it and of the well-worn revolver and clamshell holster.

The most exciting part, however, was the $565 a month that I was going to be paid. It was more than double my former salary. I found an apartment in Lemeta next to Creamer's Dairy, and as soon as I received my first paycheck, I sent for my wife and daughter to join me.

The Fairbanks Detachment was under the command of Lieutenant Bill Trafton at the time, with Sergeant Emery Chapple as his deputy. After spending two shifts with Archie Barber as my training officer, I was turned loose. I was on my own on the graveyard shift. The car assigned to me was a 1959 Ford Galaxie — "Car 22" on the roster — painted the standard gunmetal gray with blue and gold State Police decals on the doors.

Ralph Shafer had "Car 21" and held down the graveyard shift with me. The next few months were exciting times.

During the long summer nights we started at the opposite ends of the "Cushman Strip" to do bar checks just prior to the 5 a.m. bar closing hour. Ralph's sweet disposition didn't deserve the nickname "that scar-nosed logger from Ketchikan" bestowed on him by the rowdy Fairbanks bar crowd.

Occasionally, when it was very "drunk out," we managed to load up both squad cars with prisoners for the State Jail. It seemed part of the local ethic at the time for the arrestee to try and test the mettle of the arresting officer, and Ralph liked that part of it.

In the winter, a lot of the arrests kept the drunks from freezing to death in the sub-zero temperatures. My first winter in Alaska in 1960-61 was a particularly cold one. Temperatures hovered in the minus 60-degree range for days, although I thought it was normal at the time.

In addition to Archie Barber and Ralph Shafer, some of the men stationed at Fairbanks during those years were Claude St. Amand, Bob Redston, Gene O'Brien. Bill Nix, Hal Hume, Gil Hagan, Jim Barkley, Mike McRoberts and Jim Calhoun.

Along the Richardson Highway from Eielson Air Force Base to North Pole was an area known as the "Dikes." The road was nearly straight from the Boon Dox Cafe at Milepost 33 to North Pole. It was at mid-day in January during my first winter that I was at an accident scene at Moose Creek, with lights flashing, engaged in directing traffic around a tank retriever in the process of recovering an overturned military personnel carrier from Fort Greely. It was minus 50 degrees with no wind. Passing vehicles were leaving contrails of ice fog like what could be seen when high-altitude aircraft flew overhead.

Unexpectedly, I saw a vehicle approaching headed north at a high rate of speed. He didn't slow down and passed us on the single open lane at around 70 MPH. The back of his vehicle was discharging a cloud of ice fog that made him look like the first stage of a Saturn V rocket during lift-off.

I jumped into my patrol car to give chase and accelerated to 90 MPH. The closer I came to the pursued vehicle, the poorer the visibility became.

All of a sudden, I saw two vehicles in front of me that were broad-side to each other with one coming head-on in my direction. It didn't seem there was anywhere to go, but I instinctively jerked the wheel to the right and heard a "thunk" as the back of my vehicle passed the oncoming car in my lane.

I went into a high-speed broadside skid, with snow flying in every direction, and fought for control. After turning around a half-dozen times, I managed to straighten out and continued my pursuit.

As I closed in on the driver, the fog seemed to be clearing, and when he could finally see my red light he pulled over and stopped. I didn't trust myself to stand up as my legs were shaking so I called the driver over to the squad car with the PA speaker and had some difficulty controlling the shake in my pen long enough to write him a negligent driving ticket.

He said that his car didn't run very well at speeds lower than 60 MPH, and he was trying to get it to a garage at North Pole. The engine had blown a head gasket and was allowing the antifreeze to vaporize on the cylinders, which accounted for the dense ice fog. He had run out of antifreeze as I came up behind him, and his engine quit and he stopped. The "thunk" I heard turned out to be my back bumper barely touching the front bumper of the oncoming vehicle. If I had been a half- second later reacting, it would have resulted in a horrible collision.

This incident and another that happened a few weeks later inspired Gene "O.B." O'Brien to begin calling me "Lucky."

One day he asked to see my notebook and confirmed that I had stopped a pickup with a tail-light out earlier that week at Mile 3 of the Richardson. The occupants were coming from a burglary and thought when I pulled them over that they were being arrested.

A Canadian who later turned informant was one of the three men in the vehicle and "didn't want to be involved in shooting a cop." He grabbed the .44 magnum away from another occupant who was aiming it at me as I stood with the driver in the headlights at the front of the vehicle.

I suppose the worst part of the job at the time was the never-ending paperwork that was made even more difficult by the old military-surplus manual typewriters in the squad room. Three carbon copies had to be made of everything, and correcting an error and re-aligning the sheets again was a headache. I could type fairly well, but there were some like Shafer who had large calluses on the index finger of each hand and kept overlapping the adjoining keys. (I'm not sure if they were from the typewriters or poking his finger into the chest of rowdy drunks!!)

Warmer spring weather meant it was time to qualify with firearms again so we went to the Birch Hill Range. I was standing on the firing line along with Emery Chapple, preparing to fire the seven-yard sequence. When the range officer blew the whistle, we were to draw and fire.

When the whistle sounded, I started to draw but was distracted by an explosion along-side me. Chapple's weapon had discharged as he was taking it out of the clamshell holster. He shot himself in the knee, was taken to the hospital and was laid up for most of the summer.

The old clamshells were an aluminum shell covered by leather with a button in the trigger guard which operated a spring. They jammed frequently, and some officers even carried a small screwdriver to pry them open. Another big minus was that your finger was in the trigger guard before the revolver could even be freed from the holster. It was five years before the department had enough money to replace them, and in the meantime a few officers started to 'bootleg' their own holsters. The holsters issued to Judicial Services were even worse. The revolver wouldn't stay in place, and frequently fell out.

September 1993

Robert Penman was appointed to the Alaska State Police on June 1, 1960. During his 20 years with the Alaska State Troopers, he worked in Fairbanks, Juneau, Sitka twice, Palmer, and Anchorage twice. He retired in September of 1980 as a Captain. After retiring in 1980, he spent more than 20 years working security at Prudhoe Bay. In September of 2002, he gave that up for full-time retirement. He and his wife still live by Campbell School off Arctic, are active with their church, and are busy with their large family. He still enjoys the outdoors, pistol shooting, river trips, rafting, family get-togethers, and cycling the great Anchorage bike trails. They have 21 grandchildren (15 boys & six girls) and one great-granddaughter, with more on the way. Laraine and Robert have been married since October of 1958.

Alaska State Police Recollections: Part II

Captain Bob Penman, Retired

In April 1961, I was transferred to Juneau, under the command of Lieutenant Wesley Gilman and Sergeant John P. Monagle Sr. I was to be the first State Police contract officer stationed at Douglas, where the town reimbursed the department for four hours of police service each day.

The contract stipulated that I would live in Douglas so we rented a one-bedroom apartment in Mark and Mamie Jensen's home next door to Mike's Place. The other officers assigned to Juneau at the time were Pat Wellington, Hal Hume and Ken Dubber. Shortly after my arrival, Gilman retired. Sergeant Monagle replaced him in charge of Southeast Alaska, and Sergeant Jim Goodfellow was transferred in as his deputy.

Goodfellow was a stickler for report writing and used a red pencil to mark spelling, punctuation, or grammatical glitches. That red pencil was the nightmare of a lot of officers, Charlie Soriano for one. Soriano replaced Bob Erskine at Wrangell and had a particularly difficult time with one report that had been back and forth between Wrangell and Juneau several times.

Charlie became so exasperated that he typed the entire report over, without punctuation of any kind, and then placed the punctuation marks at the end of the report with instructions to put them in where it seemed appropriate.

Juneau was busy for the number of officers assigned there, with accidents, homicides, suicides, fires, drownings, and bear maulings, etc. It was a stormy night on January 20, 1962 when I took my wife up the hill to St. Ann's Hospital where our first son was born.

I was transferred to Sitka in May, 1962, to replace John Broderson who lived on Webb Island across the narrow channel from Castle Hill where Lord Baranof's castle had originally been constructed. Broderson had been somewhat unavailable for routine emergency calls, especially when a storm was blowing in the harbor. As I look back, I can see now why John lived out there because my routine was usually an average 16-hour day, seven days a week. I even needed help from my wife, who acted as dispatcher and issued driver's licenses out of our kitchen at 625 DeGroff St.

Sitka had a small police department headed at the time by Burt Doucette. There was also a jail. A couple of bars in town were lively, especially when the fishing fleet was in town.

Out of town was the infamous 3-1/2 Mile Bar on Saw Mill Creek Road. It was open later than the town bars which closed at 2 a.m. Loggers, fishermen, and mill workers frequented the place. It was the source of a lot of my activity along with the logging camps, canneries, and the villages of Angoon, Kake, Pelican, Elfin Cove, Sitkoh Bay, Baranof Warm Springs and Port Alexander, which were all part of the Sitka Post area.

Travel was mainly by floatplane, but a boat was sometimes used.

There were a number of interesting incidents that come to mind and one at Jamestown Bay was probably typical. A middle-aged fisherman lived there alone, a man who liked youthful company and would provide area teenagers with alcohol and a place to bunk down. In return, he took sexual advantage of the young girls who stayed with him.

A mother's complaint resulted in a warrant being issued and I went to the suspect's residence to serve it. When I knocked on the door, the curtain was pulled aside, and I saw the suspect pointing a .455 Webley at my face. It was obviously loaded. The hammer was cocked and his finger was on the trigger.

He ordered me to "Go Away," and at that time a dog came up behind me, barking his head off. My adrenaline was pumping buckets, but it occurred to me to say that my call was occasioned by neighbors complaining that his dog was getting into their garbage.

After a moment's hesitation he opened the door, and I went inside. He still held the revolver pointed at my chest while we continued to talk. I kept moving towards him with the intention of trying to grab the gun away. (FBI Agent A.B. Clarke used to demonstrate the technique, but I was always skeptical. Being left-handed, this meant using my gun hand to effect the take-away, and this left me unable to draw my own weapon.)

After moving in close enough, I swept the Webley to the left away from me and at the same time grabbed the top of the cylinder to keep it from revolving. At that moment, the hammer fell and the prominent firing pin on that old-style British military weapon pierced the web of my hand between my index finger and thumb. This kept the weapon from discharging, and I was able to twist it out of his hand.

The suspect yelled, "You tricked me!" He reached into a drawer for a butcher knife. I was having my own troubles because I couldn't release the grip the hammer had on my hand. I couldn't draw my own weapon with my right hand because the clamshell was on my left side.

I finally kicked him in the groin. He went down hard, allowing me to free the Webley. After that, there wasn't any trouble with the prisoner and he served a couple of years in Juneau.

New Year's Eve, 1963, involved a series of incidents which were not particularly noteworthy in themselves, but the fact that they occurred within such a short space of time was a bit unusual. Police work seems to go in cycles with occasional spurts of activity followed by a prolonged lull. Like a lot of law enforcement officers, I have always suspected some type of correlation between the full moon and people's strange behavior.

The day started pretty much as usual, checking Civil Process papers that had to be served and driving out to the end of the road in both directions to see if there were accidents or vehicles in the ditch. My wife was expecting a new baby at the time and was a week overdue.

I was staying close to home for a few days, particularly since New Year's Eve would be active locally. After supper, I started checking the bars. Things were quiet until 11 p.m. when I encountered a DWI and took him to jail.

It was nearly midnight when I received a radio message from my wife who asked me to come home because she needed to get to the hospital. I went home and bundled the children over to a neighbor's, called the hospital, and took Laraine there where her doctor was going to meet us.

He was delayed, so the nurse and I delivered our second daughter without a hitch. After the doctor arrived and was conducting his examination, I heard a loud crash against the window and ran outside to find a group of three drunks fighting.

After neutralizing the situation, I called for the Sitka paddy wagon, and we bundled them off to jail. At almost the same time, a call came through that there was a fight at the 3-1/2. By the time I arrived at the scene, the fight had nearly died down except for one fellow who wanted to fight me instead of going back to drinking quietly.

While en route with him, a call was broadcast that there was an accident and fire at Thimbleberry Bridge. I left my prisoner with a fireman who was opening the doors to the fire station and fell in behind the fire truck responding to the emergency call.

It developed that a group of teenagers had stolen an automobile and drove it up to Blue Lake for a party. On the way back to town they lost control, jumped the road, and crashed into a motor home, routing the four sleeping occupants and breaking loose the propane tank lines, which allowed the gas to leak out.

I rounded up the juveniles while the fire department took care of the propane. I had dropped the youngsters off with the Juvenile Officer and was en route back to Jamestown Bay when I observed an approaching car weaving all over the road in front of me. I activated the red light and was stopping the patrol car when I saw the passenger-side door on the approaching vehicle open, and someone jump out of the car. It was a woman. Her dress flew up, and she started rolling along the road. By this time I was stopped, and the oncoming car was also.

Running over to the woman, who was now lying on the road, I found she was conscious but confused and skinned from head to toe. She was drunk as was her husband, I found, as he staggered over from his car. I put them both in the patrol car and started for the hospital.

When I got it sorted out later, I discovered she became upset with her husband at a party and they continued the argument on the way home until she finally decided to step out without waiting for the car to come to a stop. It was noon before I got through with the reports and court proceedings and could return to the hospital to see my wife and new baby daughter.

I spent a lot of time travelling and transporting prisoners to Juneau from Sitka. When the Grand Jury convened, the number of felony cases being generated from the Sitka Post area seemed to surprise them. They asked to review my activity reports and found that I had worked more than a thousand hours of "voluntary" overtime during the previous 10 months.

Commissioner Underwood, a former FBI man, was deeply ingrained with the Bureau practice of recording "voluntary" overtime. Every Alaska State Police officer knew that his own hours of "voluntary" overtime would be carefully scrutinized when promotions were being considered. The Grand Jury recommended another officer be assigned to Sitka, and a few months later Dick Dubell and his family arrived. I expected more leisure time with my family but it seemed we really weren't much better off. Now, both of us were working "voluntary" overtime.

Not all the activities were grim, and there were lighter moments. I recall deer hunting in Rodman Bay with Bob LaGuire of Fish & Game and Ray Stratton, the FBI agent assigned to Southeast Alaska. We reached the bay in an open skiff on a cold, blustery fall day. Each time the skiff needed to be beached, I'd volunteer to wade in the thigh deep water and pull it up on the shore. After several changes of location and some mediocre hunting, we were ready to head back to town. Ray had been miserably cold and wet all day, and his foul smelling pipe was chattering in his teeth.

I allowed as how the FBI didn't have very tough agents assigned to Alaska and that his nicotine habit probably contributed to his poor circulation. For his part, he couldn't believe I could stand being wet through clear up to the waist on this miserably cold day.

There was a secret I never told him. I had the bottom portion of my wetsuit on under my hunting clothes. Standing in the water was almost a welcome and cooling relief.

Stratton was a personal friend of Special Agent Joe Sullivan for many years. Sullivan, later an FBI Inspector, was the man J. Edgar Hoover sent to clear up the disappearance of the Philadelphia, Mississippi civil rights workers. In the movie "Mississippi Burning," Gene Hackman more or less portrayed the part of Joe Sullivan in real life. Ray Stratton later had a falling out with the SAIC who replaced Sullivan and was transferred to Chicago, where he ended up in charge of the FBI's bank robbery detail.

December 1993

Alaska State Police Recollections: Part III

Captain Bob Penman, Retired

Don McQueen was stationed in Haines during the early 1960s and came to Sitka occasionally to fill in. On one of those occasions I had gone to Pelican with the Magistrate and Dr. Tom Moore to hold a presumptive death hearing on a fellow whose body was recovered on the tide fiats. Delbert Brown was living in Pelican at the time and was an associate of the deceased.

A few years earlier, Mel Personnet had investigated another disappearance of one of Brown's partners in Yakutat. Brown pulled a gun on Personnet and was convicted of ADW but got a reversal — in one of the earliest cases decided by the Alaska Supreme Court — on the grounds that he was absent during a critical stage of the proceedings when his common law wife was being examined as a potential witness.

Delbert Brown's associates had a habit of turning up dead, but on this occasion, as on others, there wasn't enough evidence to charge him. A couple of years later I not only had the pleasure of arresting him for "felon in possession of concealable weapon," but also prosecuted the case against him personally when the DA got weathered in at Juneau.

On this occasion, we got weathered in at Pelican by a big 'Sou'easter' that blew in from the Pacific Ocean. A lot of the fishermen looking for a safe harbor had congregated in Pelican and spent most of their down time in the local bars.

In one of these, Eino Wiirta, a fisherman with some others, was dancing the Limbo. Instead of going under the pole, as he was supposed to, he jumped over it and fractured both the long bones of his leg below the knee.

I was making bar checks and came on the scene moments after the accident. After wrapping the break with bar towels I sent someone to find Dr. Moore, who was using his free time making house calls. Moore, an orthopedic surgeon of considerable reputation, had no difficulty reducing the fractures. He was short on painkillers but recognized that Eino was pretty well anesthetized already. Dr. Moore was worried about complications arising from the injuries and requested that the 180-foot U.S. Coast Guard Buoy Tender Sorrell be sent to transport Wiirta and the three of us back to Sitka.

Winds in the Lisianski Inlet were gusting up to 100 mph and the seas were running 40 feet and more. Our patient was strapped to the wardroom table during the 14-hour trip, and it was a welcome relief to all of us seeing Sitka that night.

In March 1964, just after the Good Friday earthquake, I was promoted to Sergeant and sent to Palmer to head up the Matanuska Valley Detachment, as well as carry out the contract for policing the City of Palmer. In effect, I was Chief of Police for the community.

Dorothy Saxton, the Magistrate, was a wonderful person to work with. A long-time Valley resident, she had been the U.S. Commissioner before Statehood. Dorothy knew everyone in the valley by their first name and tempered mercy with justice and a lot of common sense thrown in. Howard Luther, Ray Rush, Ed Jones, Pete Heddell, Terry Fillingim, and others were assigned to the Valley Detachment and we handled the whole spectrum of problems from murder to stray dogs and cattle rustling.

The Valley became a burial ground during those years, a reputation that it retained. The bodies of a lot of missing spouses were found there in out-of-the way places. Noe Flores, later convicted of multiple murders, used the Valley to bury some of the members of the burglary ring he operated in Anchorage. One member of the gang, who was present when one of the murders took place, came to the conclusion he might be next and turned informant.

Harry 'Mac' McLaughlin and I excavated the remains of two of Flores' victims in the Wasilla area and another by Wolverine Lake on Lazy Mountain. By making use of the principle, "The grass always grows greener over the septic tank," we were able to locate the graves and recover the bodies. Later, of course, Robert Hansen the "Butcher Baker" continued the pattern of burying his numerous murder victims in the Valley.

All the early Troopers will recall that in the lean days of early statehood, we had to do most of the Coroner's work. Not a few bodies had been buried on the beach or at some other inaccessible location, so an Alaska State Police officer's signature appeared as the attending mortician on the death certificate.

Transporting frozen bodies occasionally also required ingenuity, especially getting them into an airplane cabin or automobile. But the expedients that sometimes had to be resorted to are best left for the imagination.

Once I had to transport a man who died from a heart attack in Moose Creek Campground. He had frozen in such a position that he was not suitable for transporting inside the patrol vehicle and was secured to the trunk, covered with blankets for his trip to the funeral home. Unknown to me and the Magistrate who was riding along, the blankets flew off just enough to expose the cadaver with his pants down, and he 'mooned' all the people who happened to see us from Bailey's Hill on into Palmer.

Unquestionably the most bizarre case I ever dealt with began with an individual who wrote a number of no-account counter checks around Anchorage and the Valley area in order to outfit himself for a prospecting trip into the mountains. About the same time, a grave was dug up in the Wasilla cemetery and the body removed from the metal sealer casket in which it had been interred several years earlier.

We apprehended the suspect on the check case, after some resistance, in the Palmer Laundromat. His vehicle was impounded and he was taken to the Palmer PD for interview. After patient questioning, it developed that he was the person who had disinterred the body from the Wasilla cemetery. He also purchased horses, gear, and all the necessary supplies to go prospecting for gold. These had been paid for by his check-writing activities.

He was convinced that all he needed to complete his "outfit" was a "partner" and he found his "partner" by reading the headstones until he located someone who was just about the right age. He intended to mount the cadaver on one of the horses to accompany him in his prospecting venture.

We had a measure of difficulty convincing him to tell us where he had cached his companion. Following his directions, we located the missing cemetery resident behind a berm along the Parks Highway which was in the process of construction. We identified it by means of a tattoo located on one of the cheeks on his backside. He was in a surprisingly good state of preservation.

The body had mummified since Ray Rush recovered it in a drowning accident a few years earlier. I suspect that there might have been some additional bizarre chapters in this man's background, but his ramblings were difficult to follow. API accepted him for a short time but not much was accomplished in the way of psychiatric treatment before he walked away on his own and was never heard from again.

1967 was the Alaska Centennial Year; 100 years had passed since the purchase of Alaska from Russia. It was also the year of the big Fairbanks flood and the renaming of the Alaska State Police under Governor Wally Hickel. The Alaska State Troopers, as they were now known, changed the patrol car colors from dark blue to white and we also got new uniforms, including jodhpurs and riding boots to go along with the new leather gear. The uniforms were impressive, but the boots and jodhpurs didn't last long because they were extremely uncomfortable and impractical to work in.

I had always been active in conducting First Aid training classes for police and volunteer firemen. Regularly faced with the problem of arranging for the transportation of seriously injured persons, I was well aware of the magnitude of the requirement for EMT training that existed in rural Alaska. When, in 1968, I was reassigned once again to Sitka, this time as a member of the Academy Training Staff at Sheldon Jackson College, I hoped it would be possible to begin to address these needs.

We had only a short time to sell our home, load our household goods onto a truck, and drive with our family to catch the ferry at Haines. We moved into the only apartment that was available at the time in Sitka.

I have to stop and reflect at the strength of my wife, Laraine. The uprooting, packing and unpacking, living out of boxes for months, the basement apartments, the isolation, the being at home for hours, and days on end alone, always wondering if she would ever get "that" call; of having a husband who was home very little and who was also married to his job, and having to raise children without the type of support she should have had in nurturing our family. She answered phones, listened to calls of complaint and harassment, yet was always there when I came home, a refuge from the "unreal" world of law enforcement.

The dining room at North Pacific Hall became our main classroom in the new Trooper Academy, and there was a mountain of work to do before our first students began to arrive. Jerry Williams was the Commander and John Monagle Jr., Mike Korhonen, and John Guzllak filled out the staff for the next couple of months. Janie Reeder, our clerk, kept the mountain of paperwork moving.

Busy is the only word that describes the next few years. With Trooper Academies, New Career Training for Native Alaskans, in-service schools and a full blown assault on the task of providing EMT training to all fire and police departments in the state, our time was fully taken up.

Of particular pride to the original Academy staff members is the success that we had in instituting the first Alaska Emergency Medical Technician training program in Alaska. The first Federal Highway Safety funds allocated to Alaska were a miniscule $40,000. We structured a proposal for training 40 volunteer firemen from throughout the state in EMT procedures and convinced Juneau to back the program.

Academy EMT training expanded rapidly, and within seven years, more than 900 EMT technicians from every corner of Alaska were trained at the Academy. At the time, we probably had the best First Care training program in the country. It was a tremendous accomplishment in a short period of time and would be continuing today if it weren't for the fact that the success of Trooper EMT training attracted the envy of the state health bureaucracy.

When Jerry Williams left to attend law school in the spring of 1970, I was promoted to Academy Commander. Terry McConnaughey and Harkey Tew were transferred in to augment the staff, and we continued at the same frenetic pace.

In the fall of 1970, Lowell Parker and I were selected to attend Northwestern University Traffic Institute, and when I returned to Alaska the following spring, Col. M. E. Dankworth asked me to accept an assignment on his Anchorage staff.

The "10 Detachment Plan" was being implemented and much of my time during the next few years would be devoted to drafting new policies and procedures and also acting as Division Review Officer. This assignment kept me travelling much of the time, and I was at Barrow when my 40th birthday came around. Later, Commissioner Burton made me an Inspector and Departmental Review Officer.

All during this period, I continued to maintain my interest in EMT training as well as the Breathalyzer program, and I participated actively in the annual pistol shoot with the Royal Canadian Mounted Police. We made a lot of friends in the RCMP over the years and had some good memories. My personal highpoint was the year I shot back-to-back "possibles" on both the AST and the RCMP courses, using Canadian weapons for the RCMP cycle. Dennis Clark, an excellent RCMP shooter, also shot a "possible" on the RCMP course, but I edged him out with 50 Xs to his 33 in the second round of the competition.

When I retired in September of 1980, twenty years had come and gone. The youngest of our six children was nearly three years old, and finally it appeared that I would be home to help Laraine and also see the children grow up. Working as a Prudhoe Bay security officer for the past 10 years – which involves ample time at home – has allowed me plenty of opportunity to work in my shop and enjoy the Alaska outdoors with my family. There are a lot of stories, anecdotes, and tales of heroic deeds which still remain to be told, and these comprise the real history of a fine organization whose personnel with the help of their spouses have helped make Alaska what it is today.

February 1994

Showing the Flag

Agent Ray Tremblay

Prior to statehood, the U.S. Fish and Wildlife Service was responsible for the management of all fish and game resources in Alaska. Enforcement of the game laws and regulations was delegated to USFWS under the Alaska Game Law created by Congress in 1925.

When I began my career with the Service in 1953, my title was Alaska Enforcement Agent. In Fairbanks at the time we had a total of four agents and two planes, a Piper Pacer and a Gull-Wing Stinson to patrol all the area north of the Alaska Range. We were continuously visiting the villages in our enforcement efforts, developing contacts with all the key people to assist us in our efforts.

The U.S. Marshal's office and the FBI were responsible for enforcing most of the other federal laws throughout the Territory. The Territorial Police provided law enforcement in the major cities and along the road and highway system. We were frequently asked by the U.S. Marshal's office and the FBI for assistance with our aircraft to help locate fugitives and to haul prisoners and bodies from the outlying areas.

My first request for flight assistance from the Territorial Police came from Lieutenant Bill Trafton. Territorial officials had determined it was time to make territorial laws and police known throughout the villages of the Interior. It was in the spring of 1955, and we were flying to all the villages sealing beaver skins. Taking a police officer along posed no problem.

At the time, there was a limit of 10 beaver per trapper. In order for a trapper to sell his skins, he or she had to have them either tagged or sealed. A tagged beaver could be sold locally but had to be sealed before it could be shipped out of the Territory. At the time, over 10,000 beaver skins were being sealed out of the Fairbanks office alone.

Prior to the season, which began on February 1 and ended on March 31, we appointed a beaver tagging officer in each village. Usually this was the postmaster, teacher or some other responsible person. They received 10 cents per skin, payable at the end of the season. Trappers would take their skins to the tagging officer and fill out an affidavit stating the location and dates the beavers were taken. The officer would then put the affidavit in a tagging envelope.

A special string was passed through the rear leg of the beaver skins, then through an eyelet in the envelope and into a leaded seal. The officer would clamp the lead seal with coded pliers and return the skins to the trapper. The trapper was then able to sell his beaver to the local trader or to traveling fur buyers.

Every other week, we would travel around to all the villages where the buyers had tagged beaver ready to be sealed. At times there were as many as 2,000 skins piled up in warehouses.

We would cut the string, remove the affidavit, and list on the top the numbers of the individual seals we placed on the skins. The seal was passed through a leg and then locked in place. They were very similar to box car seals. Once sealed, the buyer could then ship them to fur houses in the states, usually in Seattle.

I agreed to take a police officer on one of our trips in April. Since Lieutenant Trafton wanted to make the proper impression, he picked his biggest officer, Ray Hill, to make the trip. On April 11, I departed Fairbanks in the Gull Wing Stinson on skis — with Ray Hill in full uniform — to make a tour of all the villages down the Yukon River from Tanana to Kaltag and then up the Koyukuk to Bettles.

It was warm, with the snow soft and melting. Most of the winter landing strips were on the river in front of the villages. We had no problems until we arrived in Nulato. The strip on the ice was narrow and, except for the packed-down snow from other planes and activity, there was a considerable amount of overflow moving underneath the deep snow along the edges.

The Gull Wing is a good-size airplane with a radial 300 horsepower Lycoming engine for power. On skis, it was difficult to steer because it did not have a steerable tail ski. In order to get turned around in a narrow place, it was necessary to have the passenger get out and push against the fuselage just ahead of the horizontal stabilizer as the plane moved forward.

This led to a caste system in the Fish and Wildlife Service of blasters and pushers. Best to be the pilot (blaster) and not the pusher, because pushing from behind on the Gull Wing's tail surface with the big Lycoming blasting away was not the best of places to be. In fact, when we went into uniforms for a short period of time, Clarence Rhode, the Regional Director, suggested wings for the lapels of the pilots. The pushers asked for their own insignia of crossed snowshoes on the sleeve with a hash mark for every time the tail of an airplane ran over them.

I explained to Ray the procedure and warned him that if we didn't complete the turn and get back on the packed surface we would be there indefinitely getting the plane out of the overflow. Ray dutifully got out and – with most of the villagers standing on the bank watching – I proceeded to make a turn with my Trooper pushing the tail around. As the turn progressed, I realized it was going to be nip and tuck, so I advanced the throttle all the way to get back in the ski tracks. I knew Ray was in big trouble back there, but felt I had no choice.

Sure enough, Ray could not get away from the tail when the plane surged forward and got wrapped over the horizontal stabilizer. Good thing it was a stout aircraft! When I finally got back on the runway surface, I looked back to see a most disheveled officer limping back in the tracks to retrieve his clip-on tie and whatever else had been blown off his uniform.

I wish there was some way I could describe the guffaws and knee-slapping that was going on up the river bank. I'm sure this is not what Lieutenant Trafton had in mind when he envisioned his hand-picked officer walking into a village for the first time.

Ray rose to the occasion, however, like the real trooper he was. He put his tie back on, straightened out his uniform, put on his Police Stetson, and walked tall up the bank to introduce himself to all the folks. This was the first uniformed officer many had seen and they were dutifully impressed. He held a brief meeting to explain who the Territorial Police were and how they would function in the outlying areas in the future.

I remember a remark from one of the villagers in Nulato as we were departing "He's a big 'un, ain't he!" He sure was, and still is in all ways.

We traveled to all the other villages with no further troubles, gaining recognition for the future State Troopers, and returned to Fairbanks on April 18— mission accomplished.

May 1997

Ray Tremblay came to Alaska in the late 1940s after serving three years in the U.S. Marine Corps during World War II. After spending several years on the Yukon and Tanana Rivers working and running riverboats and fishing and trapping in Interior Alaska, he joined the U.S. Fish and Wildlife Service in January 1953. He served with that agency until April 1978 when he came on board with the Alaska Department of Public Safety in charge of the Aviation Program. Ray retired for the second time in 1983. After retirement from the state, Ray wrote several books including *Trails of an Alaska Trapper* and *Trails of an Alaskan Game Warden*, and also developed a consulting business on outdoor survival training. He passed away on August 23, 2004.

A Split Foot and Duct-Taped Airplane

Agent Ray Tremblay

It must have been the summer of 1957 or 1958 when I was stationed at McGrath as an Enforcement Agent for the U.S. Fish and Wildlife Service.

Another request from Lieutenant Bill Trafton in Fairbanks: would I take Sergeant Emery Chapple to Kaltag to investigate a reported rape case? No problem. When will he arrive in McGrath?

I met Emery's flight and we immediately departed for Kaltag in the Service's Cessna 180 on floats. At Kaltag, I stayed in the background while Emery talked to the girl who had filed a charge of rape against a friend in the village. With great diligence, Emery explained to the girl how serious the charge of rape was and asked her the circumstances.

She said the encounter occurred behind her cabin and she hadn't been intimate with him in the past. Emery was very patient and let her tell her story. After listening to everything she had to say, he suggested that maybe it wasn't rape but just poor timing on the man's part. She finally agreed and said she would drop the charges if the Trooper would talk to the individual involved and make sure he left her alone. Emery complied with her wishes and we departed with everyone friends again. What a negotiator; no wonder he became Commissioner in later years.

We decided to stay at the Vernetti's roadhouse in Koyukuk for the night since it was getting late. The Yukon River was extremely high due to heavy August rains, and there was a great deal of driftwood running in the current. Koyukuk is situated at the junction of the Koyukuk and Yukon Rivers and the drift, which had many uprooted trees and logs, was running nearly bank full in front of the village. After looking it over very carefully we set the floats down where there was the least amount of debris, happy that we had plenty of daylight to help us pick out the right spot.

We enjoyed one of Dominic Vernetti's dinner specialties that evening: spaghetti with homemade sauce and lots of meatballs. Later, we were all sitting around enjoying a good bull session when a villager was brought into the store, a man who had split his foot open with an ax. It was a nasty wound, and we agreed he would have to go to a doctor or at least a nurse with suturing capabilities.

That meant a trip to Galena. Here it was getting dark and we would have to take off and land in the debris-choked river. Not the most pleasant way to end the day.

We taxied around in the drift and finally found a place to make a take-off. I radioed to Galena for assistance. We landed on the opposite side of the village where there wasn't any driftwood and taxied across to the riverbank (dodging the floating debris), where there was a vehicle waiting for the patient.

By now, it was very dark. We taxied back across to the clear area and took off. So far, so good. Now, all we had to do was land in the Koyukuk and miss all the logs waiting for us. As I recall, we made a couple of passes using the landing light to check the drift.

Again, we were able to make a successful landing without hitting anything big enough to do any damage. We tailed the floats on the bank in front of the store and tied the plane up with the assistance of the villagers that were watching. If we were pleased with the first landing earlier in the evening, we were now elated with our good fortune. It was two happy campers that went to bed that night.

The next morning we said our goodbyes and accepted the thanks of the family of the young man we had taken to Galena. After warming up the engine, I added power to slide off the bank and taxi out for take-off. The plane immediately tilted to my side and the left float started to go underwater. A hasty turn and we were back to the bank wondering what was wrong.

We had a large hole in the float that wasn't there the night before, and wondered how that happened. The culprit was an old engine block that had been thrown over the riverbank to help stabilize the embankment from erosion. In the dark, we hadn't seen it and had set the float down on the block, which was hidden underwater.

Fortunately, there were several men on the bank willing to help. We were able to pull the plane's float out of the water and up on a log to get at the tear, which was quite large.

Good old duct tape! We laid a patch inside and out, using up most of a roll of the great stuff, and decided it would hold long enough for a take-off. Sure enough, it worked, although we took on more water than I wanted before we were airborne. Knowing we would only be able to make one landing, we loaded up on gas in order to make a direct flight to Anchorage. We landed at Lake Hood where the mechanics at the FWS hangar were waiting for us. The plane was taken out on a dolly and into the hangar for permanent repairs.

Emery took a commercial flight back to Fairbanks and two days later, I returned to McGrath with a new float on the port side of the aircraft.

I sent in my report to headquarters in Juneau. The reply was something to the affect that while we were very willing to assist the State Police with their efforts in the Bush, it could be damn expensive at times!!! Were these the good ol' days or what!

November 1997

The Shrunken Trophy

Agent Ray Tremblay

Who among you old-timers can't remember being "had" by Walt Sinn, that fun guy of the old Territorial days? I think Walt was a Trooper; at least he had a uniform, badge, gun, and a patrol vehicle, which were the prerequisites.

The reason I have a problem knowing exactly what he did was that most any time I patrolled the Big Delta-Tok area for game violators in the winter I would run into Walt running his trapline from a patrol car. In the trunk was an assortment of traps and snares and any fur he happened to pick up that day. Talk about subsidized trapping!

He always assured me that everything he did was legal. I thought that someday I would catch him doing something nefarious, however I was dealing with a master and he covered his tracks better than the famous "Rat River Trapper," who defied the entire RCMP of the Yukon Territory in 1932.

Probably the only person that knew how he conducted his activities was Gene Morris, the Trooper at Big Delta. But then, Gene also ran a trapline from a patrol car so he wasn't much help. I'm sure they had some kind of "Trooper trapper" code of honor.

Walt was finally transferred to Point Barrow. My troubles were over, right? Wrong! He now became the great white hunter, killing polar bears, including knocking one out with the tail of an airplane. Ask him about that one at the next gathering. Seems like he and the pilot had to use wire to hold the stabilizer together to get back to town.

My next encounter with my friend Walt was at Point Lay. I was on a patrol along the Arctic Coast with Agent Stan Fredrickson. Walt was in the village conducting an investigation of a break-in at the local Post Office.

After Stan and I conducted a meeting with the villagers, we stayed overnight with the teachers and shared some Scotch we had brought along. The next morning, Walt requested a ride back to Point Barrow with us in the Cessna 180 to check for polar bears along the way. This posed a problem since the rear of the plane was full of wing covers, engine cover, fire pots, and emergency gear, plus our own baggage. "No problem", said Walt. He would send some of the gear to Barrow on the mail plane that was just landing.

This seemed okay, so we proceeded along the coast, checking bear activity. It was okay until we arrived at Barrow and found out we had to pay freight on our baggage in order to have the privilege of taking Walt and his personal gear home. What a guy!

He then proposed that we take our baggage to his house for lunch and a 'short one" before we checked into the hotel. Sounded okay, again. We were slow learners.

At his house, he poured each one of us a Scotch and water. Nice guy, I thought, and obviously knows what brand of Scotch to keep on hand. When we opened our bags at the hotel, we realized why it had taken him so long to pour the drinks. They were from our bottle that we had shared with him the night before! He had to go through all our luggage to locate the Scotch.

Then, in Fairbanks years later, things finally went my way. Walt had killed a large grizzly that he felt would go into the record book, and asked if I would take the skull to the University "bug cage." These special bugs were used to clean the meat and cartilage from the skulls and other bones of critters being studied by biologists. The method took time, but was preferred over boiling to remove gristle and other tissue, because it didn't damage the skulls.

I prevailed with the powers that be at the museum and Walt's trophy was placed in the cage. After several months, I was told it was ready, and I advised Walt. Deciding that this trophy needed to be shared with friends, he invited a group to his house on the afternoon I delivered the bear skull.

This was the golden opportunity I had waited for all these years. I arrived at the gathering with a large box as Walt was entertaining everyone with the story of the bear hunt. He proudly placed the box on the table and opened it for everyone to observe and to receive the accolades he felt were forthcoming. When he brought out the skull, it turned out to be the smallest bear skull on record, a newborn cub. Never did I witness Walt at a loss for words, but there he was, holding up this miniature skull, his lips moving but nothing coming out. I assured him that this occurred at times when the bugs got really hungry. I let him cry for a while and then felt sorry for him. I brought in his real trophy. Tears turned to laughter and everyone there agreed that maybe he really did have a tender side after all.

So ended the story of Walt and the shrunken bear head. We shared many laughs and stories since, and he has told me he still considers me a friend, but then, you know Walt!

February 1999

Justice Without the Law-the First Murder Trial in Alaska

Lieutenant Gerald O. "Jerry" Williams, Retired

On August 21st 1992, the Alaska Court of Appeals affirmed the murder conviction and life sentence of Fairbanks resident Michael Alexander. A young Fairbanks High School student was the victim in this kidnap/murder that occurred in March 1987.

Trooper investigators who arrested Alexander developed the evidence used at the trial relying heavily on blood, hair, fiber, and other trace evidence to link him to the crime scene and body of the murdered girl.

Sergeant Jim McCann, the principal investigator, testified to the importance of trace evidence transferred to and from the crime scene. The scientific proof was introduced by FBI laboratory technicians, who were experts in serology, hairs, and fibers.

The jury, convinced by this circumstantial evidence, subsequently rejected the defendant's contrived alibi and convicted him of kidnapping and first-degree murder. If you read the decision, it is evident that even the court was impressed with the thoroughness of the Troopers' crime-scene examination, and the case is a good example of the remarkable progress made by Alaska's justice institutions.

It is a far cry from an earlier time, within the memory of many of us, when law enforcement organizations relied primarily upon confessions and felt that both the public and the courts were watching too much TV when they expected police agencies to utilize scientific crime investigation techniques.

The changes that have occurred in the 100 years that have passed since the first murder trial was conducted in Alaska are even more noteworthy because Alaska started from ground zero. A total absence of law, as well as law enforcement, characterized the history of Alaska during the first 17 years of United States rule over the territory. And the situation did not improve markedly during the next 16 years. Alaska was a frontier area much less endowed, even in terms of the pioneer settlements of the West, with the minimum attributes of law and order. Murder and other crimes occurred, and the criminals often remained unsought, unapprehended, and their crimes unpunished.

In 1880, a Revenue Marine Officer who visited St. Michaels reported the murder of two white traders on the Yukon River. He observed that "the guilty parties are still at large... they are well known, and can be easily reached. I believe that they would be readily given up should an officer of the Government go and make a demand for them."

A year later he remarked that still no effort had been made to affect their apprehension. At the time, there wasn't a single law enforcement officer in the entire 500,000 square miles of Alaska and the nearest judge was 3,500 miles away in Portland, Oregon. A major complicating factor in Alaska was the absence of means of communication and transportation, even by the primitive standards of the 19th Century.

The skippers of the revenue cutters that patrolled the Bering Sea were primarily concerned with protecting the fur seals from Canadian poachers as well as accompanying the whaling fleet in its annual voyage to the Arctic. But they were frequently called upon to act as peace officers and even administer a rough form of justice. To do this, they relied upon the extra-legal force that they possessed, in the form of the armed vessels under their command, and their own forceful personality.

Captain Mike Healy was one of the best-known of these early officers. As the only representative of the United States government north of Unalaska, Healy felt he had an obligation to protect life and property. The law and order afforded by Healy and his vessel, the famous Bear, was essential to the security of thousands of Native and white inhabitants along the coastline of Western and Northern Alaska.

When crimes were committed on the whalers, Healy arrested the miscreants and took them onto the Bear, where he either confined them or put them to work. At the end of the voyage they were usually set ashore in San Francisco without being prosecuted. Sheldon Jackson, the pioneer Presbyterian missionary, was a passenger on the Bear in 1890 when a prisoner was brought aboard after the nearly fatal knifing of an officer on one of the whalers. Jackson remarked that "When the ship arrives in San Francisco, the man can go ashore a free man."

Some years later it became customary to appoint the revenue cutter commanders as U.S. Commissioners to support their actions with a modicum of judicial authority, a practice that was continued until the advent of World War II.

Strange as it may seem, a person charged with a crime in Alaska during the first 14 years under the American flag couldn't legally be charged, tried or convicted of committing a crime.

When Alaska was first transferred to U.S. jurisdiction from Russia, it was assumed that the only law that was needed to govern the new possession was provided in the "Trading with the Indians Act of 1826." This federal statute gave the Army authority to control commerce, make arrests for criminal offenses, and in some cases allowed trials to be held before military courts.

Secretary of State William H. Seward thought this statute was sufficient, and Congress wasn't much interested in passing any more laws for an "icebox" in any event. But even the limited authority the Army thought was provided by the 1826 Act proved illusory when U.S. Territorial Judge Matthew Deady, in Portland, ruled that the 1826 Act didn't apply to Alaska unless Congress specifically extended it to the District.

The upshot was that a whole series of earlier convictions were overturned, including several for murder, and the Army officers involved were sued, successfully, for false arrest. By 1879, the Army was more than happy to get out from under the burden of administering justice and keeping order in Alaska.

When the Nez Perce Indian War broke out in 1877, they pulled up stakes and ordered the Alaska garrison of 52 soldiers south. All that was left was the collector of customs at Sitka who tried to organize a militia among the white shopkeepers to keep some kind of order.

The U.S. Navy was forced to fill the gap between 1879 and 1884, after the embarrassment that followed when residents of Sitka appealed for protection from the British Navy at Victoria, because "their own government had deserted them."

The Navy governors who ruled Alaska from 1879 to 1884 also complained about the absence of laws or courts. An attempted murder occurred at Sitka shortly after Commander Lester Beardslee arrived with the U.S.S. Jamestown, in 1879. A board of naval officers recommended that the suspect be sent to Portland, Oregon for trial. At Portland he was indicted, but the case was dismissed on the grounds that no code of criminal laws had been enacted for Alaska, and there was no federal statute under which the offense could be prosecuted.

Judge Deady in delivering his opinion observed: "By this ruling the defendant will escape punishment for what appears to have been an atrocious crime, but the court cannot inflict punishment where the law does not so provide."

Drunks and minor miscreants were easily dealt with by the Naval governors, who customarily sentenced them to terms in the Sitka Guardhouse or put them to work on chain gangs repairing the streets of Sitka, Juneau, or Wrangell. They were in a quandary however, when more serious crimes were involved.

In May 1880, Commander Beardslee requested instructions from the Navy Secretary concerning the disposition of two felony prisoners that had been confined in the Sitka Guardhouse for a long period of time. There is no record that he received a reply. The Navy Department expected not to be asked for answers to unanswerable questions. Thereafter, felons were usually released upon the appointment of each succeeding Naval governor and told to "get out of the territory."

While both the revenue cutter officers to the westward and the naval officers in S.E. Alaska felt they could in good conscience punish misdemeanor behavior, they hesitated to inflict punishment for serious crimes even when these involved only Natives, whose standing was lower than whites. They frequently resorted to "customary justice" or allowed it to take its course.

In most instances Captain Healy found crimes among the Eskimos and Indians were settled by revenge or restitution, and once the balance had been righted, there was little that civilized forms of justice could contribute. This precedent was firmly established as the tenuous rule of the United States government made its fitful progress.

A typical incident occurred at Sitka in August 1880. An Indian killed another who had committed adultery with his wife. The slain man's brother took revenge by killing the murderer. Under Indian law, the families were even, and the Naval governor allowed the situation to stand. Restitution in the form of blankets for assault, or even murder, came to be an accepted practice. Captain Beardslee, at one point, explained the basis for his action:

[Until] Congress sees fit to furnish a substitute I am compelled to recognize the only law of this country—the Indian law, founded on the old Mosaic—and when a murder among themselves is fully atoned for, according to their ideas, either by death of the murderer or payment for the life, and I am ensured that all parties are satisfied, and no further troubles will spring up, to do as I did in this case, lecture the criminals and let them go.

Both the revenue cutter skippers and the Naval governors occasionally rounded up drifters, drunks, and petty criminals and shipped them south. Although authority of law, it was evident quite early in Alaska's experience that a large group of destitute white men, in a lonely Arctic post or shoreline community, could constitute a danger to the few inhabitants trying to eke out a living in the harsh environment.

At Nome, in the late fall, the Deputy Marshals in that booming gold rush community, aided by soldiers from the nearby military post, rounded up the drifters, prostitutes, gamblers, and vagrants, and "blue ticketed" them out on the last departing passenger steamer. The "blue ticket" was a practice still followed by police chiefs in S.E. Alaska communities until the early 1950's.

It was with considerable relief that the Navy, in 1884, welcomed the first Territorial District Judge and District Attorney, newly appointed to posts created under Alaska's First Organic Act. At the same time, Congress also extended the Laws of the Territory of Oregon to Alaska, "insofar as they are applicable."

But even this two-man team of officers, assigned to stamp out crime in Alaska, found something was lacking. The huge expanse of the territory and the almost utter absence of transportation made it difficult for the new justice system to function very effectively.

The impediments to effective law and order were summarized in an observation by a long-time resident reported in the *Sitka Sentinel* in 1890.

...A murder is committed at Kodiak. A month or two later a sailing vessel arrives. The murder is reported, and on its return to San Francisco, word is sent to the deputy marshal at Unalaska, also by sailing vessel, or possibly a revenue cutter, or steamer of the Alaska Commercial Company, which makes semi-annual trips. He then reports to his chief at Sitka, via San Francisco, and if the vessels are not lost in the course of a year or so, he may get a warrant for the arrest of the malefactor. If he is in haste to arrest him, he will take the first vessel for San Francisco, thence to Kodiak - as this is the shortest and usually the only route between the ports. If he is lucky enough to find the man still alive, he will arrest him; and by this time the last vessel for the season having probably sailed, he and his prisoner will wait quietly another six months, when by schooner and steamer by way of San Francisco and Puget Sound, prisoner and marshal may arrive at Sitka to find that in the change of administration the case [has been] forgotten, and the deputy marshal salted for all his expenses.

The difficulty of transporting witnesses was one of the problems involved in the first prosecution of a white man charged with murder in Alaska. The man was Frank Fuller, and his victim was Charles John Seghers, Catholic Bishop of British Columbia and Alaska. There were in fact an unusual number of churchmen who met a violent death in Alaska during the late 1880s and 1890s, and the New York Times pointed out that with three missionaries murdered, "Alaska presented a state of affairs which was comparable to the worst incidents in darkest Africa."

The Presbyterians under the energetic Sheldon Jackson had more or less dictated a division of missionary areas in Alaska and the Catholics had drawn the lower reaches of the Yukon River. Bishop Seghers was anxious to establish a chain of missions in this area beginning at Nulato. Early in 1886 the bishop and Fuller, a Canadian Catholic layman who volunteered to accompany the expedition, and two Jesuit priests, entered the Yukon Territory via the Chilkoot Pass on a journey to scout locations for the new missions. Fuller began exhibiting paranoid symptoms very early in the trip and the two priests tried unsuccessfully to convince Seghers to leave him behind.

Early in September the Jesuits wanted to establish a winter camp, but Seghers was anxious to push on to Nulato, and insisted on having Fuller accompany him. Segher's diary recorded Fuller's increasingly bizarre behavior, and the bishop's certainty that he had a sick man on his hands. On the morning of November 28, Fuller fired a single shot into Segher's back, killing him instantly. The two indians who accompanied them tried to wrest the rifle from Fuller, but he resisted and they finally gave up. They pushed on to Nulato, leaving the bishop's body where it had fallen. Later a party from Nulato recovered it.

A few days before Christmas, Fuller arrived at St. Michaels, in the company of a Nulato trader, with Bishop Seghers body. Fuller admitted to the Alaska Commercial Co. agent that he killed the bishop, but gave no reason. He roamed at large, a prisoner of the geography, until the Jesuit priests arrived on June 20th. One took passage for Unalaska to search for the revenue cutter and returned with Captain Healy and the Bear to take Fuller into custody.

Fuller waved to the bystanders on shore as he was transported in manacles out to the cutter. Bishop Segher's murderer didn't display any overt signs of his insanity to the Revenue Marine officers while in their custody, but later accused them of attempting to drive him to commit suicide.

Fuller's murder trial was convened at Sitka in November, 1887. His court-appointed attorney was convinced his client was insane and felt confident he could convince the jury. During the trial, Fuller acted irrationally, occasionally standing to interrupt the proceedings. Testifying himself, he changed his story from what he had originally admitted was an intentional shooting. Now he claimed it was the result of an accident while defending himself from an attack by one of the Indians.

A local physician testified that in his opinion Fuller was insane. The jury was confused and probably irritated as well. There was no autopsy, and testimony was in conflict regarding where the bishop had been struck by Fuller's bullet. Only one of the Indian witnesses was brought to Sitka for the trial, and his account was sketchy and uncertain. Judge Lafayette Dawson was compelled to explain that the cost of transporting additional witnesses, who would have had to come via San Francisco by commercial steamer, would have been prohibitive.

After nineteen hours of deliberation and 40 ballots, the jury was still undecided. A minority held out for murder and the death penalty, a majority for not guilty by reason of insanity. The jury asked Judge Lafayette Dawson for additional instructions and he informed them that they could return a verdict of manslaughter if they found he did not intend to kill Seghers. This compromise was chosen.

Although his sanity was doubted, no one wanted him to go free, and a manslaughter verdict would send him to prison. At his sentencing, Fuller insisted he was innocent and even suggested that the Catholic Bishop had died of "natural causes." Judge Dawson told Fuller to count his blessings because the jury had been merciful.

The lack of transportation support for law enforcement was one of the greatest shortcomings of the Alaska justice system. The Navy tried to rectify this by stationing the armed tugboat U.S.S. Pinta at Sitka, but the vessel was incapable of operating on the open waters of the Gulf of Alaska. After the murder of a missionary-teacher at Kake in 1892, the Secretary of the Interior concluded that Alaska's greatest single need was law and order. He addressed a memo to the President suggesting more judicial officers be appointed and vessels be provided for the transportation of the handful of Deputy Marshals.

> [We must] immediately establish through the Governor, the power to appoint Justices of the Peace, Constables, and confer sufficient jurisdiction to adjudicate offenses... supported by a seaworthy vessel, if not two, manned by experienced officers to be selected by the Governor... The whole community should be compelled to recognize without delay the existence of a superior and formidable power to preserve the peace and advance the welfare of that country.

No action was taken then, or later, as successive governors pleaded for a vessel to serve the law enforcement needs of Alaska. In 1899, Governor John Brady, testified before the U.S. Senate Committee on Territories that: "If all of (Admiral) Dewey's fleet were up there they could not keep order."

The colonial-style justice system of Alaska in its early days lacked manpower, machinery, and resources to function effectively over such great distances and among such widely dispersed communities. This lack of law enforcement probably impeded the territory's development until well into the 20th Century. Alaskans were also slow to develop their own institutions and continued to rely on the penurious allocations made by the federal government. Whatever excesses of authority Mike Healy and the early Navy governors may have been guilty of, their actions seemed to have been justified in retrospect.

December 1992

Gerard O Williams graduated from Washington State

University with a B.S. in Police Administration in 1950. He worked a short time as a police officer in Washington State then joined the Alaska Territorial Police in 1953 attending Academy Class # 1 in January of 1954. He wrote Alaska's first Safety Responsibility Law and in 1963 graduated from Northwestern University as a Kemper Insurance Fellowship Student. After 18 years with the Alaska State Police he returned to college and graduated from Willamette Law School in 1972. He returned to Alaska and worked as a District Court Judge for 10 years. In 1987 he returned to Oregon and earned a Masters Degree in History from the University of Oregon . He was a prolific writer on all aspects of law enforcement history and, among those writings he was author of the 50-year history of the Alaska State Troopers. He passed away in July of 2001.

The Short Violent Life of Gary Zieger

Lieutenant Gerald O. "Jerry" Williams, Retired

NOTE: Johnny's Girl by Kim Rich, a story of the Anchorage Underworld in the 1970's, has been a bestseller in Alaska. Earlier this year, local night club owner Jimmy Sumpter died, and both events have caused old time Alaska coppers to reminisce about the crime story surrounding the career of Gary Zieger. The following is a reconstruction based primarily upon interviews.

Soldotna resident Bill Stock was enroute to Anchorage approaching Potter shortly before 10 p.m. on November 28th, 1973, when he observed what appeared to be the body of a man sprawled in the middle of the highway. After confirming the man was dead, Stock drove to Rabbit Creek Lodge to report his discovery. When Troopers Brad Brown and Drew Rotermund reached the scene, it took only a moment to confirm the identification. It was Gary Zieger, and the gaping hole in his chest was made at close range by a shotgun.

Joe Hoffbeck, involved in several of the murder investigations Zieger was implicated in, lived on Rabbit Creek Road. He was the first CIB man to reach the scene. Hoffbeck recalls, "Zieger's body was still warm. There was a large pool of blood on the road not far from where he was lying, and more blood on the bottom of his shoes, as well as that big hole in his chest and handcuff marks on his wrists.

Our biggest headache was trying to work the crime scene in the middle of the road. I remember radio and television personality Herb Shaindlin coming by and leaning out of the window of his car snapping pictures of the body as we motioned him on by."

The execution-style death on the highway ended the story of one of Alaska's most brutal killers. Zieger, only 20 years of age when he died, one of four children, was born and raised in Anchorage and lived there all his life. He frequented the party spots and ran with a fast, hard crowd, and was as fast and hard as any of them. Working in construction as a heavy equipment operator, he wasn't known to be employed or even have a permanent address at the time of his death. Zieger was suspected of having participated in at least seven murders; several were executions, the same as his own ending.

Retired Major Walter Gilmour, then a Sergeant assigned to CIB, recalls his first encounter with Zieger several years earlier: "Zieger and a friend, James Batie, killed an Indian boy named George Nudlasch by shooting him nine times with a .22 and then cutting his throat. They picked him up hiking along Northern Lights Blvd. near the old Woodland Park Apartments and killed him when he refused to perform oral sodomy on Zieger."

Zieger and Batie buried Nudlasch's body at the old Borough car dump near the airport, but Batie bragged about the murder to friends who later reported the location to the Troopers. Batie copped a plea and served a year for manslaughter, Gilmour recalls, "but Zieger never gave us the time of day, and Batie was much too afraid of him to involve him in the murder." As a result Zieger was never prosecuted.

A couple of years later, in 1972, Zieger turned up again during the investigation of the murder of Zingre 'ZeZe' Mason. ZeZe, as she was known to her friends, was an attractive 20-year-old who lived with her parents in the Sand Lake area. Last seen leaving her home on August 22nd, her body was discovered six days later, on the 28th, by children playing in a gravel pit near Kincaid and Sand Lake Road.

The body was completely desanguinated from multiple knife wounds in the chest. There was no evidence of rape and the autopsy conducted by Dr. D.R. Rogers indicated that she had died within 48 hours of the time her body was discovered. Suspicion immediately centered on her boyfriend, a hippie type, because of the unexplained four-day time interval between her last being seen and the discovery of the body.

C.J. Cedarborg, a former Army explosives expert assigned to Anchorage CIB, helped conduct the crime scene search. Near the body, he discovered an unusual set of truck tire tracks. The tires were a heavy industrial type, with lugs on the outside, but the right front tire was mounted with the lugs on the inside making the marks distinctive. Cedarborg proceeded to widen his search and found similar tracks a mile or so distant in another part of the gravel pit.

Except for the tire tracks, other clues were scarce. It was suspected that the murder occurred at another location and the body had been transported to where it was found. The investigation team headed by Don Church consisted of Gilmour, Joe Hoffbeck, and Mark Troutman.

A neighborhood canvass didn't turn up anything except a truck driver who was delivering asphalt for the paving of the Minnesota Bypass and recalled seeing a girl meeting 'ZeZe' Mason's description walking beside the road the day she disappeared.

She was observed getting into a pickup truck with two young men. He saw the same pickup in the gravel pit on a return trip. Since the sighting occurred on August 22nd, the information seemed a slender lead, indeed, at the time.

The investigation was going nowhere when Gilmour received an unusual telephone call on September 1st. It was from a young lady who refused to identify herself, but accused the Troopers of harassing her boyfriend. The accusation evidently grew out of the murder investigation.

She gave her boyfriend's name only as 'Ralph,' which didn't strike a bell with Gilmour. When his anonymous caller was asked why she thought they were hassling Ralph, she replied, "Because he was in the truck when ZeZe was picked up."

"If you mean on August 22nd, we don't have any problem with that," Gilmour answered, "because the murder didn't occur until almost a week later." Gilmour tried to tell her that she could quit worrying. But then it struck me. Did we miss something? And I asked, "How can you be so sure Ralph wasn't involved?" She replied, "Because he got out of the pickup at the fire station and left Gary Zieger with the girl."

This was the first time Zieger had come up in the investigation. A quick check revealed Zieger drove a light colored four-wheel-drive pickup, and later Gilmour located a friend of Zieger who worked in a tire shop and admitted mounting four stolen tires on Zieger's truck. In the process he put the right front tire on backwards, corresponding with the marks found in the gravel pit.

At the crime scene a large quantity of blood was discovered to have soaked into the sand under the body. It began to look as though the girl might have been murdered in the gravel pit, and her body not just dumped there. Dr. Rogers also reviewed his findings and concluded that death could have occurred several days earlier than his first estimate. The fresh appearance of the body could have been attributable to unseasonably low night temperatures and the blood loss.

Although Colonel Ed Dankworth suggested employment of a local clairvoyant, the investigation followed a more conventional course and a search warrant was obtained. Zieger's car was seized, dismantled and examined with the help of laboratory technician Charles O. King.

The inspection, Hoffbeck recalls, took place in Dankworth's garage, "because that was where all of our equipment was located." The pickup was extraordinarily clean, but human bloodstains were found under the floor covering, and behind the handle and panel of the right passenger door.

On September 2nd, Zieger was arrested and charged with murder. There was no evidence of rape, and no discernible motive. Zieger himself was characterized as sexually dysfunctional.

The prosecution case was based exclusively on circumstantial evidence, with more than 210 individual items, photographs, casts and lab reports. As Hoffbeck recalls, "I thought it was a strong case, and we did some innovative things.

Zieger was working in the area, which accounted for his tire tracks, so we had to establish the relative recentness of the marks found near the body. For this we enlisted the assistance of university botanists and geologists. We also found what could have been the murder weapon in Zieger's car, an unusually sharp, double-bladed dagger. But the evidence of blood traces was too slight to be very helpful."

The Public Defender representing Zieger obtained a change of venue to Kodiak, and the trial commenced there in the middle of January, 1973.

Prior to this, a series of stories under the byline of Howard Weaver, a young cub reporter, appeared in the Anchorage Daily News suggesting that the Trooper theory of the murder had changed since Zieger's arrest. The stories tracked closely with the argument of his lawyers that the case was "weak and circumstantial," and the investigators acted in haste to make an arrest because of public pressure to solve the murder. Weaver pointed in particular to the modified autopsy report prepared by Dr. Rogers. Zieger's youthful appearance also belied the claim by Asst. District Attorney Bill Mackey that Zieger was in fact a "cold-blooded killer."

Gilmour was on the witness stand when defense attorney Phil Weidner, participating in one of his first criminal trials, objected to the Trooper investigator characterizing a rock found at the scene as "blood-stained."

"Rephrase your answer then, Trooper," said Mackey. Gilmour replied, "The rock was covered with a sticky, gelatinous, red-colored, blood-like material."

But it was during the cross-examination of the prosecution witnesses that the case began to fall apart. The laboratory technician who testified the blood he found was human was asked if it was correct that the test would also prove positive for non-human blood. The answer was 'yes,' but the technician wasn't allowed to explain that only higher primate blood (chimps and monkeys) would give the same reaction.

An FBI technician who matched Zieger's tires with a cast made at the crime scene got confused. If the vehicle backed up, the pattern would be reversed. Mackey recalls the incident. "It was a 100 percent circumstantial case, but a good one. I prepared a diagram for the FBI expert to use and asked him to draw the tire tracks and direction of travel. When he was finished, it didn't look right. It was backwards, so I asked if he was sure of this, and he said he was.

The jury was having difficulty following the testimony and one juror stood up and said, 'I'm a trucker, and if you want to know the right answer, I can tell you that the outside radius always follows the direction of travel.' I think we lost the case at that point," Mackey remembers. "All of our evidence was circumstantial, and if we were wrong on this issue, we could be wrong on a lot of others as well." The end result was an acquittal for Zieger.

Hoffbeck recalls they had a problem getting convictions in cases tried before Kodiak juries. "We lost the case of Wesley Ladd's murder of Ferris Rezk in Cindy's Massage Parlor because the jurors believed Boyko's ludicrous story of a sinister hand with a gun, reaching out from behind a curtain to shoot Rezk. They ignored the testimony of two eyewitnesses and chose to believe a fantasy world picture of an organized crime plot to dominate the Anchorage underworld.

With Zieger, the jury could never bring themselves to believe this clean-cut-appearing 20-year-old really was a dangerous psychopath."

Hoffbeck, who first encountered Gary Zieger during the Nudlasch investigation, described him "as the most cold-blooded individual I ever met... There was nothing warm or human about him. He was devoid of any personality- just hollow."

Zieger returned to Anchorage to demand the return of his pickup which was still in its dismantled condition. His picture standing alongside the vehicle was published on the front page of the Daily News with a caption intimating that law enforcement officers were "picking on him."

Having confronted the system and beaten it, Zieger became bolder. Even before the chain of events that led 10 months later to his body being left on the Seward Highway, he burglarized an explosives warehouse in Cordova and committed at least one murder for which there is conclusive evidence.

He is suspected of two more, that of a young woman whose frozen, naked body was found in McHugh Park as well as the owner of the construction firm that employed him – and testified on his behalf during the Kodiak trial.

Jimmy Sumpter had owned bars and nightclubs in the Anchorage area since the late 1940's. He ran the Last Chance on Post Road behind the old Territorial Police Headquarters on E. 5th Ave. before it was destroyed by the 1964 earthquake. It was his practice to make the rounds of his clubs early in the morning hours to pick up the day's receipts, and usually he left his home on Greenland Drive in Spenard about 2 a.m.

This Monday morning November 28th, 1973, the temperature was hovering at 10 below when Sumpter walked out to his car enroute to his two clubs, the Kit Kat on the Old Seward Highway and the Sportsman's Too Club on Muldoon.

He noticed the front gate was standing open. Glancing around, Sumpter saw fresh tracks in the snow and would tell investigators later that it looked like someone had been prowling around the house, but that he wasn't unduly concerned because he expected to be back within an hour. He was also sure the house in which his wife Marguerite, 40, his stepdaughter Jody Justice, 16, and his stepson Michael Merck, 13 were, was securely locked.

Sumpter made his calls, stopping off at the Pancake Palace for a cup of coffee before starting home. Enroute he was passed by Anchorage fire trucks responding to the area where his home was located. When Sumpter turned onto Greenland, he realized they were stopping at his house.

Police officers were already at the scene, and Sumpter could see his house was on fire with the flames centered on the master bedroom. When firemen were able to enter the house they found two bodies, Sumpter's wife in the upstairs bedroom, and his stepson in the basement. The stepdaughter was located in a nearby neighbor's home. Preliminary indications were that both victims died from gunshot wounds to the head.

Sumpter's stepdaughter was able to help reconstruct the tragedy. Asleep in her bedroom on the first floor, she was awakened by a series of gunshots at approximately 2:30 a.m. Managing to escape out the front door, she ran around the side of the house and kicked in the window of her younger brother's basement bedroom, lacerating her leg in the process.

Finding his lifeless body on the bed, she climbed out again and ran next door. Money and jewelry valued at $20,000 was missing from the upstairs bedroom where the fire was started in a clothes closet.

Sumpter at first told Anchorage detectives assigned to the investigation that he thought the murders were tied to trouble he was having with the Brothers, a motorcycle gang that was trying to take over the prostitution and drug business in Anchorage. Sumpter's problems with the Brothers centered around the Kit Kat Club.

He claimed this involved extortion of protection money, repeated disturbances and destruction of club furnishings, as well as vandalizing customers' cars and other acts. "They have succeeded in taking over other clubs, but not mine," Sumpter said. "But my wife and son had nothing to do with my business activities," he added. "In all the years I have been in business in Anchorage I have never let my wife visit my nightclubs."

"The people who have been trying to take over my club are no good. They are involved in drugs, robberies, pimping. They're dirt."

"Those who killed my wife and son and burned my home did so because they didn't want any witnesses. They stole some money and jewelry. But those things don't count. It was my wife and son who meant everything to me. But human life doesn't mean anything to them," Sumpter declared.

Retired Trooper Colonel Tom Anderson, CIB commander at the time, recalls that, "it was an interesting period. The pipeline was getting ready to start up, and a lot of new faces were appearing in Anchorage. Johnny Rich disappeared a couple of months earlier — we were sure he'd been murdered. The Brothers moved in to take over prostitution and drugs, and for the next couple of years they were a major headache. It's not unreasonable for Sumpter to have suspected them. He was stubborn and wouldn't roll over and play dead for the Brothers or anyone else."

Walt Gilmour was patrol supervisor and on duty when he was informed of the Sumpter murders. His immediate suspicion, he recalls, was that Gary Zieger did it. "I had no reason in particular. It was mostly because I didn't like him and thought he was capable of just about anything." Talking with APD detectives at the scene, Gilmour noticed someone was watching them from the house across the street. It had been checked earlier, but there was no response from the occupants.

With APD detective Ron Rice, the two walked over and knocked on the door, which was opened by an elderly woman who admitted she had not answered when other officers had come by earlier. Replying to Gilmour's questions, she said she heard a car drive up the street that morning and park beyond the Sumpter residence. It was a pickup with a camper on the back. Later, at approximately 2:30 am, it started up and sped away, almost careening into another neighbor's fence. She had written down the license plate number.

The previous evening while Trooper John Myers was taking his wife to the movies he noticed Gary Zieger at a gas pump filling the tank of a pickup truck with a camper on the back. It was a vehicle Zieger hadn't been seen driving before, so Myers wrote the number down. Zieger had made threats against several police officers, Gilmour for one, and Myers called him to relay the plate number and vehicle description. It corresponded with the license plate on the truck seen parked outside the Sumpter residence.

After he was acquitted of the Zingre Mason murder at Kodiak in January, Zieger went back to work for his former employer, Arctic Pipelines, in Cordova. On June 28th, Don Church took a call from the Trooper stationed in Cordova informing him that a large quantity of explosives was stolen in the burglary of a warehouse there. Zieger was a suspect and left the same evening with his vehicle on the ferry to Valdez. Church didn't tell anyone else, but headed straight for the Valley to intercept Zieger's pickup truck with the stolen explosives. Later, Zieger boasted that he intended to use the explosives to blow up the Trooper offices behind the Sears Mall.

Church was no longer in charge of CIB Major Crimes at the time of the Sumpter killings. "Some think," Hoffbeck says, "that Church had a hang-up on seeing Zieger behind bars. I think it was more likely that he was uncomfortable with any case not being solved." Bill Mackey took on the task of prosecuting Zieger for the theft of the explosives and vividly recalls the Fairbanks trial. While it was in progress, Mackey received word that Wesley Ladd and Benny Ramey had come to town, and the rumor was that if Zieger was convicted they would attempt to rescue him. "Judge Van Hoomisen had an unusual way of conducting bench conferences," Mackey said. "Van Hoomisen insisted that counsel meet in a small room with only the defendant present. Frankly, I didn't want to go into that room with Zieger unless Don Church accompanied us. I tried to communicate my uneasiness; to emphasize my point and impress the judge with my belief that Zieger was extremely dangerous, I told him that I carried a weapon in the courtroom. It was only a small .22 cal. pistol, but I showed it to the judge. Van Hoomisen looked at me and said, 'and what makes you think I don't?' as he lifted his robe to expose the biggest revolver I've ever seen, strapped on his hip."

According to Mackey, Zieger was an absolutely dead fish, who had the unusual characteristic of giving off a distinctive odor when he was upset. "It was very noticeable if you were standing alongside of him. I don't know whether it was sweat or something else, but it was a foul odor, and it occurred when he became angry or agitated."

While Zieger was waiting to be sentenced following his Fairbanks conviction, he participated with Wesley Ladd and Benny Ramey in the murder of Johnny Rich. The motive was the disputed ownership of Cindy's Massage Parlor on Spenard Road. Zieger shot Rich first with a .357 and Ladd, in his nominal role as leader, administered the 'coup de grace' with a .45 automatic. Ladd would later admit to this, assuming that it had been Zieger's shot that actually killed Rich. "You can't convict me for murder if all I did was fire a bullet into someone who was already dead. Unknown to Ladd when he made his admission was the fact that the autopsy report established conclusively that the fatal shot had come from Ladd's weapon.

Zieger was out on bail pending an appeal of his 'receiving and concealing' conviction and also waiting for another trial on drug charges scheduled to begin in Fairbanks. District Attorney Mackey managed to keep Zieger in custody for six months prior to the Zingre Mason trial. From this experience Zieger decided he didn't want to spend any more time in jail. His motive in the Sumpter murders is practically impossible to know for sure. There was speculation at the time that it may have been to obtain money to finance his appeal and pay for his drug trial. Reportedly Duncan Webb, an attorney who later went to jail in connection with the Johnny Rich murder, wanted $10,000 up front to file the appeal on his 'receiving and concealing' conviction. Gilmour for one wouldn't credit this, "Zieger always had money and would steal whatever else he wanted. He also had done very well by the criminal justice system. The state always provided the best defense attorneys, and his frequent trials didn't cost him a penny."

Zieger often associated with the Brothers motorcycle gang and may have wished to become a member but wasn't accepted or trusted by them, although he shared an apartment with two members of the gang. Whether his commission of the Sumpter killings was intended to strengthen his credentials for membership will never be known. Almost everyone who came into contact with Zieger at this time agrees that he had developed a 'Billy the Kid' attitude and thoroughly enjoyed the newspaper publicity which contributed to his image of being dangerous and unpredictable.

Jim Vaden thinks it was Zieger's reputation for being unpredictable that played a part in his execution-style slaying. "Even the Brothers were afraid of him because he gloried in his reputation as a contract murderer and had no qualms about killing anyone... He could have done the Sumpter killings as a favor or just on a whim, because Jimmy had angered him in some way."

The same afternoon that the murders occurred, Sumpter offered a cash reward of $10,000 to be paid in $20 bills for information leading to the apprehension of the killers. "Pretty soon Sumpter was building an army," Gilmour recalls. "Not only did Sumpter have plenty of contacts of his own, but his wife Marguerite was formerly married to Ed Merck, and the second victim, the boy, was Merck's son." Merck, well-known in the Fairbanks underworld, came to Anchorage that same afternoon with his own muscle.

Sumpter, when questioned by newspaper reporters, said that he wasn't sure what he would do with any information he might receive from his reward offer. "I'm sure there are some people who know something about the murders. They are not the people who will go to the police with the information. But they might come to me. They can reach me through my club, and then I can return their call."

An Anchorage detective says, "Once we learned of Zieger's connection, we tried to keep the information from Sumpter because we knew the money he was offering for information was really a contract for a hit. It was impossible to keep it a secret. He found out within a matter of hours."

Next day, Anchorage investigators obtained a warrant to seize Zieger's vehicle and spent hours going over it for evidence of a homicide. The next step would be to charge Zieger with the murders, but there was a noticeable reluctance to hurry the process. Larry Kulik, Zieger's public defender, requested a hearing from Judge Moody seeking to quash the search warrant. The motion was opposed by Anchorage District Attorney Joe Balfe and Asst. D.A. Mackey. Zieger was present. He appeared nervous and expressed his fear that his life was in danger.

Mackey offered Zieger a polygraph exam. "If you're innocent of the murder of Sumpter's wife and son, the exam will help to protect you," said Mackey. "If the results are favorable, I'll tell Sumpter personally. Even if you fail the test, it couldn't be used against you in court." Mackey also offered protective custody at the Jail, but Zieger wanted no part of it. He left with Kulik just before 5 p.m. Five hours later he was dead.

According to acquaintances, Gary Zieger spent his last day with a growing certainty that he was marked for death by a professional killer. Friends and others who saw him say that by 5 p.m. Tuesday, Zieger was certain a contract for his death had been made. During the morning hours Tuesday he had heard from friends his life might be in danger. Throughout the day, his knowledge of the danger grew as he heard more about the contract from friends and local underworld sources.

"He was terrified. His hands trembled and he cried," a newspaper reporter who had befriended him earlier said.

With his truck in police custody, he asked a friend for a ride. "No way," was the reply. He said Zieger was in too much trouble, and riding with him might not be healthy.

That same Tuesday evening, Jimmy Sumpter asked Colonel Ed Dankworth to meet him at the Captain Cook Hotel. "I knew that he wanted an alibi witness to be able to say where he was in case something happened to Zieger," Dankworth recalls. "I'd known Sumpter for a lot of years and sat drinking coffee with him until 9:15 p.m. when he got up and left, saying he was going to a friend's house. After I arrived home, the dispatcher called to tell me Zieger's body had been found on the Seward Highway." Sumpter himself couldn't be reached.

Hoffbeck says Zieger called Don Church several times on the day he was killed asking for help, but all Church could offer him was protection in a jail cell. "We know Zieger went to Kulik's office where he telephoned his roommates 'P. J.' and 'Big Jim' to come and pick him up. He left with them, although I think he knew they had a part of the contract. The shotgun that killed him was stolen from Cindy's Massage Parlor, and was owned by Johnny Rich. I'm not sure what the symbolism is, but the shotgun turned up again at Cindy's a few days later. "Jim Vaden doesn't agree. In his opinion, Zieger had no idea that 'P. J.' and 'Big Jim' were out to kill him, and in fact had told Public Defender Kulik that they were the only people he trusted when he called them at the Barbecue Pit from Kulik's office.

"The hit was put together by a matchmaker who set up the contract for Sumpter, and we know who that was," Vaden says. "When they left the restaurant they had the shotgun with them. They picked up Zieger at the Police Department office and took him to a house on 44th Ave. where he was kept in handcuffs until taken down the Seward highway and executed there on the road. I don't think he had any idea his friends had the contract."

Investigators thought at first that two people might have been involved in the Sumpter killings. The information from the step-daughter seemed to indicate the gunshots in two different parts of the house might have been simultaneous. Suspicion centered on Zieger's friend Benny Ramey, who went underground in the Wasilla area, where he was hidden out by friends. Some of the jewelry stolen from the Sumpter house was thought to have been offered for sale by Ramey, who was a heroin addict and needed money to support his habit.

A warrant for receiving and concealing stolen property was issued and six APD officers arrested Ramey without resistance. Ramey's complicity was never proved, and he later cooperated with Troopers in locating Johnny Rich's body, which he had helped Ladd and Zieger bury. Jim Vaden believes there was a second killer in the

Sumpter house that morning, and that he left Anchorage immediately afterwards with most of the loot. Vaden followed this lead to Oakland, California before it petered out.

Vaden, lead investigator on the Zieger killing for the Troopers, recounts another bizarre twist to the story. "I received a telephone call from the 'Vending Machine King' of Alaska the same day Sumpter's wife was killed. He said he had information but couldn't talk on the phone and wanted me to meet him. He suggested the Black Angus where he insisted I get into his car, which he then drove to a house in Spenard where an APD detective, among others, was waiting for us. The conversation that followed was not altogether friendly. We had been pressing Benny Ramey pretty hard in connection with the Johnny Rich killing and they wanted us to back off because they hoped to use Ramey to pin the Sumpter killings on Wesley Ladd. They had already told Jimmy that Ladd was involved. Their primary interest, apparently, was to get rid of Ladd because they were afraid he was moving in to gain control of the Anchorage massage parlors."

Ramey later pled to kidnapping charges in connection with the Rich slaying, and Wesley Ladd was convicted of the murder. Ramey recently died of cancer in Cordova, where he has lived since his release from prison. At least one of Zieger's killers is still living in Alaska. Walt Gilmour has retired, as have Don Church and Jim Vaden. Church is selling real estate in Wasilla and Vaden, currently residing in Washington, D.C., travels around the world selling fingerprint computers to police departments for a Japanese firm.

June 1993

White Collar Criminals-An Alaska Tradition

Lieutenant Gerald O. "Jerry" Williams, Retired

White-collar crime is a part of the history of Alaska. The only two vigilante movements in the state's history occurred at Skagway in 1898 and at Nome in 1902, not as a result of violent crime, but because of frauds perpetrated by men who would be described today as "white-collar criminals."

Unfortunately, official efforts to reduce the incidence of these crimes have been uneven, if not ineffective.

Real estate scams began in 1867 when the U.S. took possession of the Territory from Russia. Almost immediately, promoters in San Francisco, working with the steamship companies, began to advertise free land available in Alaska. Even lots in the center of Sitka, part reserved military land, were sold to the newcomers, and some had to be forcibly evicted by federal authorities.

Soapy Smith made his reputation as a Colorado conman before he landed at Skagway in 1896, to set up a range of fraudulent schemes. As soon as the Klondikers stepped off the boat at the Skagway wharf, they were encouraged to make use of Soapy's "cable office" to notify loved ones of their safe arrival.

Soapy had a wire running out into the water, supposedly a telegraph cable running all the way to Seattle, but Alaska's first telegraph cable link with Seattle wasn't laid until four years later. Soapy pocketed the money from the gullible newcomers, and took whatever they had left later when he "outfitted" them, contracted to pack their gear to the White Pass Summit, or sold dog teams culled from strays on the Seattle waterfront. Con artists got short shrift from the Mounties at the border, so Soapy never had a chance to expand his operations into Canada.

Rex Beach's novel 'The Spoilers,' depicting the turn of the century Nome Gold Rush, was made into a motion picture with Marlene

Dietrich and John Wayne. Beach's story portrays the machinations of Arther Noyes, the first Nome Federal judge. Noyes owed his appointment to political friends in the Midwest who he paid back by milking the Nome gold mines and diverting production into the pockets of his cronies.

Claim jumping began almost as soon as gold was discovered. Noyes ordered the disputed claims turned over to Alexander McKenzie, a friend from North Dakota who was instrumental in obtaining the federal judgeship for Noyes. As Special Commissioner for the court, McKenzie supervised working the claims while the litigation was pending and pocketed the proceeds.

U.S. Marshals finally were sent from San Francisco to put a stop to the operations of the corrupt court officials. The District Attorney, the Clerk of Court, McKenzie, and several others received jail terms. Noyes himself escaped prison, but was sacked by President Teddy Roosevelt.

Everyone who had dealings with E.T. Barnette, the founder of Fairbanks and its first mayor, thought he was just a sharp trader. Others suspected there was something shady in his background. Barnette was tried before a miner's meeting for theft and acquitted, but this experience didn't daunt him. He went on to found Fairbanks' first bank, and it was a shock when it was revealed in 1906 that he was convicted in 1886 of grand larceny in Oregon where he operated another bank. But Fairbanksans continued to put their money in his bank, and when it collapsed in 1911, depositors were out over $1 million.

Barnette was indicted for fraud and embezzlement; he was tried at Valdez in December 1912 because it was conceded that a Fairbanks jury would not likely be unbiased. Barnette was only convicted of making false reports, a misdemeanor, and kept a $600,000 Virginia horse ranch purchased the year before. Fairbanks journalists, who historically have not been enamored of 'due process,' characterized the trial the "rottenest judicial farce the North has ever witnessed."

In 1960, when Barnette School was dedicated, a search was made for a photograph of Fairbanks' first citizen. It was discovered that Barnette had never been anxious to have his picture taken and only a fuzzy group shot existed. Barnette disappeared from Alaska, but those who knew him figured he was continuing to "do something to somebody, wherever he was."

After the gold rushes petered out, Alaska settled down and Federal law enforcement administered by a handful of U.S. Marshals and Deputies served the needs of Alaska adequately until WWII. Confidence men weren't likely to thrive in an environment where there were so few opportunities of eluding one's outraged victims. During the war, travel to Alaska was rigidly controlled by the Military authorities and anyone with a criminal record was denied passage.

But from 1948 onwards, when the billion dollar Cold War construction boom shifted into high gear, there were a wealth of opportunities for conmen operating spurious employment agencies promoting non-existent construction job opportunities. Phony job offerings peaked again during pipeline construction.

Statehood in 1959 sparked a new interest in Alaska on the part of some colorful big-time conmen. Bethel, for a time, was the stage for a new act by Ferdinand Waldo Demara, who achieved a measure of fame during the 1950s as the Great Imposter, masquerading successfully as a Canadian Navy surgeon, banker, psychiatrist, and even as a Texas penitentiary warden. With forged credentials, Demara obtained appointment as School Principal at Bethel.

After he was found out as a result of drunken boasting in a Bethel watering hole, he kited a check on Pacific Northern Airlines to pay for his flight out of the territory. Later he wrote a spurious story about his adventures in Alaska including an account of crossing the Bering Sea to Russian Siberia.

Another white collar criminal, Thomas S. Browder, came north from Texas to run what perhaps still ranks as the largest confidence game ever carried on in Alaska. Fresh from milking the assets of one of Texas' largest insurance companies, Browder founded the First Alaska Investment Co. and the First Alaska Insurance Company and then proceeded to skim Alaskan investors of more than $5 million in a giant 'Ponzi scheme.' Browder was indicted and convicted of embezzlement and securities fraud in 1962 in a trial that was notable for what was not said about the Alaska politicians who helped Browder obtain the insurance license he needed to carry out his fraudulent schemes.

During much of its history, Alaska has been isolated from the rest of the United States. White-collar crime schemes developed in the Southern 48 had little impact on Alaska or took a long time to get here. When construction of the Trans-Alaska Pipeline began, conmen, grifters and syndicated crime interests took a new look at the 49th State. There was also concern over the possibility that organized crime would put its roots down, and traditionally they had begun their operations in other areas by first forging an alliance with legitimate businessmen,

In the spring of 1971, Col. Ed Dankworth convinced Commissioner Emery Chapple that it was time to organize a statewide Criminal Investigation Bureau to upgrade and centralize trooper investigative performance. Dankworth didn't like the idea of creating specialized investigative units. "I always felt," Dankworth recalls, "that the Troopers were too small an organization to have specialization. There is a tendency to call your cases too close when you begin specializing and a backlog is going to build up in other areas."

Dankworth, however, felt that since white-collar crimes in Alaska had been ignored, a special unit was needed to develop expertise that was neglected earlier. Sergeant Don Church, an experienced investigator, was appointed first head of the White Collar Crimes Section when it was organized in 1971.

Progress was slow at first. Chuck Reid, Loren Thomas and Tom Zaruba worked White Collar Crimes from the beginning but the unit came together when Maurice Christie was assigned. Christie, a former Trooper with a degree in accounting, had left to try his hand as a school teacher at Seward. Recruited back to CIB he provided the much-needed expertise for conducting financial investigations and was one of the few outside law enforcement officers to attend the FBI's prestigious Fraud Investigation training program.

During the late 1970s, the White Collar section began to pick up steam, and by 1979 Alaska had what some described as the "best State Police Fraud Squad in the country." A number of their investigations resulted in convictions including- several prominent politicians, an assistant attorney general, a judge, and the director of a community college. An investigation of the Alaska Housing Authority also revealed the involvement of prominent political figures in fraudulent home financing practices.

With Christie's early death from cancer, White Collar investigations went into decline. The early 80s was also a time of budget tightening, and CIB was reduced sharply as Commissioner Sundberg and Colonel Kolivosky concentrated on putting men back into uniform. Kolivosky recalls some of his frustrations during those years.

"I'll admit," said Kolivosky, "that I didn't know a lot about what the White Collar Crime Section was doing. I just assumed that it took them longer to make their cases because they were more involved and time consuming. But after a while, it didn't appear to me that anything was getting done or that anybody was going to jail. I decided that we had better things to do with our personnel."

During the 1980s, the White Collar Crime section was cut back sharply, as were most CIB investigative units, except for Narcotics. This was also the period when emphasis was placed on creating General Investigation Units (GIU's) under the supervision of Detachment Commanders. In 1991, the pendulum started to swing back again. The Anchorage GIU was dismantled and its personnel were transferred back to a reorganized CIB. The White Collar unit was reconstituted and personnel expanded. The WC unit under Sergeant Warren Grant now consists of four investigators together with Valerie Van Brocklin, of the Office of Special Prosecutions, assigned as their legal advisor. Business has also picked up.

As in the past, a large part of the White Collar Crime unit activities are devoted to investigating frauds that arise in government, and these seem to be proliferating. They vary all the way from ferry system pursers who skim ticket sales, for a loss of $48,000 in State revenues to the persistent use of jail telephones by prisoners engaged in carrying out credit card scams, or the front-page allegations of high-level contract fraud in the Alaska Power Authority.

More recently, the unit inherited the Charlie Hamel "whistle-blower" case involving Alyeska, Wackenhut Security, and a Congressional Investigating Committee. They are sifting through affidavits to determine if any State law violations occurred. Environmental Crime itself is a new branch of White Collar Crime Unit interest, because prosecutors are using the criminal law to reign in repeated violators. "It is a whole new area where there is a critical need for developing in-house expertise," according to Sergeant Grant.

The private sector is not being neglected, but there is a constant challenge to keep up with the creativity of the present-day conman. Several real-estate equity skimming frauds, including the Vanguard Case, which cost Alaska banks and property owners in excess of $100,000, prosecuted in 1992. Investigators Dave Kilpatrick and Ed Stauber have developed on-the-job expertise in handling real estate and financial crimes. Both, as well as other members of the unit are graduates of the FBI Basic and Advanced White Collar Crime training programs. Sergeant Grant feels the new emphasis on White Collar Crime prosecution is important, "because everyone is a victim in this type of case." He almost wishes it were possible to mount signs at major airports of the type that vigilantes placed on the Skagway dock in 1898:

A WORD TO THE WISE SHOULD BE SUFFICIENT. ALL CONFIDENCE SHARKS, BUNCO MEN, SURE-THING MEN, AND ALL OTHER OBJECTIONAL CHARACTERS ARE NOTIFIED TO LEAVE SKAGWAY. FAILURE TO COMPLY WITH THIS WARNING WILL BE FOLLOWED BY PROMPT ACTION.

September 1992

The Typical Cordova Moose

Sergeant Mac McKinley, Retired

I could bore you folks for hours with tales that soon become old. But some are so doggone funny they really must be told.

Cordova's weather was cold and windy, and the snow was falling down. All the people were in attendance at a basketball game in town.

Rod had received a tip this day. About a moose being shot on the flats. So he called the Trooper and Police Chief and gave them all the facts.

By God! This will take strategy. We'll get them, that's a cinch. A quick and efficient plan was made on a place to make the pinch.

We can't have any vehicles around; that would tip them off, I'd say. Okay, the Trooper would drop Mills off near where the poached moose lay.

Rod took off with a white sheet, to camouflage his place in the snow. It wasn't long before his talky squawked; get ready! Because here we go.

A station wagon pulled off the road, and two men slipped out the door. They pulled the white tarp off the moose, and began loading, like never before.

Their work was fast and furious, so dark you could hardly see. One guy suddenly quit backing. Good Lord! He was going to pee.

He took a few steps to the left, and he let his water fly. Wouldn't you know, Rod was there, and got soaked above the eye.

Mills could hardly contain himself, until the car backed out in the road. He called the Trooper to come on in. Rod was puffed up like a toad.

The poachers buzzed off quickly. They were headed back to town. But the Police Chief had the road blocked and they couldn't get around.

Rod and Trooper Hoffbeck soon appeared, and the bandits were taken to jail. The old moose had to be cared for. It had reached the end of the trail.

Their wagon was driven to a freezer, and the rear door was opened wide. Rod and the Trooper began unloading the moose that was packed inside.

Don't think the story ended there, and you should have heard Mills squawk. This cussid moose had eight legs when they hung it in the box.

September 1993

Ovid R. 'Mac' McKinley passed away on December 9, 2007, at Harbor Hospice Hospital in Beaumont, Texas. In his youth Mac traveled by boxcar across the Southwest. He served in the Civilian Conservation Corps in 1940-1941 and came to Kodiak by boat in 1946. He was joined there by his wife Nita and their oldest daughter, Dale. During his 26 years in Kodiak, Mac worked as a taxi driver, a Kodiak Police Department Patrolman and acting Chief of Police. He joined the Marshal's Office as a Territorial Deputy Marshal and upon Statehood joined the Department of Fish and Game as a Protection Officer. That job took the family to Fairbanks and then to the Mat-Su Valley. In 1970, Mac and his family moved to Cordova where he established the city Police Department, became Chief and served as Customs Agent.. He also worked construction, drove the airport shuttle and ended his working years providing security on the Alaska Pipeline for American Guard and Alert. Mac was also a private pilot. He resided in Texas for his last five years. During retirement in Anchorage he was a weekly volunteer at the Alaska Law Enforcement Museum.

Ode to "Whirl Winn"

Sergeant Mac McKinley

A kid came North from Sunny California in the year of '71.
He joined the Department of Fish and Game - he thought it would be fun.
The name of Winn may not be known to all who read this poem,
But from Prince William Sound to Old Kenai, this boy will surely roam.
His deeds of daring are not the thing this man is known for best,
But what he has become so famous for really tickles all the rest.

Now Winn made the trip across the Sound to Whittier by the Sea.
A lad named Carpenter assisted him and told this tale with glee:
A charming lady vessel was riding the soft sea crest,
And "Whirl" Winn approached the vessel to check for the license she should possess.
He slammed the Bertrum back and forth trying to maneuver to her boat rail,
But the water would not cooperate and Winn could only hale.
She could not understand his words as he shouted at this girl,
And that was the time that the trouble began to pile on the kid named "Whirl."

The Bertrum was seven feet away as Winn waved his arms and cried.
He made a jump for the lady's boat but landed three feet from its side.
Now a lonesome flea that was on his coat was caught as the water arose,
And run to the top as fast as it could and there it stood on "Whirl" Winn's nose.
The trusty aide then grabbed our friend from the icy water's grasp,
And our stalwart officer just shook his head; he was too cold to gasp.

It was in mid-July in '72 that "Whirl" took his patrol boat out to sea.
It's a thing these officers do a lot; it's their job you see.
A Chitina aircraft came on the scene with Wayne Smith at the stick.
The plane landed close to "Whirl" Winn and once again this did the trick.
Officer Mills was in the plane; he and Winn discussed the fisheries plight.
Winn said, "I'll get the chart and show you the place we must guard with all our might."

As he dashed along down the patrol boat's deck to get a chart from the cabin's chest.
In his haste returned on the outside again, and I'm sure you guess the rest.
Mills could not believe his eyes as he saw this great big "splash,"
And once again Winn was in the drink; he did that really fast.
Officer Winn never missed a word as he grabbed for the bell buoy's rail.
He had sunk about half way down and this caused his lips to pale.
Now of all the requests that Mills ever heard, this must be the one.
Winn said to Mills in a very calm voice, "Will you please take my gun?"
As Winn pulled himself from out of the sea he was very wet and damp.
This would never do with a fisherman. This boy had been their champ.
May I use your aircraft Winn said to Mills, I must take a very short trip,
And I believe I'll land at my camp and change clothes; these garments are beginning to drip.

Now history will repeat itself if one will give it the chance.
The Russian River on the Kenai caused Winn to do his little dance.
The California Kid was strolling along down the Russian River Bank,
When he walked completely out in space; this couldn't be called a prank.
The land dropped away to the Russian River's wave
As Winn fell through space and went ker-plash; his thought would be a grave.
Whirl Winn landed on his back and the bubbles all flew free.
He grabbed the very first branch he saw and hung on to that tree.
Now once again a dripping mess the officer climbed to shore.
"I'll be damned," Officer Winn exclaimed, "I'm wet enough to pour."
February 2008

The Micronesian Connection

Trust Territory of the Pacific Islands

After World War Two the United States entered into an agreement with the United Nations to administer and support the Trust Territory of the Pacific Islands. The four largest Districts within TTPI included what later became known as the Republic of the Marshall Islands, Federated States of Micronesia, Republic of Palau and the Commonwealth of the Northern Mariana Islands.

The U.S. was responsible for various aspects of civil administration, including law enforcement in remote communities which previously had little interaction with more urbanized areas of the South Pacific. Prior to 1980 very little progress had been made on law enforcement. The U.S. Department of the Interior became aware of significant achievements in dealing with similar problems experienced by Native people in Rural Alaska.

Providing law enforcement in the remote and often isolated rural communities of America's northernmost state is the job of the Alaska State Troopers. Though the villages of Alaska were no more crime-ridden than comparable American communities were in their earliest years, they did have the usual share of those who preyed on the weak and vulnerable, broke the law and otherwise made life less livable for others.

Enforcing the law in Rural Alaska is sometimes complicated by the fact that many residents still live a relatively primitive lifestyle – and their language and culture are often quite different than that of Alaskans from more distant communities. The men and women of the Alaska State Troopers meet that challenge.

Though the Trust Territory of the Pacific and Alaska are almost literally at opposite ends of the Earth, and their weather represents two extremes, the problems of law enforcement in their remote communities are remarkably similar.

Because of the Alaska State Troopers' experience and notable record of success, the Interior Department proposed that AST conduct training in the TTPI. The Alaska/Micronesia connection proved to be one of the most unusual and successful exchange programs in modern police history.

The following article is the personal account of an AST officer who played a key role in development of the TTPI program. It was written for The Banner, quarterly newsletter of the Fraternal Order of Alaska State Troopers in the humorous vein retired officers often adopt when communicating with their peers.

Major Mike Korhonen, Retired

On January 10, 1980, Commissioner Bill Nix responded to a request for Alaska State Trooper training assistance by Dennis Lund, Administrator of the Trust Territory of the Pacific, Justice Improvement Commission, in Saipan. As it turned out, Jim Messick, ace grant writer and word merchant, had worked with Denny in Alaska prior to Denny returning to Michigan and obtaining his PhD, and then accepting the Trust Territory position.

The two kept in touch and Jim mentioned the State Troopers' success in village training and the Village Public Safety Officer program, which was then in the planning stages and would bring village residents into the law enforcement community as what became known as the VPSOs. Denny recognized the potential of utilizing the AST training experience by the Micronesian Police and thus developed the letter to Commissioner Nix.

Bill Nix was intrigued and replied, in part, "If I could pass myself off as a line-level trainer, I would quickly assign myself to assist you in this endeavor. But alas, commissioners being as they are, you know, relegated to the head table where I can recite to myself the multiplication tables until it is my turn to expound on some subject, leaves me little time to fantasize about going to the Trust Territory."

The Commissioner pledged support and forwarded the letter to Colonel Tom Anderson to find two Troopers to send. Tom selected me and we agreed that First Sergeant Glenn Godfrey (later AST's director) would also be a good representative. In May of 1980, Glenn and I traveled to Saipan for an orientation. The Trust Territory of the Pacific Islands (TTPI) paid travel and per diem. The state paid our wages. No fees were charged for our time.

Brian Vila, the law enforcement specialist of the TTPI, briefed us and we went on to Truk, where Chief of Police Bill Stinnett met us and introduced us to the real Micronesia (which Saipan is not). We taught a two-week class to 18 new officers hired under the Comprehensive Employment Training Act.

The Alaska training was invaluable. Most of the Micronesian officers had limited formal education and poor English skills. The techniques involved in utilizing interpreters, role playing and hands-on training were used with great success. The students, local police officials and Saipan bureaucrats all spoke highly of the training.

We were then invited to conduct a second class in Majuro, Marshall Islands in August 1980. Colonel Tom Anderson and First Sergeant Ron Cole traveled with me to Majuro for the second class, which was attended by 50 Marshallese officers. Tom taught Crime Scene Investigation; Ron, Practical Accident Investigation, and we all taught in the classroom.

This class was also given high marks by students, local police and Saipan headquarters TTPI. The appearance and demeanor of the AST officers always added a great deal to the overall success of the program.

The story of one young onlooker illustrates the impact of the Trooper program: In Majoro we taught in a screened-in, open-air classroom of the local Catholic school. To make way for our class, the local kids were moved out of their classroom for two weeks. A young boy, about 13 years old, kept peeking back into his classroom to see what was going on.

The now-grown boy says today that he was so influenced by the Troopers that he decided then that police work was his life's goal. Vincent Tani has since graduated from Marshall's High School, earned an A.A. Degree in Police Science in Portland, and is currently Chief of Operations of the Marshall Island's Federal Police.

July 1994

Major Mike Korhonen became an award-winning intern at the Juneau Police Department in 1961 and began his career with the Alaska State Troopers on October 10, 1964 when he attended the Public Safety Academy in Sitka. Between then and his Alaska State Trooper retirement on May 1, 1987, Mike was also stationed in Bethel, Juneau, Sitka Academy and Anchorage Headquarters. After retirement he spent several sessions in Micronesia training local, state and national police. Upon moving to Washington State, Mike and his wife bought a 30-acre farm and for many years raised show dairy goats. He was a Director on the National Board of the American Dairy Goat Association, representing Alaska, Washington, Oregon, Idaho, Montana, Utah, Hawaii, Guam and Russia. Mike Korhonen and Joe DeTemple have hosted the Retired Alaska Law Enforcement Officers Annual Reunion in Chehalis, Washington, for 23 years. Major Korhonen was awarded FOAST's Life Time Achievement Award on October 29, 2014.

The Micronesian Connection - Part 2

Major Mike Korhonen, Retired

Following the success of the Marshall Islands training, the Trust Territory of the Pacific Islands expanded its training request of Alaska and scheduled a comprehensive in-service class in Pohnpei. We gave Investigations, Management and Basic classes to officers from Pohnpei, Yap, Palau, Kosrae and Truk.

In October 1981, a larger training team accompanied me to Pohnpei. Lieutenant John Lucking, Corporal Dan Weatherly, Trooper Gary (Big) Lewis and I taught the classes in three classrooms, running simultaneously. The classes were again praised by all. Governor Leo Falcom hosted a Sakau party for the Alaska State Trooper personnel in his private naus. I have since learned this was a high honor, as it is seldom done.

By this time, Bill Stinnett had moved from his Truk job to Saipan to join the Micronesian Bureau of Investigation. He, Brian Vila and I agreed that a logical follow-up to the expanded police training would be the establishment of a Basic Academy in Micronesia. We worked with the Micronesian officers to develop a five-year plan. Two groups of the most talented and motivated officers would be selected from the entire area. This core group would be trained at the AST Academy in Sitka.

During the third year, the AST academy staff would travel to Micronesia and conduct a Basic Academy there, using the core group as assistant squad leaders. The fourth year, the Academy Commander would be an Alaska State Trooper and the Micronesians would fill the rest of the staff positions. In year five the Micronesians were to run the entire class with an AST representative on hand to offer advice.

The five-year plan was presented to Governor Jay Hammond through Commissioner Nix. Following the state election in 1982, Alaska committed to the plan. I was promoted and transferred to

Anchorage. Captain Joe DeTemple took over the Micronesian program. In January 1983, the State and TTPI agreed on the first two Micronesian Academies, which were conducted in Sitka.

The Micronesian Chiefs of Police selected the Micronesian Occupational College at Palau as the site for the first class to be conducted in Micronesia. Bill Stinnett was the coordinator for that third Academy.

As the time for the class approached, then-Commissioner Bob Sundborg decided that dwindling federal funding and the AST manpower requirements of the program were a problem and withdrew his support. Stinnett contacted me and asked my advice on how to proceed. I asked Deputy Commander Jim Vaden to intercede on the Micronesians behalf and brief the Commissioner in more detail on the five-year plan. There was no change in position by Sundborg.

Eventually, I agreed to take annual leave for 15 weeks, travel to Palau, and be the Academy Commander. The Squad Leader, First Sergeant and Deputy Commander would be graduates of Micronesia One and Two in Sitka. Colonel Mike Kolivosky, recognizing the position the Micronesians were in, granted my leave. For 15 weeks my deputy, Lieutenant George Pollitt, and Lana Hobson ran Administrative Services.

The Micronesia class was a huge success. Two TTPI Presidents and the High Commissioner participated and the Micronesian Chiefs voted to continue with the plan.

As an aside; it was during this school that the President of the Republic of Palau was assassinated. The class and I personally were involved in the investigation; however, that is another story for another time.

As I could not give another 15 weeks to the fourth Academy, we modified the five-year plan. The school would be shortened to nine weeks. I would travel out to Palau, work for two weeks with the Micronesian Commander to get the school started, then return to Alaska. I would again travel to Palau for the last week of the Academy to help with the wrap-up, graduation and accreditation paperwork.

This class started on July 5, 1986 and I departed as scheduled, leaving the Micronesian staff to run things, but there was an unexpected interruption in the plan. About 90 miles north of Whitehorse, B.C., I fell on my motorcycle and severely broke my leg. Morris Rodgers, who was riding south with me, babysat for two days until we could get back to Anchorage, leaving the bikes with the Mounties in Whitehorse. I never got back to finish the class in Palau. Sergeant John McGhee taught Accident Investigation and some Traffic Law to the group.

During the critiques of this class, the Chiefs of Police agreed that the all-Micronesian staff had been unable to maintain discipline among the class and insisted I participate full- time in future schools or they would withdraw support. As it turned out, this became no problem because I retired prior to the class in 1987. I became the advisor to the Micronesian Academy, which placed a local officer as Commander but made me available to answer questions and be visible as a disciplinary stabilizer.

Following the '87 class, we moved to the Community College of Micronesia in Pohnpei. In 1988, Walt Gilmour traveled over to assist. I read the galley proof of his book *"Butcher, Baker"* while he was there and we had long hours of remembrances on the hot tropical nights. Our running partner that year was John Haglequm, President of the Federated States of Micronesia. The President's bodyguards were in such poor shape that they had to follow along in the car.

In 1990 and 1991 we elevated the level of training to managers and conducted nine weeks of intensive management classes. The 1992 class was a basic class to catch up on new hires. This was class number 10. More than 350 officers were trained at the Basic Academy level during the course of the 10 academies.

U.S. federal agencies - FBI, DEA, Marine Fisheries (represented by Ed Eckhoff), Postal Service, Secret Service, Coast Guard, Naval Investigative Service, and Customs all participated at one time or another during the academies.

As a final step in training we worked with representative senior officers from each of the jurisdictions and put together a six-week Basic Academy, complete with lesson plans, exams, visual aids, handouts, grade sheets, and all other materials necessary to start their own academies.

Although I will miss the associations and challenges in Micronesia, I believe it is time for them to take responsibility for their future development in law enforcement.

With my withdrawal from the Micronesian Law Enforcement community, I consider my active police career ended. 1961-1993. It has been good.

October 1994

Baby Bear Flies Coach

Trooper R.M. 'Ron' Costlow, Retired

March contact with the curator of the Alaska Zoo reveals Tuffy, the former mascot of the Alaska State Troopers, has survived his 26th year. The saga of Tuffy goes back to April 1969 when Trooper Ron Costlow, posted at Aniak, received a call from Anvik that village hunters had shot a mother bear, and one small cub survived. The cub was transported to Aniak and the Costlows took him into their home. The bear was a 12-inch, approximately two-week-old cub that initially acted tough and could only be handled with leather gloves.

Upon receiving baby bottles of milk, the lively cub, dubbed Tuffy, fit into the household. On the first night, he was placed on the porch and growled and screamed so loud that the Costlow family had to bring him inside. He immediately made a beeline for the bedroom, jumped on the bed, and promptly fell asleep.

The Costlows had the cub seven days and, according to Mrs. Costlow, it seemed like several months. The cub went from docile to mischievous, getting stuck in a drain pipe, climbing on the furniture, biting the nearest human when he didn't get his way, but most of the time being a character and fun to have around.

The Department of Fish and Game directed that the cub be brought to Anchorage. Trooper Costlow booked space on Wien Airlines and on the day of departure, was advised that Tuffy, being an animal, had to be placed in a case and transported in the baggage section of the aircraft. The airline policy did not allow for exceptions until Tuffy began screaming, growling and making such a noise that the airline staff asked what could be done. Trooper Costlow requested and obtained permission to carry Tuffy into the airplane in a blanket and, as soon as he arrived on board, gave Tuffy a bottle of milk. The little bear slept the entire flight.

Upon arrival in Anchorage, Trooper Costlow was met by Sergeant Tom Anderson and other Troopers who had heard the story of Tuffy. The news media was there and before anyone knew it, the Alaska State Troopers had a new mascot. The Fraternal Order had been formed in 1969 and immediately began to raise a fund to care for Tuffy, who lived at the Costlow family home.

For several months, Tuffy was taken to Trooper functions such as auto races, baseball games, and even toured grade schools. As you might expect, Tuffy got too big for demonstrations and display, and during the late summer of 1969, the Alaska Children's Zoo took Tuffy in as the Zoo's second animal, preceded only by Annabelle the elephant, its first. Until the Zoo facility opened four months later, Tuffy lived in the home of its founder, Sammye Seawell, and won Sammye's heart.

Tuffy has been a popular animal at the Zoo and although he's now getting old, the curator of the Zoo indicates he continues to be friendly — somewhat arthritic, but overall a great asset to the Zoo.

April 1996

Trooper Ronald M. Costlow joined the Alaska State Police in September 1966. He attended the 10th State Trooper Academy in Anchorage, took a leave in '67, and was rehired in June 1968 and assigned to the 14th State Trooper Academy. That Academy was the first held at Sheldon Jackson College in Sitka. Costlow pulled out and reported for duty halfway through due to two things: a manpower shortage and previous experience. He was assigned to Anchorage Patrol, and then sent to open a one-man remote Bush post at Aniak on January 1, 1969. (He also did temporary duty in the Bethel & Dillingham Post). Ron later served at the Fairbanks Detachment. He is a Charter & Lifetime member of FOAST, and was issued his Retired Trooper I.D. card in August 2001 by Commissioner Glenn Godfrey. He worked at a number of law enforcement departments in Washington State and became a Business Representative and President for a Teamster's Local in Seattle, WA. He was recognized by the Seattle Chamber of Commerce & *Time* magazine in 1978 as "One of 100 News Makers of Tomorrow."

First One

Trooper R. M. "Ron" Costlow, Retired

On January 1, 1969, I was selected as the first Trooper to open and man the Aniak post. With no Bush or one-man post experience and still on probation as a recruit Trooper, I accepted the assignment.

However, not knowing just what I was supposed to do, I asked Sergeant Harry "Mac" McLaughlin. He said, "Just take your fishing pole and shotgun, and go out and enjoy."

It's one thing to be assigned to a one-man remote Bush post that had been established by those who have gone before you. However, Aniak was a brand new post. No official office or office equipment, files, records, evidence log, and locker; no emergency equipment, no radio, or telephone; no patrol vehicle or supervisor; and your nearest back-up was 350 miles away, weather and personnel permitting.

What does it take to handle a one-man post? Well, anyone who has done it can tell you that it's not just about enforcement of the law or doing a shift on patrol in Anchorage. You are it! You are the representative for state government assigned to protect and serve.

You also represent every other federal and state agency, handle all law enforcement problems, health and social service issues, and any other matter generally handled by city, state, or federal governments. In other words, you can act as a Trooper, a bailiff, a coroner, a minister, and you are your own crime scene investigator, medical examiner, records clerk, secretary, the whole nine yards.

In those days there was very little or no direct supervision. You had to set up your own living quarters, (in a vacant federal

DEW-line[1] house), not to complain as I found out the trooper station in Bethel had honey-bucket service. We at least had flush toilets. No beds, no furniture. Try furnishing an apartment from stores in Aniak. There were none. I was able to scrounge a couple of mattresses and an old couch from some of the FAA employees living in the complex at the time, to use until I was able to have some furniture shipped out from Anchorage on the National Guard plane, along with my patrol vehicle, an old WWII military Jeep outfitted with a bubble-gum light mounted on the roof. Lieutenant Bill Nix was able to commandeer some office equipment— typewriter, file cabinets, IBM pocket recorder, and "how" manuals with procedures for setting up the evidence log, locker room and so forth.

With it came emergency equipment and supplies from the Civil Defense headquarters in Anchorage, (folding military cots, blankets, first aid and survival equipment). It was a challenge getting it all into my space. The building was a duplex; I took over the small apartment attached and turned it into an Aniak Trooper office and jail, with no bars. This all happened within days of arriving, and at the same time I was handling calls that were coming in from ham radio operators and on the only phone line, which was located at the lodge. A call would come in and someone would run across the air strip and give me the message.

The Aniak post consisted of 57,581 square miles with villages up and down the Yukon and Kuskokwim Rivers plus a number in the Interior. The activity was such that there was no time for me to use my fishing pole or shotgun. At the time, the Aniak post was one of the most active posts in Alaska and, in addition, there were TDY assignments to Dillingham and Bethel posts during the time these posts were vacant or Troopers were on vacation. There were many incidents where a back-up would have been welcomed: the fishing strike in Dillingham, summer of '69; a stabbing, shooting, and a plane accident, all going on in three different villages at the same time. Backup was something you only dreamed about.

And then breakup at Aniak on the Kuskokwim River! An ice jam backed up on the road and was just inches from breaching the

1 Distant Early Warning Line, a Cold War radar system

dike. What to do? Contact Civil Defense and Air National Guard for possible evacuation of the village.

Aniak is almost an island— one-half mile wide and one and a half miles long, with a population of approximately 250 people at the time. It was a 24-hour vigil, but the ice finally broke up and the river receded.

The experience at Aniak was challenging and a period in my life I will never forget.

June 2009

Police Flying in the '50s

Trooper Marc Stella

In the early 1950s, the Alaska Highway Patrol inherited some rural enforcement functions from the U.S. Marshal Service which were above and beyond routine traffic control activities.

There was early recognition that airplanes were a valuable tool in effective law enforcement. Pilot and Highway Patrolman Phil Ames, assisted by Officer Tom Roberts, provided a good demonstration of this while conducting a search for a violent escapee from the federal jail in Seward ,Third Judicial District. Most of the flying was performed by Patrolman Ames in Cessna N4244N, a Cessna 140, at his own expense as no funding was available.

When the Territorial Legislature created the Alaska Territorial Police, they recognized there would be a need for an aviation section. Unfortunately, they did not obtain funding for an aviation section as money was limited and was dedicated to training and fielding police officers. With the prospect of being able to use his flying skills and qualifications, Marc Stella allowed himself to be lured into resigning from the U.S. Air Force, and joined the Alaska Territorial Police upon completion of the first Territorial Police class in Anchorage.

Officer Stella was assigned to the Fairbanks post in what was then a booming community of nearly 10,000 citizens. He took Cessna N4244N to Phillips Field, where it was very seldomly used, and ultimately traded it for a Piper PA16 Clipper, formerly belonging to the Presbyterian Mission from Point Barrow. The Piper PA16 N577AH was often operated at personal expense, although some monies were made available by the U.S. Marshal Service and the Alaska Railroad.

Ladessa Nordale, the U.S. Commissioner, Fourth Judicial District, recognized the value of aircraft and managed to find and direct funds to cover expenses for some rural investigation and body retrieval work. She eventually convinced the Territorial Legislature to allocate money specifically for aircraft use. During those early days there were many individuals who did not fully appreciate the value of aerial law enforcement and were slow to accept the concept.

Alaska Territorial Police who did put aircraft to good use included Officers James Goodfellow, M. E. Ed Dankworth, Emery Chapple, Cyril Wood, Marc Stella, "Tank" Anderson, Sergeant Sherman Edwards, Walt Sinn, Dispatcher Bob Sundberg, Lieutenant Bill Trafton and Lieutenant Emmett Botelho.

The early success of aircraft during territorial days relates directly back to individuals such as Marc Stella and Phil Ames, who out of their own pockets, contributed to the utilization of aircraft. Their success, coupled with the funding from the railroad, the U.S. District Court, and the Marshal Service, laid the foundation for the very successful aviation program of the Eighties and Nineties.

February 1997

Marc Stella served in the 2nd U.S. Marine Division in the Pacific Theater during World War Two. After the War he joined the U.S. Air force (formerly Army Air Corps) obtained his pilot's license and was assigned to Elmendorf Air Force Base. He joined the Civil Air Patrol in 1953 and is still a member. In 1954 he resigned from the Air Force and joined the Alaska Territorial Police (ATP) attending academy number one. He was the first ATP pilot. After several years he left the ATP and continued to fly in the private sector. In 1965 he went to Saigon as a medevac pilot, flying 56 missions. Since that time he has held numerous flying and aviation positions including Air Traffic Controller, NTSB as Air Safety Investigator and aviation safety consultant. Marc has won numerous aviation related awards including the prestigious Wright Brothers Master Pilot Award in 2006 making him one of only 12 in Alaska who have received the award. Marc lives with his wife Val in Anchorage.

The Case of the Phantom Piddler

Trooper Marc Stella

It was a dark but not stormy night when Bob Sundberg ("Sundy") and I arrived at Ruby, Alaska on the evening of August 9, 1954. We were then Territorial Policemen en route from Unalakleet to Phillips Field in Fairbanks and stopped at Galena Air Force Base to refuel and check the weather at the CAA station.

Fairbanks was still "klaggy" with post-frontal rain but Tanana weather was good. It was nearly dark when we departed Galena and, about 20 minutes later, flight service called to tell us that the Tanana Low Frequency "A" range was out of service

With my minimal night experience, I had no trouble convincing Sundy that the strip on the hill above Ruby was a preferred choice. Lights in the village served as an invitation for sanctuary.

We found no tie-down facilities after landing and spent considerable time securing the airplane while waiting for a ride to show up from the village. After a long, unrewarding wait, we decided to walk the two miles to Johnny May's Trading Post before it got too late. By the time we got down the hill, there wasn't a light showing anywhere, and Johnny's light plant had been shut down. It was almost midnight, so we walked on to Mamie Olson's Roadhouse at the far end of the village where there was a sign at the entrance: "Closed till September 15."

At this point, we decided that, rather than awaken anyone, we would just go back to the strip, roll out our sleeping bags and "siwash" it until first light, then head east. It was after 1 a.m. when we finally crawled into our bags and spread out under the left wing of the airplane.

During the night, I was vaguely aware that it had turned quite cold and that Sundberg was thrashing about and, I thought, snuggling his bag up to mine (probably subconsciously seeking warmth).

I awoke at the first hint of dawn and crawled out of my bag to seek relief across the Poorman Roadway. On returning to the airplane, I made enough noise to awaken Bob and, when he poked his nose out of his bag, he asked if it had stopped raining. I replied that it had not rained and that it was a clear, soon-to-be bright morning. He said he distinctly remembered rain and wind during the night, and that was why the bottom of his sleeping bag was wet from sticking out beyond the shelter of the wing's leading edge.

I walked over and saw that his bag was indeed wet, and that there was a small puddle around the bottom. I urged him to climb out of his bag, look at the weather, and see the marks in the frost on the ground. The readily recognizable paw prints indicated that a bear had arrived from the south during the night, explored the whole airplane and focused on Sundberg's bag, which it had pawed and anointed.

Then it ambled between our bags and on down the road in the direction of the village. Suddenly, Sundy was very wide-awake and alert, so we broke camp and took off for Manley Hot Springs.

In recounting our experience to the roadhouse cook where we stopped for breakfast, we could discern his skepticism. However, the description of the size of the bear tracks got his attention. He said we had to be talking about a 300 pounder at least, and how lucky we were that, so late in the summer, the critter must not have been too hungry.

Fortunately for us, our bear had a preference for salmon over Sundy's feet! I'm just glad that Sundy hadn't been wearing fresh, clean socks because it was obvious that his apparently aromatic socks made good bear repellent. After leaving Manley heading for Phillips Field we agreed that, if we refrained from relating the event in Fairbanks, we would not have to endure any joshing, teasing, or ridicule.

Forty-four years later though, we have agreed that since we have now reached a certain maturity, we had best relate the story while we still can, and have a good laugh at the event.

NOTE: Bob Sundberg and Marc Stella served together at the First Territorial Police post on Cushman Street in Fairbanks. Bob went on to become Commissioner of Public Safety, and Marc went on to get into all kinds of mischief.

December 1998

The Seizure and Protective Custody of Alaska's Last Floating Fish Trap

Lieutenant Eugene (E.L.) O'Brien, Retired

When Alaska became a state in 1959, the first act of the new Legislature outlawed floating fish traps. The traps had been mostly owned and operated by Seattle-based canneries and were widely hated by Alaska's commercial net fishermen. The traps had been used for many years, starting well before Native contact with white civilization, but their modern designs were so efficient they could wipe out the productivity of an entire stream in a single season.

Since enforcement of fish and game law in Alaska was no longer the responsibility of U.S. Marshals or the U.S. Fish and Wildlife service, enforcement of the new fish trap law fell to the State Police.

Anticipating that the canneries would challenge the new law, a task force of four or five officers - myself among them - were assembled in Juneau under the command of Lieutenant Turk Mayfield. In a few days, word was received that a trap had been put in place at Pybus Point at the entrance to Pybus Bay outside Petersburg. The task force went into action.

We were painfully aware that placement of the fish trap pitted the fledgling State of Alaska against the federal government, the powerful Seattle fish packers, and several of Alaska's own villages. And rumor had it that seizing officers could expect armed resistance.

The problem was further complicated by the fact that the fish packers had recently sold many of the canneries— and their fish traps— to Native villages in Southeastern Alaska, apparently in the hope that Native ownership would forestall state action against the traps. And the sales had been financed with money advanced by the federal Bureau of Indian Affairs. The villages were thus deeply in hock and felt they needed to keep the traps operating to pay down their debts. Some Natives supported the traps, others opposed them.

Because of the rumors that fighting could erupt over the traps, the raiding party was sent to Pybus Bay in the Blue Star, a stout steel vessel leased by the state and well-known in those waters as a floating machine and welding shop. A second vessel of wood construction was sent along but was ordered to remain in the background, beyond the range of rifle fire.

Since I was an experienced boat handler and aircraft pilot, I was ordered to stand by in Juneau until the advance party determined what equipment would be needed. The rest of the task force boarded the Blue Star during the evening of June 15 and headed for Pybus Bay. There they found the offending trap and seized it without resistance from the cannery crew operating it.

The trap had been taken without firing a shot and without casualties to either side, but now another problem became apparent. The officers had closed the trap's mouth to keep it from catching fish, but they now had possession of a multi-ton object for which they were responsible until the courts ruled in the case. The massive trap had to be both kept safe and prevented from resuming fishing. They decided to keep a security force in place.

I was dispatched to Ketchikan to bring the Fish and Game boat Okeeda to Pybus Point to house the security force. I arrived with the Okeeda on the afternoon of the second day and found that the task force had been through a tough ordeal. They had been surviving for more than a day on the bounty of the sea. At that point, they had captured more crabs than they could eat and had converted the revenue cutter's lifeboat into a holding tank for the extras.

It was at that point that I learned that the security force to be left at the trap consisted of Officer Lloyd Howard and me. After instructing us to guard and protect the trap at all costs, the rest of the task force departed to return to their respective duties. Officer Howard and I set up a routine in which we took turns surveying the area with binoculars in order to spot any possible hazard before it got too close.

You may wonder what could pose a danger to a structure made with logs and chicken wire, but anyone familiar with that area knows that icebergs sometimes drift out of the bays and into these waters. Also, humpback whales have been known to get tangled in the traps and destroy them. Neither icebergs nor whales approached our position, but we noticed that hungry, vicious, herring-eating salmon were passing below us at all times. We soon found that these fish would attack any shiny object that happened to fall into the water. Due to the passage of years, I don't recall why we had two fishing rods with us, but they must have been issued as a defensive weapon or survival equipment.

We resorted to catching as many of these vicious fish as we could, releasing them on the upstream side of the trap, thus preventing them from doing damage to the facility for which we were responsible. We also found that we could supplement our food supply by filleting an occasional fish.

In checking out the area, we also found that a small island at the mouth of Pybus Bay was so loaded with clams that we only had to scoop them up with a bucket. The clams did not appear to be a threat to the fish trap in our custody, but we made several pots of great clam chowder anyway.

After about two weeks of this stressful and hazardous duty, we received word that Officer Howard was needed back in Anchorage, and a plane would pick him up and drop off a replacement officer. After almost 40 years, I can't recall the name of the replacement, but together we continued to protect the trap for another two weeks. Every day at 5p.m. we tuned in to the news on a Petersburg radio station, hoping to hear something about disposition of the trap. One night the news carried word that the matter had been settled and the cannery had agreed to dismantle and remove the trap from Pybus Point.

The following day a crew from the cannery arrived, but we had received no instructions from our office in Juneau. I got on the radiophone and tried to contact Lieutenant Mayfield, whom we assumed was still in charge of our operation. The Juneau office said they didn't know where he was. They never admitted it, but I think they forgot we were out there. Eventually I did get in touch with Superintendent Bob Brandt, who instructed us to get a receipt for the trap and turn it over to the cannery crew, then return the Okeeda to Ketchikan.

As a result of this operation, I had the honor of witnessing the demise of the last of the infamous floating fish traps and of being the first Alaska State Police officer assigned to skipper a patrol vessel, though the assignment lasted only one month.

December 1998

Lieutenant E.L. (Gene) O'Brien, also known as "OB," was born in Chehalis, Washington and spent four years in the U.S. Navy. He started law enforcement with the Bremerton, Washington, Police Department in September 1950, and in 1955 came to Alaska to join the Alaska Territorial Police. During his career, he worked in Ketchikan, Juneau, Fairbanks, Anchorage and various other assignments. OB had a reputation for being a top-notch, no-nonsense investigator, which from time to time rubbed politicians the wrong way as he was unbending in enforcing the law. OB flew a number of planes for the Alaska State Troopers and during that time was in charge of statewide search and rescue operations, including the famous search for Alaska Congressman Nick Begich and U.S. House Majority Leader Hale Boggs, who disappeared on a flight from Anchorage to Juneau in 1972. OB is a long-time member of the Alaska Peace Officers Association and the Elks. He raised three boys in Alaska and presently lives in Chehalis, Washington.

Trooper Higgins Gets Badged

Sergeant George B. Cole, Retired

"He had me jumping through my shorts" was how Trooper Quentin Higgins explained it to me.

Quentin and I were standing on a beach about 10 miles north of Wales where Trooper Bill McMillan had dropped us off. Bill flew us there in the Trooper plane from Nome so we could make a search and recovery dive on a downed plane. As Quentin and I were checking our dive gear, he told me about the time he nearly got fired.

It seems that Quentin had been working in the Anchorage Metro Drug Unit for about a year when he got orders to call Col. Tom Anderson. Quentin mentally ran through his career to date and couldn't think of anything good or bad enough to rate a call from on high.

"Where's your hat badge?" was the question Col. Anderson had for Quentin. Now, you have to understand that it had been nearly a year since Quentin had even looked at his uniforms. They were carefully folded and put away in plastic bags in the top of his closet at home. He sincerely hoped they were still there.

"My hat badge? It's at home in my closet on my hat."

"I want to see it."

"Yes, sir."

Quentin went home and with a great deal of panic, dug out his uniforms. He heaved a great sigh of relief when he pulled out his hat and right there, centered perfectly, was his hat badge. Trooper Hat Badge Number 58!

Quentin showed his hat and badge to Col. Anderson. He said the Colonel looked a bit puzzled and pulled open a drawer and took out an identical hat badge and letter. They examined both badges. Yep, they were identical; two Alaska State Trooper Hat Badges Number 58.

Col. Anderson explained to Trooper Higgins that the badge in his desk drawer had been sent to him from Wisconsin. The letter with the badge explained that the son of a Wisconsin police officer found the badge while playing in a sand pile in a construction site. The boy showed the badge to his dad, and they decided to mail it back to the Alaska State Troopers.

Like all policemen, Col. Anderson loves a good mystery. Where in the heck did the badge from Wisconsin come from? A quick check of departmental records showed that only two Troopers had been assigned Badge Set Number 58 - Quentin Higgins and George Cole. Since Higgins did not know anything, maybe Cole did. Actually, I did know part of the story. It was 10 years earlier when the mystery began.

Trooper Joe DeTemple and Wildlife Protection Officer Keith Rulison were to blame. I quickly gave them up.

The winter of 1969 was a bitterly cold one in Tok. I was the only law enforcement officer between Delta Junction and Whitehorse that could keep his car running. Every night, I put my 1969 Plymouth to bed with an electric blanket wrapped around its engine. I placed a small catalytic heater under the differential. The block heater was plugged in.

The other two officers, DeTemple and Rulison, did not take such elaborate care of their much older vehicles. The Wildlife Protection vehicle wouldn't start when Mrs. Rulison went into labor at l a.m. that cold November night. Keith called DeTemple, who was on call. DeTemple's car wouldn't start, so Joe knocked on my door to borrow my lovingly well-maintained superior vehicle.

Now, I had been a Tok Trooper for nearly two years. I kept cold weather stuff in the vehicle at all time - the Eddie Bauer down parka, the two military mummy bags, the mouton fur Trooper hat with Trooper Hat Badge Number 58.

Trooper DeTemple took off for Glennallen Hospital in my patrol vehicle with Mrs. Rulison in the back seat. Near Slana, the baby refused to wait any longer. Trooper DeTemple made Mrs. Rulison comfortable by laying her on my parka, mummy bags, and mouton hat with Trooper Hat Badge Number 58.

Later, DeTemple returned the birthing room to me and suggested I get the mess cleaned up before Sergeant Hal Hume came down for a post inspection. Seeing the logic in this, I packaged up the swaddling materials, removed Trooper Hat Badge Number 58 from the mouton hat, and sent the whole shebang to Alaska Laundry in Fairbanks.

A couple of weeks later, the parka, hat and mummy bags came back to Tok, clean as the day they were made. I went to get Trooper Hat Badge Number 58 to put it back on to the mouton hat. No can find!

Searching my memory, I recalled the last time I could actually remember seeing it was the moment I took it off the hat and set it on the dashboard of my patrol car. The car, including the heater vents, was thoroughly searched. No luck. The house was searched. No luck.

Memo to Sergeant Hume: Sir, I seem to have misplaced my hat badge.

$22 and a reprimand later, I was issued a newly manufactured replacement — Trooper Hat Badge Number 58.

In 1974, I was promoted to Corporal. Trooper Badge Set Number 58 was turned in and issued to Trooper Higgins. Five years later, in 1979, the original hat badge turns up in the mail from Wisconsin. When Col. Anderson heard this story, he handed me the original badge and said, "Sergeant, you paid for this, I suppose it's yours."

Oh, how I wish that badge could talk! How did it get from the dashboard of a patrol car in Tok to a sandlot in Wisconsin?

I related all this to Quentin Higgins as we stood together on shore of the Bering Strait, two Alaska Troopers alone together in a remote and wild place, engaged in manly business, serving the public. After the foot race and knuckle rub, I pointed out to Trooper Higgins that he should not do that to a Sergeant.

June 1999

Sergeant George Cole joined the Alaska State Police in June 1966 as a radio dispatcher in Juneau. In January 1967, he was commissioned as a State Trooper. During his career he was stationed in Fairbanks, Tok, Ketchikan, Juneau, and Anchorage. He was also assigned to statewide narcotics, was a long-time member of the tactical dive unit and was honored for valor in 1980. After retiring from the Troopers, George worked for seven years as a VPSO coordinator for Southeast Alaska. George's last endeavor in the workforce was with the City and Borough of Juneau, administering a domestic violence grant. He is presently retired at his cabin in Petersburg.

Constable Gallen Gets Fired Up

Sergeant George B. Cole, Retired

Once again I found myself the victim of circumstances brought about by others. Thanks to Constable Jim Gallen of Northway, I survived.

It was all Fish and Wildlife Protection Officer Mike Roscovius' fault. He was very interested in Alaska history and read lots of books about it. Well, he read one book. Okay, he looked at the pictures. Most of them, anyway.

One autumn day in 1977, we were having a Tok Post meeting. We had a rather spirited debate on the qualities of beverages made with toasted hops vs. non-toasted hops. This led to several samples of each being consumed by everyone present, except Roger Whitaker whose personal convictions prevented him from drinking anything containing the letters B, E, E, or R.

During the post meeting, someone remarked that Roscovius was reading a new book. He discovered Judge James Wickersham made the last law enforcement patrol down the Yukon River from Eagle to Circle to Fairbanks in 1908. We were astounded and immediately calmed our surprise by quaffing some more hop-flavored libations.

I was idly talking with Roscovius one day about the strange habits of grouse on the Old River Road when he again mentioned how long it had been since anyone had made a law enforcement patrol down the Yukon. He thought it might be fun to retrace Judge Wickersham' s footsteps.

All winter, the topic of the Yukon patrol kept coming up. As the nights got colder and longer, any topic about being outside in daylight took on special import. Before February rolled in, the topic had taken on a life of its own and was becoming a plan. The plan became a mission. The mission became an obsession. WE WERE GOING.

After hours of debate and careful consideration, three certainties surfaced: (1) we would need a reason (2) we would need a drink, and (3) we would need help.

Trespass onto Bureau of Lands Management property would be our reason. We invited Leroy Cook , the BLM lands specialist, and Leroy Allen, the BLM enforcement officer, to ask us to accompany them on our patrol, which would be their patrol when talking to our bosses and our patrol when talking to their bosses. (Convoluted reasoning is revered in the federal government as much as it is in state government.)

Roscovius took care of drink. He arranged with Officer/Pilot Dick Hemmen to deliver a couple of jugs of foot medicine in the F&WP Supercub. It is a well-known fact that riding on snowmachines makes your feet hurt. Foot medicine was a necessity.

We took a vote and elected Constable Jim Gallen as our guide. He was born and raised in Northway and had been bragging for years about his survival skills.

I was real impressed with Constable Gallen. Jim could find his way from Northway to Tok three out of four tries. That was considerably better than Geoffrey Engleman who was once lost for a week between the bar and the men' s room at the Northway Lodge.

Jim once paid me the highest compliment. He took me on a snowmachine patrol to Tetlin to visit with one of the village Elders. I only fell off the machine one or eight times. After I made a brief speech to the Elders, they playfully threw us out of Tetlin, brandishing axes and sticks in the air to salute our departure. After we returned to Northway he told me, "Corporal, after meeting you I have a much higher opinion of former Northway Post Troopers Glenn Godfrey, Roy Sagraves, and Geoff Engleman." I thanked him, as it was obvious my poised and regal bearing did much to improve his opinion of Alaska State Troopers in general.

Constable Gallen was delighted when we told him he was to be our guide. He disguised his elation with a faux display of gruff disgust. He pretended to be reluctant to participate and jested with us, quipping, "We're all going to die," and, "You guys are morons." But in the end, he threw himself into the spirit of the adventure after Rosco told him about the foot medicine.

On March 13, 1978, the historical journey began. I had court that day, so Roger Whitaker drove my machine at the start. By vehicle to Mile 32 on the Taylor Highway, then snowmachines to Eagle.

From Eagle, Roscovius, Gallen, the two Leroys, and Whittaker began the historic first law enforcement patrol down the Yukon River since 1908. On March 15, I flew and traded places with Roger.

It was cold— thirty degrees below zero with colder nights. Jim soon earned his position. He picked out the best trail. He kept us away from thin ice. His no-nonsense stoic bearing inspired us all. Jim of the North.

The third day was the coldest. It looked like we were going to camp out in the cold when we ran into a trapper who was on his way to Eagle. He graciously offered us the use of his cabin. "She'll be cold and there's not much wood, but there's a stove and you're welcome to use her." Jim told us not to worry. He knew how to start fires in this bitterly cold, frozen land. He knew an old Indian trick his grandfather taught him.

We followed that trapper's backtrail, crisscrossing the frozen Yukon. Finally, as night was approaching, we reached his cabin, a surprisingly spacious place perched on a bank well above the river and set back up against a mixed stand of birch and fir. We were all frozen.

After we unloaded our gear, we were ready for a rip-roaring fire. We all looked at Jim and I asked if we could watch him build the fire. He grunted his assent.

In a mystical and reverent manner, Constable Gallen went outside to a birch tree. He murmured to the tree and cleared the snow away from the base of its trunk. He gathered a handful of small twigs. Thanking the tree, he went to another and again intoned a mantra. He broke off several dry, dead branches and scraped a handful of moss from its trunk. He took these items into the cabin and arranged them carefully in the stove. He then said, "Now for the secret my grandfather passed down to me to preserve our people." He sprang to his feet, rushed outside to where the snowmachines were and drained a half-cup of gas and oil from one of them.

Grinning like a bear munching on a tourist, he splashed the mixture on his twigs and moss. Standing about three feet away, he threw lit matches at the gas soaked tinder and VOILA! We had a roaring fire. In fact, we had about 11 roaring fires. After beating and stomping out all the fires we did not need and fanning the smoke from the cabin, we settled down for the night in front of the now cherry-red stove.

Everyone agreed that an explosion and impromptu fire drill caused pain in our feet and a copious quantity of foot medicine was consumed. A feeling of manly fellowship fell over the group. After Roscovius led us in group singing and a rousing game of Go Fish, we fell asleep on the floor of a trapper' s cabin on the bank of the Yukon River in the wild and frozen North. Rumors of Herculean hangovers the next day have been greatly exaggerated.

If you don't believe this story is true, just examine Jim's moustache the next time you run into him. It used to be thick and luxurious like Tom Selleck's. One of the 11 fires burned it down to the thin and scraggly remnant you see today.

September 1999

Lieutenant Lown Goes to See the Varmint

Sergeant George B. Cole, Retired

"I had one of those in-of-body experiences the other day," retired Alaska Trooper Lieutenant Robin Lown was telling me.

"You mean out-of-body, don't you?" I replied.

"Nope, in-of-body."

Many times during his 24 years with the Alaska State Troopers, Robin Lown had encounters with animals. Protected and emboldened by the badge on his chest, the gun on his hip, and the Trooper blue of his uniform, Trooper Lown rose to every animal occasion.

One time in Fairbanks he chased a moose off the road with a flare. (Okay, it was really Jay Yakopatz that was held captive in his patrol car after tossing a flare at a moose. It hit the moose and Mr. Moose responded by chasing Jay back to his car and keeping him trapped inside for 15 minutes. But this story flows better if you imagine it was Robin.)

Another time Robin helped swing-shift round up two loose goats. And don't forget the time he assisted with the runaway turkey. Heck, he is even named after an animal.

With all his rapport with animals, it was no surprise to us that in his retirement he should adopt Babs the cat and Moki the old, fat Beagle. It is quite a sight to behold, this old, grizzled, steely-eyed retired Trooper, scratching Babs under the chin or sleeping on the couch with Moki cuddled up against him.

Robin loved the old Mokester. He even put in a pet door, so Moke could get outside at night. And Moki loved Robin. That love was nearly Moki's undoing.

It was about 3 a.m. when Moki tried to awaken Robin to warn him of danger. Robin was sleeping soundly and would not stir. Finally, in desperation, the old Beagle began to howl while scratching the floor and bumping against Robin's bed.

"Go use your doggie door," Robin mumbled. But Moki was not deterred. He had to get Robin up and moving. More howling and scratching.

Finally, Robin was aroused enough to be angry. He staggered out of bed and grabbed Moki. With Moki under one arm, Robin scurried towards the front door. With all the noise Moki was making, he must really have to go.

Protected, not by Trooper blue, but only jockey shorts, Robin threw open the front door as the crescendo of Moki's howls reached their zenith. With one hand on the door now and the other holding Moki by the scruff of the neck, Robin thrust Moki through the door into the night, and right into the arms of the black bear that was rummaging through the trash.

Now everyone is in pretty much of a hum. The bear dropped the garbage. The bear headed up the hill. Moki headed down the stairs. Robin headed back to bed. There were three distinct pops as the air rushed in to fill the voids where they had been microseconds before.

"I felt a bit bad about it later," Robin confessed. "I felt a tad vulnerable standing there in my underwear. It would have been a lot different if I had been in uniform. Anyway, Moki made it around the house, through the doggie door, up the stairs and under my bed before I was halfway there."

"What about that 'in-of-body' experience you were talking about," I asked.

"Well, in the excitement of the moment, I forgot about my larynx. Some small girl took advantage of that and seized my vocal cords. She used them to scream in a high voice as I slammed the door and ran back to bed. I couldn't wrest control of them away from her until I had the covers up over my head."

February 2000

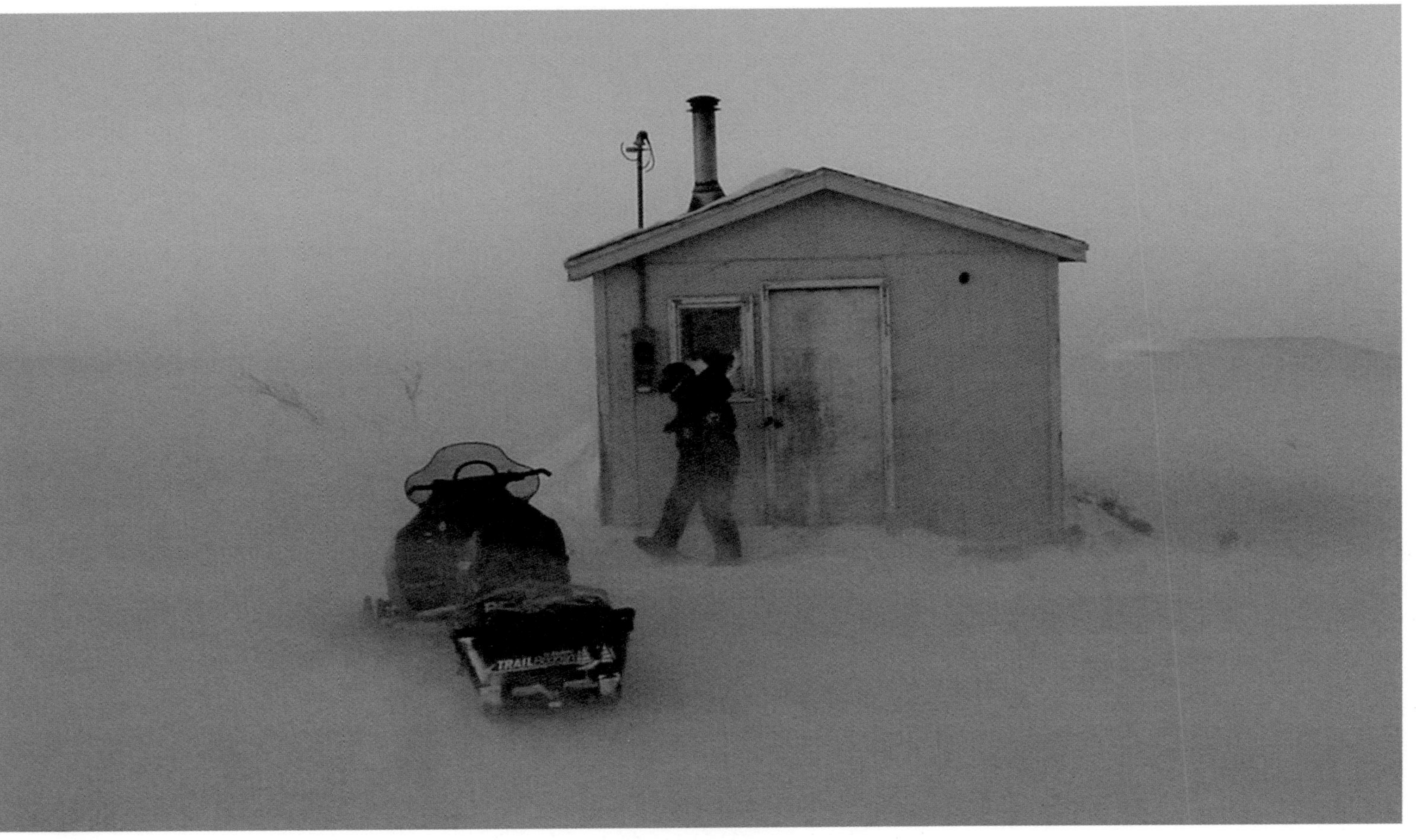

TPR Fowler in Teller AK, North of Nome

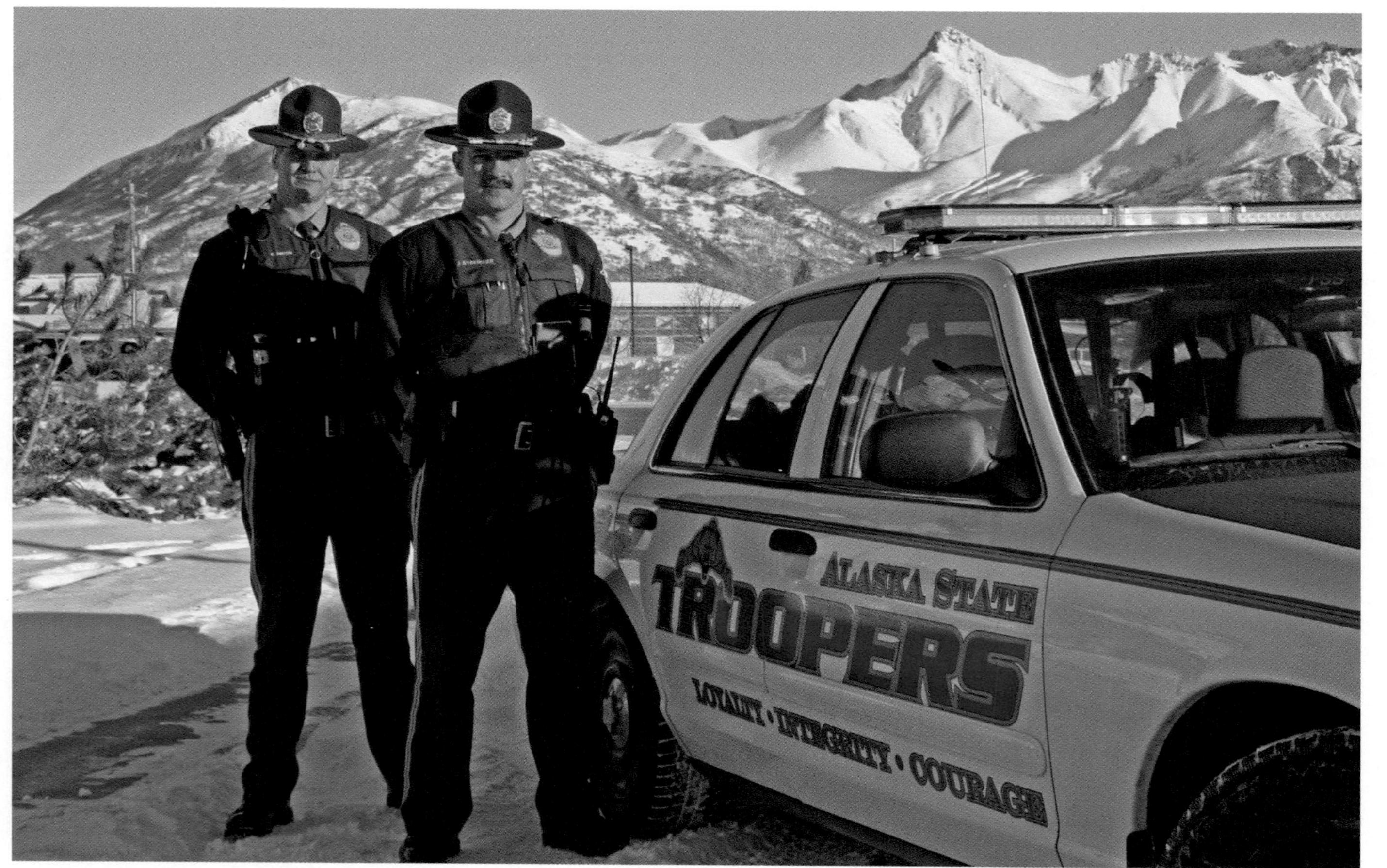

FTO Hinson & TPR Streicher with patrol car

SGT Roberts responding to call

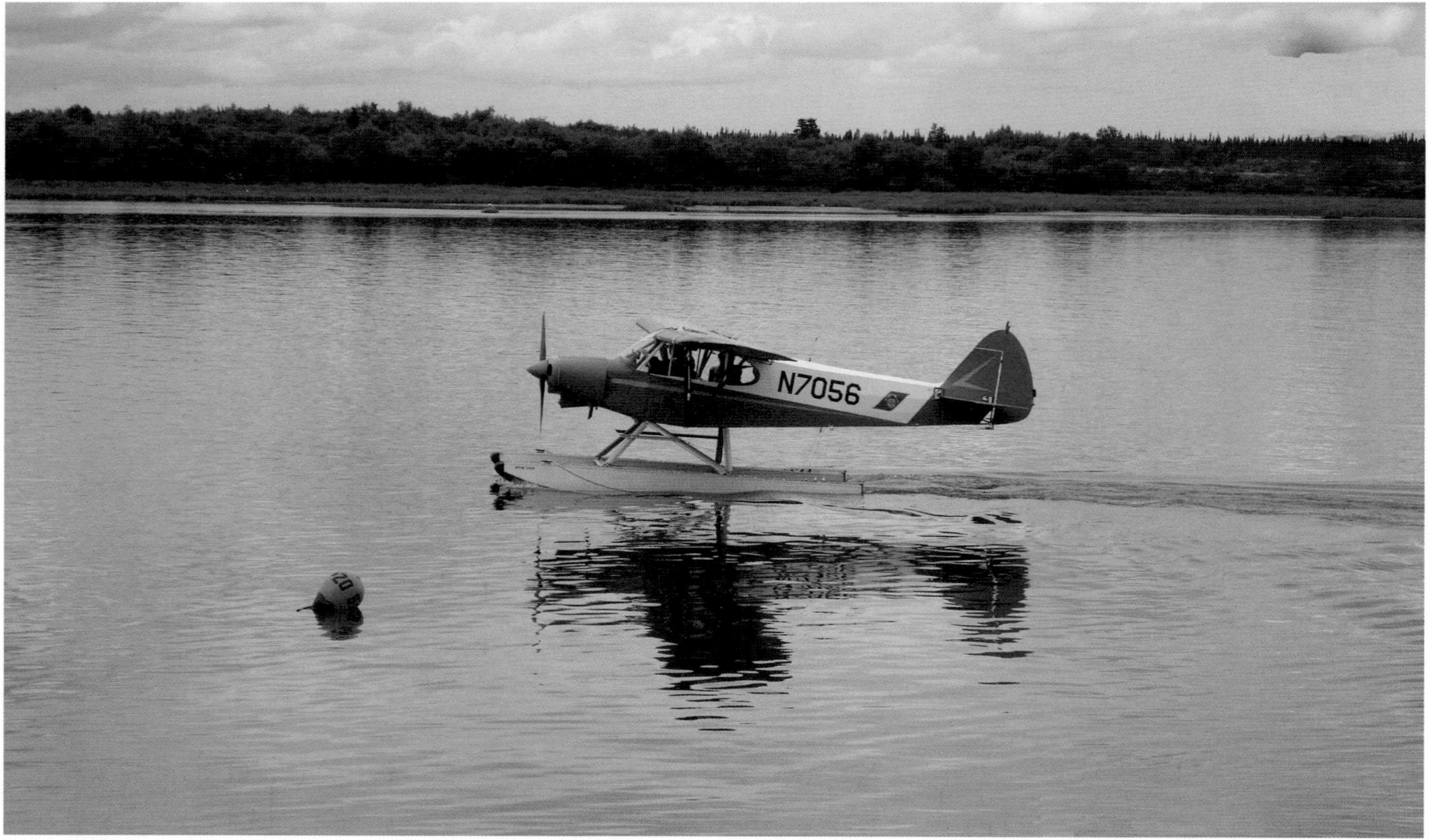

TPR Francis Fay and Capt Waldren

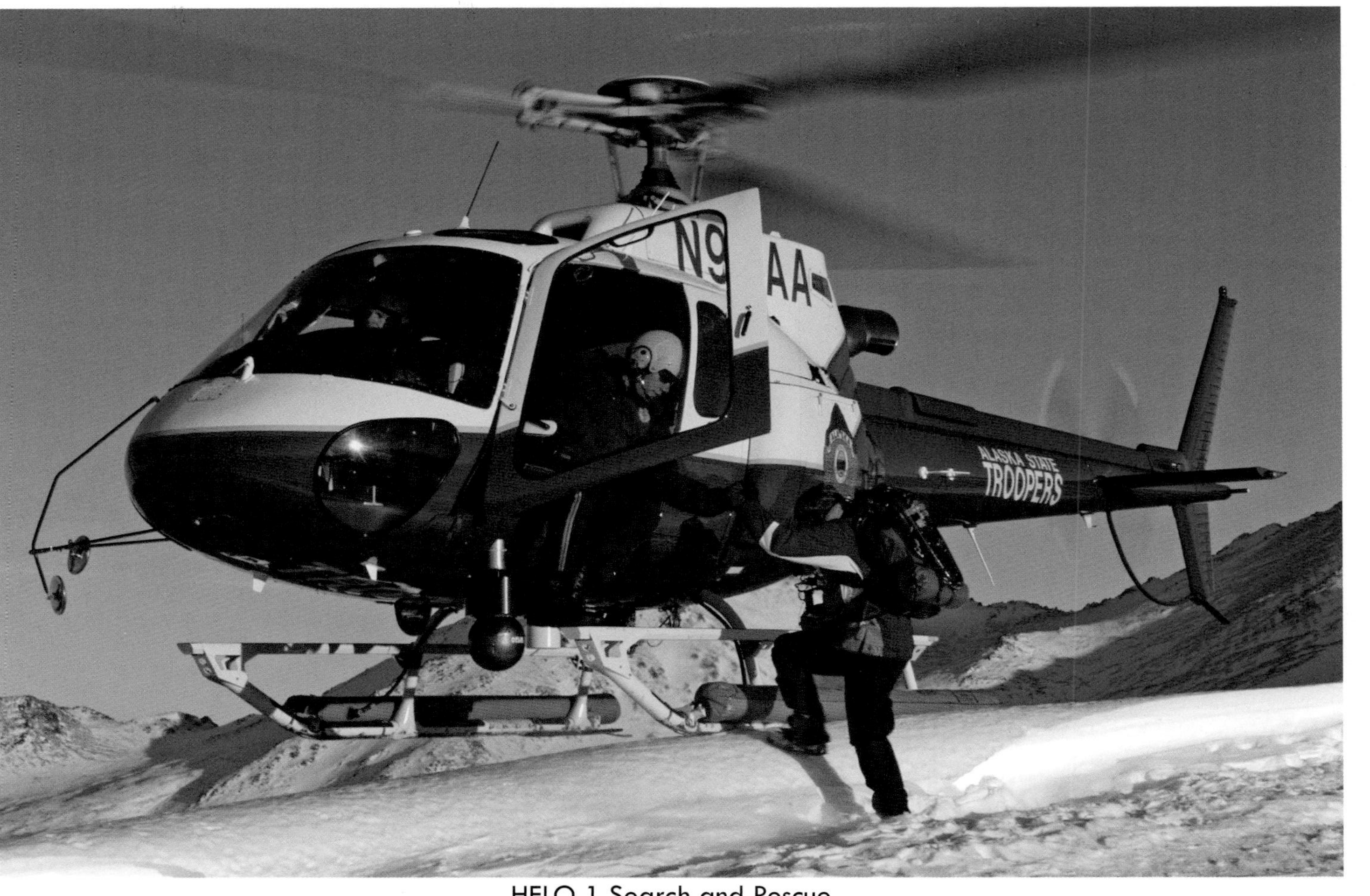

HELO 1 Search and Rescue

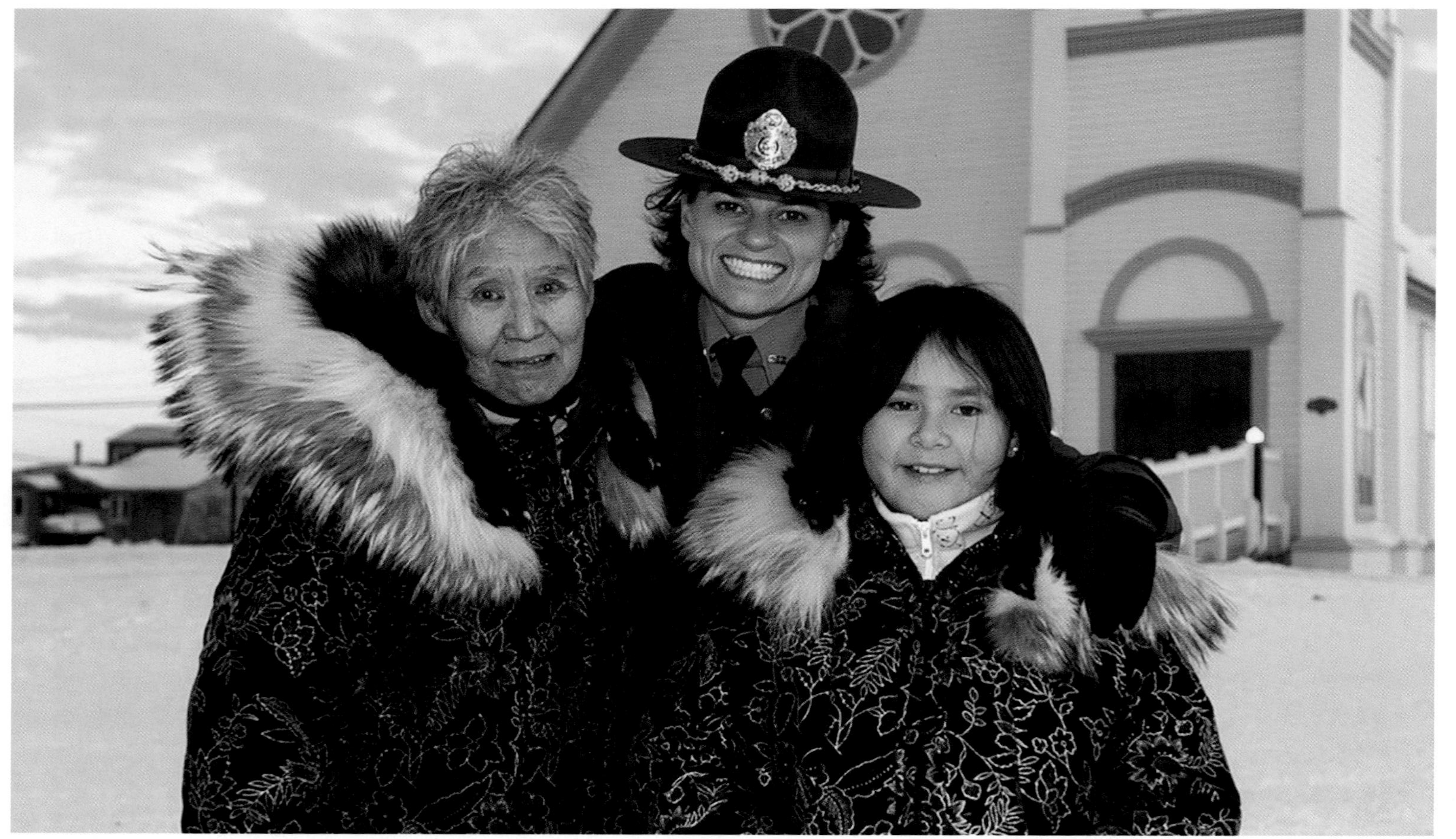

TPR Witrosky with 2 friends in Nome

TPR Shanigan recruits by demonstrating traditional dog sledding

TPR Shamhart and TPR Burton AWT on PV MOEN

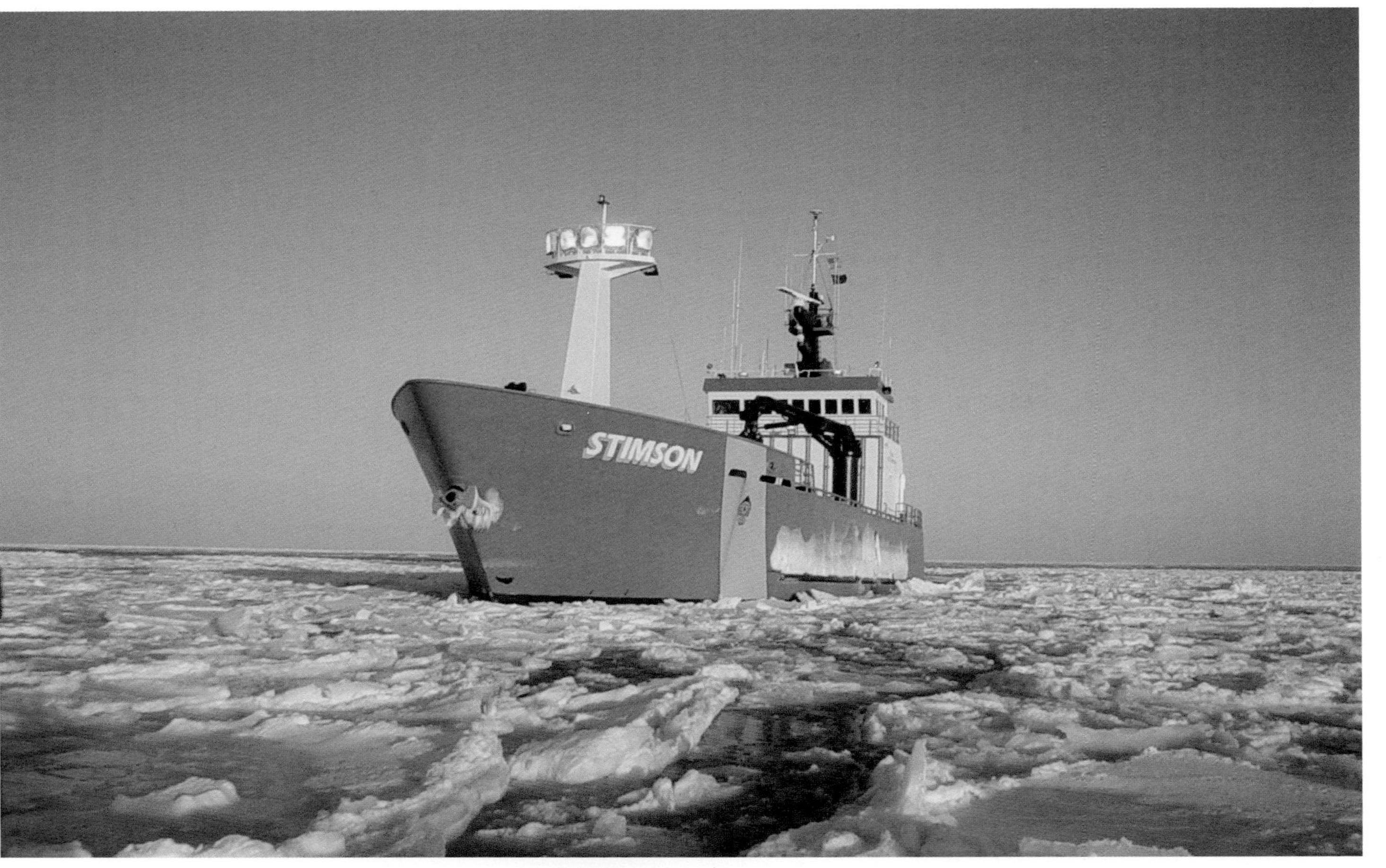

PV STIMSON in icy waters

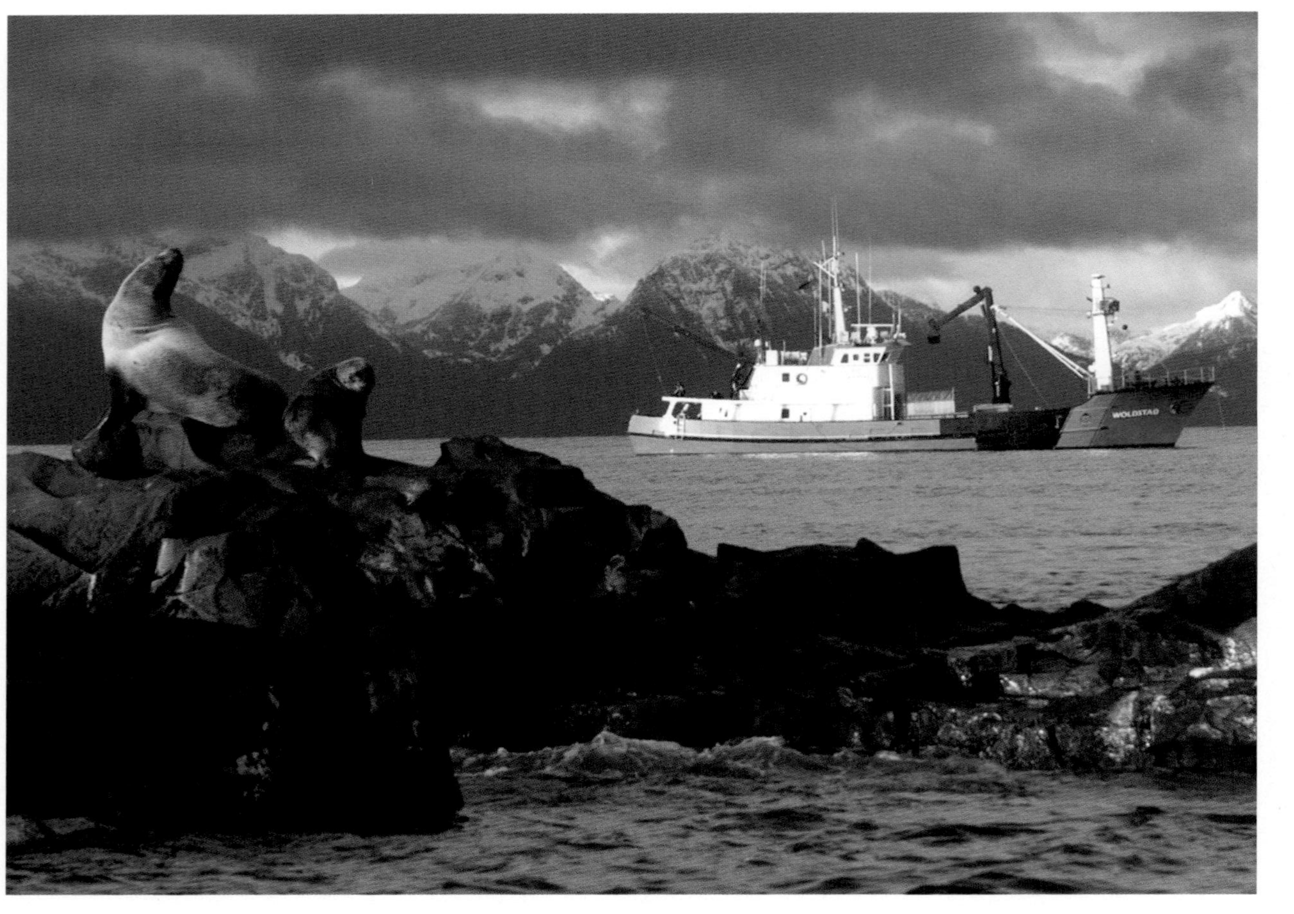

PV WOLDSTAD and sea lions

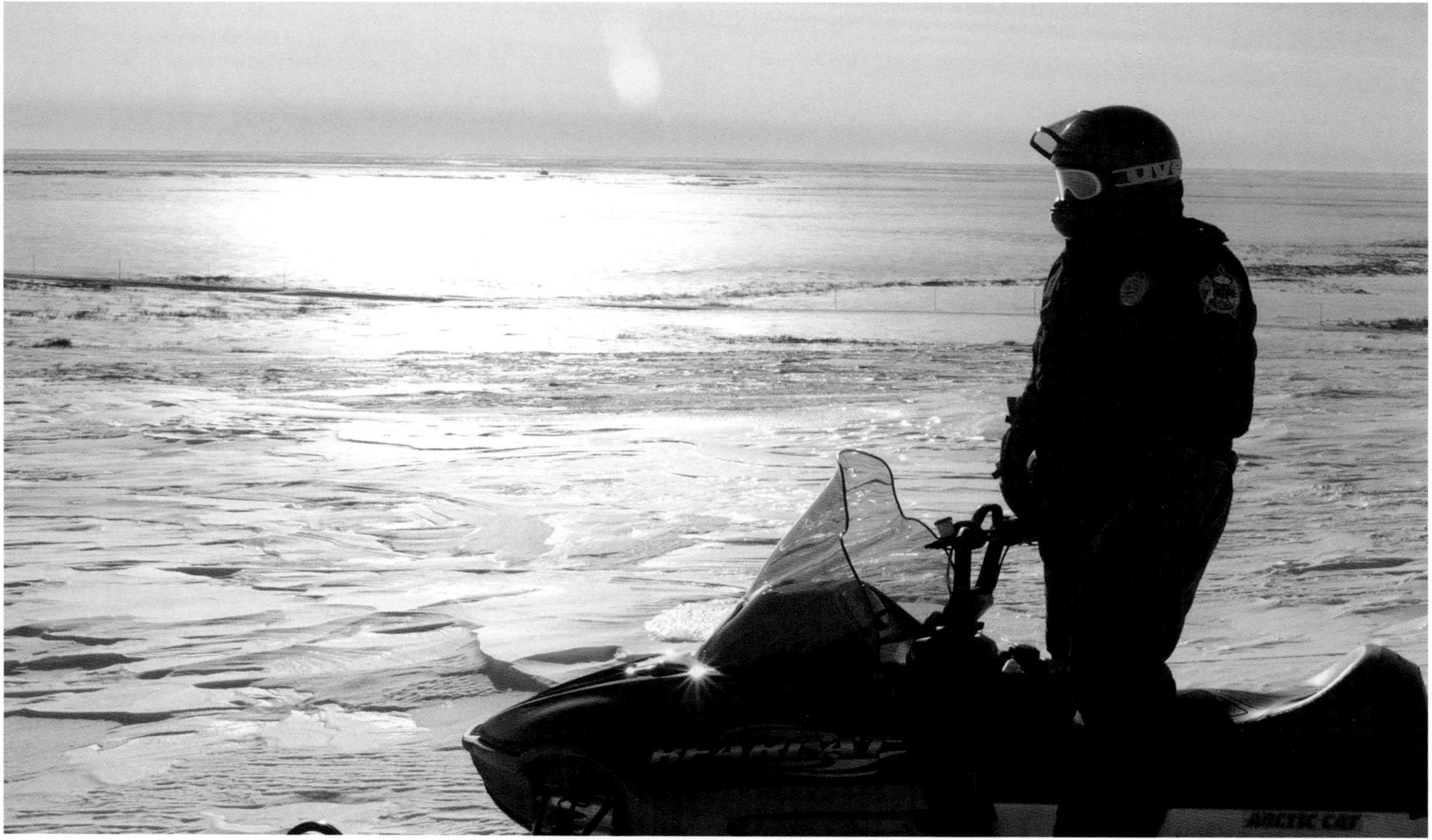

AST on snow machine viewing Nome

Contemporary AST Patrol Vehicle

Historical Patrol Car-Restored 1952 Hudson Hornet

Museum Display – Bronze of George Taft first AK Crime Lab Director

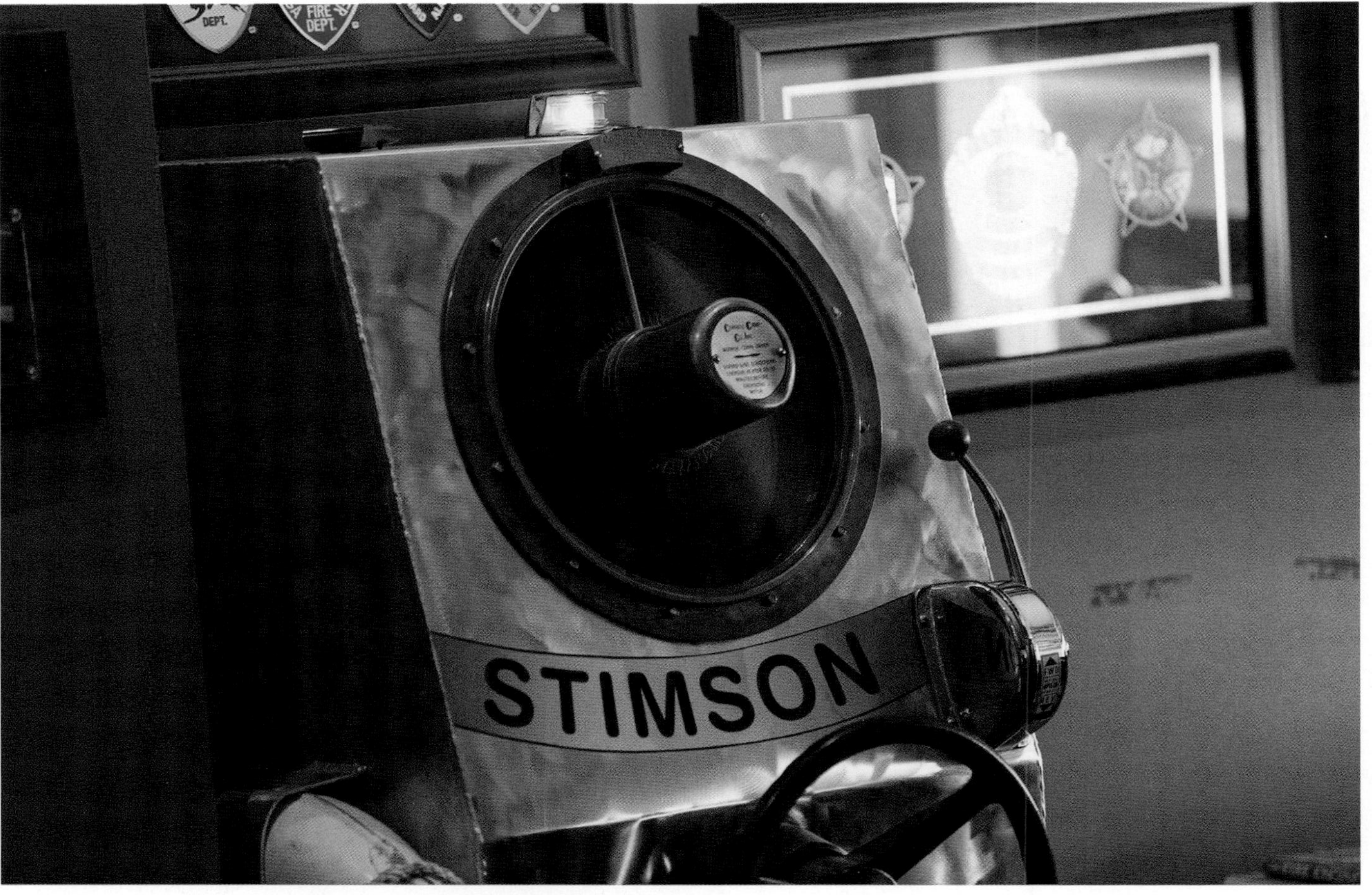

PV Stimson parts salvaged to create interactive display

FOAST Law Enforcement Museum Displays –
Safety Bear, Uniforms and artifacts

Fairbanks Memories

Sergeant George B. Cole, Retired

When I was a young man, I used to hate it when some old guy would suddenly say, "that reminds me." Now, I know it means that mental mist has momentarily lifted and the old gentleman has to get it quickly said or it will again be lost. Come on fingers; type these memories rapidly before they get lost again.

"Say, that reminds me." Sergeant Carl Schligtig could strike terror in a young Trooper's heart with those words. You could be trapped in his office for hours while he wandered among memories. You learned to quickly stride past the open door of his office with an air about you like you were hastening to an emergency or responding to a summons by Commander Shirley Johnson. Everyone below the rank of Captain snapped to attention when Mrs. Johnson issued an order. Even old Carl was afraid of her.

It is strange how seemingly unrelated events can come together to bring back memories that drifted away and became lost in the fog of time. Two recent stories about Shirley Johnston in the Banner and a visit by my father- in-law combined to dispel some of my mental haze.

My father-in-law recently visited our remote Petersburg home for the purpose of hunting the elusive buck. Since he is in his 70's, he did most of his hunting from our front porch with a libation tightly held in one hand while using the other to punctuate his tales. On the last day of our short season, he got his buck. I trotted over to it and gave it a 'coop- dee-grassy" with my "pistolover", as Joe DeTemple would say.

A dirty gun caused me to dig out the box containing my gun cleaning stuff. In the box I also found an Alaska State Police Property Envelope. Inside the envelope was Jay Yakopatz' name tag, old State Police buttons, ASP and AST collar insignia, a pin in the form of the number eight, chevrons, patches, and a pair of lead- lined gloves.

The stories about Shirley Johnston reminded me of when I was first posted to Fairbanks. I arrived on February 15, 1967. To say that Shirley Johnston dominated the office at 1616 Cushman is like saying Fairbanks is somewhat chilly in January. She ordered young Troopers around like they were assigned to her.

Come to think of it, I was assigned to work for her just after the flood. Many dispatchers were not able to get to work, and I had been a dispatcher before becoming a Trooper. While other young troops were out patrolling by boat or rescuing damsels in distress, I was stuck working in dispatch for Mrs. Johnston. Actually, she was very easy to work for, as long as your work was perfect. Thinking about Mrs. Johnston (I would not have dared call her then, or now Shirley) reminds me of three dispatchers that cause me to smile—Bernita Purdy, Mattie Flanagan and Alice Malcolm.

I was working a lone graveyard with Alice as my dispatcher. She was one of the sweetest people I ever met. It had been pretty slow when the radio repeater clicked on followed by Alice briskly announcing there was a report of an 11-88 off Sheep Creek Road. I acknowledged with a 10-4. I looked at my cheat sheet, but it did not list 11-88. So, I called back to Alice and asked her what an 11-88 was. There was a very long pause. Finally the repeater clicked on and after another long pause, Alice softly whispered, "rape." Alice, I'm sorry my ignorance made it necessary for you to utter that word on the radio.

One day I came into the dispatch area from back by the coffee pot and had a green felt marker that I was using to mark a map with locations of recovered stolen autos. Mattie Flanagan was leaning into the radio cubicle using her hand to support herself against the doorjamb. I stopped and looked at her hand and thought how pretty her nails would be if they were green. I painted one green and she did not move. She was totally absorbed in whatever was happening in the cubicle. I painted the rest of her nails, but could not get her thumbnail because it was around the corner. Finally, she straightened up and noticed her nails. I wish you could have seen the look on her face when she discovered her newly painted fingertips.

Bernita Purdy was great. She was not only an outstanding dispatcher but also a good sport. One time in January she was flying out of Fairbanks and did not want to leave her car to freeze up at the airport. I was asked to provide transportation for her. I was nearing the end of a graveyard shift and picked her up in a marked unit while wearing the full winter uniform. When we got to the airport, I helped her carry her luggage up to the crowded ticket counter. When I set her luggage down, I turned to her and in a loud, stern voice said, "And don't you ever come back!" I turned and walked away without a backward glance. She tried for years to get even with me.

The stuff in the gun cleaning box reminded me that the bunch of young Troopers assigned to Fairbanks in the late '60s and early '70s were pretty easily amused. One thing we all did was steal each other's name tags. My favorite one to steal belonged to Jay Yakopatz. I would put it on and seek him out to see how long I could talk to him before he would notice. I assumed I won the contest because I still have his nametag. But then I got to looking around for mine and I cannot seem to locate it. Hmmmmmm.

Another name game we played was to change names on the mailboxes located in the hallway between the dispatch/clerical center and the back of the holding cells. The boxes were open at both ends so mail or completed reports could be slipped in one side and taken out the other. Nametags on both ends helped route material to the correct Trooper. We began playing two games. One was to mix up the name tags and the other was to create fictitious officers or misspell real names. Ed Close became "Fast Eddie." Cole became "Coal." I drove poor Sam Barnard crazy by continuously changing his name to read "Barnyard" (Please Sam, don't sharpen your knife). No comment on John Lucking.

Later in my career we showed departmental seniority by numerical metal pins worn in a blue fabric circle on our left sleeves. The "8" pin reminded me that anyone with more than a year in the Department was considered a seasoned veteran. Roger McCoy, aka "The Phantom," was one of those old hands when I joined. He had a full year on and knew almost everything. I often rode with him after my shift to gain the benefit of his experience.

One shift found us on the way to an injury accident at Aurora Drive and College Road. Roger took the shortcut through Phillips Field and where the road makes the sharp right corner, he ran into the ditch. He never mentioned it and neither did I, until now. (A couple of years later, I ran into the ditch while responding to a call for assistance from the Nite Beat. I got out without damage, thanks to Rudy Voight who was just passing by. Neither he nor I ever mentioned it, until now).

At the accident, Roger told me to direct traffic. I got traffic moving slowly but steadily around the scene. Everyone cooperated but this one blue car stopped, and the driver rolled down the window and asked if he could help. I wondered what this rather dowdy and scruffy looking guy in his plaid wool shirt thought he could do to help and told him "no" and waved him on. Trooper Bob Crank from Nenana rolled up his window, and as he drove his marked patrol car away I noticed the Alaska State Police logo on his door and the red light on the roof. So much for my reputation as a keen-eyed sleuth. Bob could have sent us both home and handled the scene in half the time it took us. Much later, I used this lesson to watch young Troopers muddle through other accidents that I could have handled easier and quicker.

The ASP and AST collar insignia and buttons remind me of the changeover from Alaska State Police to Alaska State Troopers. There was even some consideration given to calling ourselves Alaska State Rangers! We also changed the design of our uniforms. Even after all the years, I still prefer "Alaska State Police" (Hey, are we policemen or the cavalry?) and the old "Alaska Tuxedo" uniform. Mine came equipped with a six-inch revolver in a clamshell holster.

I was happy to see the old clamshell holster go away. For those of you who never experienced this early version of a "safe" holster, this was a two-piece hard holster that folded around the barrel and muzzle of the gun. It latched shut and could only be opened by poking your index finger through the trigger guard. The holster snapped open, and the gun dropped into your hand. In the six months I wore it, I did not shoot myself. I attribute this more to good luck than good design or good sense.

As for the lead-lined gloves, they were a waste of money. I never used them, and they did not keep my hands warm on those cold Fairbanks nights. But I have to admit I slipped them on and for a flash of a moment I felt like a 21-year-old, steely-eyed protector of the frozen North.

Say, that reminds me....

February 2001

Trooper Swanson Always Aimed High

Sergeant George B. Cole, Retired

Trooper Bill Swanson (who later became Sergeant Carl Swanson in a futile attempt to disguise his identity from former friends and associates), always aimed high.

I first met Bill in Ketchikan where he was always aiming high. While most of us Troopers were taking the Corporals Exam, Bill was taking the Sergeants Exam. He intended to skip Corporal and become a Sergeant on his way to Colonel.

Bill stood tall. His head was always held high. Everything about Bill exuded a sense of loftiness. When Bill wrote a report, that report stood tall. Bill lived at the top of Carlana. Bill, and everything about him, was rising.

Bill also shot high. No matter how he tried, his groups tended to be above the X ring. He worked on it. Shot the PPC in the high nineties, but still the groups tended to be high. Right on, but high.

In the mid-70's, hostage situations were pretty rare. No one thought much about them, especially in Ketchikan, Alaska. We had no training, no plan, and very little idea of what to do if one should come our way. So we were caught pretty much unprepared when we found ourselves in the middle of one.

I think it was Trooper Leonard Krise - or perhaps Trooper Harvey Homan - that took the original call. A distraught woman had taken three people hostage in a trailer about three miles south of Ketchikan near Buggy Beach. One of the hostages was a pregnant woman. The troubled woman was armed with a rifle.

Bill Swanson and I arrived at about the same time. We quickly formulated a plan of action. Krise would take the rear of the trailer and Homan the front. Bill would back me up as I tried to get a peek inside. I went up to the side door and peered through the window.

The woman with the rifle was sitting on the floor across the room from three people who were sitting on a couch. I could hear distressed voices but could not make out what they were saying.

I retreated to talk it over with Bill. I've since learned that what I did was not correct procedure, but it seemed like a good idea at the time. I decided to trade myself for the pregnant woman if I could. This would put me inside where I had a chance of talking the woman out of anything rash.

I was sort of known for talking. One of my proudest moments up to this time was the time the 325-pound, 6'7" monster who was holding five Troopers at bay said to me, "Trooper, I'll go to jail with you if you will just shut the blank up."

I went back up on the side porch and hollered to the woman. She agreed to let me exchange myself for the pregnant woman. The expecting lady and I passed in the doorway. I left the door open behind me so Bill could continue to cover me.

I moved over next to the couch and pulled up a folding chair. I sat down and began talking to the woman with the rifle. I didn't recognize how scared I was until later when I realized I had talked non-stop for 45 minutes and could not remember a single word I said to her.

But it must have worked. After 45 minutes, she laid the rifle down. I lunged forward, grabbed it, and skidded it behind me towards the open door. Bill came boiling through the door on his hands and knees, skidding the rifle further out of reach. We both grabbed the woman and as Bill was putting his pistol back into his holster, I handcuffed her and turned her over to Trooper Homan.

Bill spoke a few words to me. I nearly fainted and had to sit down. Some might say it was reaction to stress. Some might say the adrenaline was wearing off. But, I know it was because of what Bill said.

"I had you covered, Corporal. I had a perfect shot at her under your seat, between your legs. If she had started to point that rifle at you, I was going to shoot her."

Trooper Bill Swanson always aimed high.

November 2001

'Iron Hand' Trooper Breaks the Language Barrier

Sergeant George B. Cole, Retired

Bob "Iron Hand" Stuart was a manly man. He was an imposing figure— 6 foot, 3 inches tall and weighing in at 215 lbs. He looked like the ex-Marine, ex-semipro football player he was. His craggy visage, erect stature, and piercing gaze were enough to let you know right from the start that this was not a man to mess with. When you met him in the hall in his Trooper uniform, it was like you were meeting a blue mountain. Sort of a Walt Zahn-like physical presence.

Bob was a veteran of Vietnam, where a sniper's shot took the four fingers from his right hand and the pinky from his left. He rehabilitated himself by laboriously turning himself into a leftie and designing a prosthesis right hand. He settled on an apparatus consisting of four slightly curved fingers and half a palm that nestled against the remaining stub of his natural palm and strapped around his wrist.

With the prosthesis in place, he had some use of his right hand by working against the artificial fingers with his thumb. He even taught himself to shoot his revolver with that hand by holding it upside down and pulling the trigger with his thumb. But the most unusual thing about it was that Bob chose to have his artificial hand made not out of flesh colored plastic, but out of three and a half pounds of cold, rolled steel.

When he was transferred to Tok in the summer of 1977, his reputation preceded him. He was the Trooper who painted a holding cell on the floor of his office in Prudhoe Bay. He told his prisoners to stay in the cell— and they did. He would stop a pipeline 18-wheeler in mid-winter and walk the driver to the back of the rig to talk with him. With his iron hand covered by a glove he would casually reach out and knock the thick ice buildup off the license plate— impressing the heck out of the Texan or Oklahoman driver who was shivering in his tight jeans and cowboy boots trying to look good at 40-below.

One of the first things Bob did when he arrived in Tok was to install a heavy bag and a speed bag in the storage locker area. Then he put in a full weight set in one of the empty apartments. We all got used to the sound of his workouts. The rappa-rappa of the speed bag. The thud, thud, thud of the heavy bag. The clanking and grunting of a weight room. He used them all daily, and he ran. You did not mess with Trooper Stuart.

A French-Canadian man from Quebec decided to travel across Canada and then tour Alaska. He did not have a lot of money so he thought he would finance his journey by selling drugs along the way. He had a wonderful trip. He toured Alaska with stops in Kenai, Anchorage, Denali, Fairbanks, and Tok.

His plan was simple. Contact the young people he ran into and extol the effects of MDMA. Then sell them a handful of the pills for enough money to continue his journey. In Tok, he opened his roadside shop but hit a bit of a snag when the first kid he contacted went home and told his parents. The parents contacted the on-call Trooper, Trooper Stuart, with a description of the entrepreneur and the location of his roadside business.

Bob rolled up to the man and began talking to him. The suspect spoke perfect English even if it was heavily accented. After all, he was able to conduct his business with young people who could not speak French. When Bob broached the subject of his business, the erstwhile tourist began forgetting English. After Bob found the drugs, the suspect could no longer "Parley Vois Inglais." But he did understand handcuffs.

Now Bob knows the suspect can speak English, but he refuses to respond other than to indicate he only understands French. So Bob decides to find someone in Tok who can act as interpreter. He parks the suspect in the Tok holding facility and begins his search.

A call to the school yields people who can speak Spanish and one who can get by in German, but no French. No luck with other Troopers, the Visitor's Center, the pipeline pump station, Customs, or Department of Highways. So, Bob heads out to the places where people gather. No French spoken at Tok Tesoro, Partners Pantry, or the Parker House. But his luck changes at Tok Lodge.

"Does anyone in here speak French?" asked Trooper Stuart,

standing tall at one end of the bar. No one answered as he glanced around the room. At the other end of the bar sat Tom. He looked up at Bob, nodded his head, and stood up.

"I speak French," he said. Bob explained his problem, and Tom agreed to come with him to the Trooper office. "Glad to be of assistance, Trooper."

Bob drove Tom to the Trooper office since Tom had been drinking and should not drive by himself. But, Tom seemed lucid and Bob decided he was quite capable of handling the task of interpreting.

When they got to the office, Bob got everything arranged. The rights form, the tape recorder, and his notebook were carefully arranged on the table. He sat Tom down at one end of the table and brought the suspect out of the holding cell and seated him at the other end. Bob sat down and started the recorder. "Okay," said Trooper Stuart, sternly. "Tell him he has the right to remain silent." Tom nodded his head and turned to the suspect. "You 'av zeeee rrrrite to rrreemain zilent."

The explosion of air from Stuart cleared his desk of all papers. He slammed his steel fist onto the table, causing the whole office to shake. The bear rug on the wall quivered and shook as if it was awakening from hibernation. The suspect looked like he had just experienced a heart attack. Tom looked mildly surprised.

"Get the hell out of here," bellowed Stuart, pointing at the door. "Not you," he said at the suspect who all of a sudden again understood English and was making a move to the door. "Me?" asked Tom, "but aren't you going to give me a ride back to the bar?"

May 2002

Eh?

Sergeant George B. Cole, Retired

Lately, I've been deeply concerned about my wife's hearing. She just doesn't seem to hear me when I talk to her unless we are close and facing each other. The other day she was piling seaweed on the garden and since she was facing away from the house, did not notice me sitting on the porch. I thought to myself that this would be a perfect time to test her hearing.

"Honey," I said in a normal voice, "Can you hear me?" There was no response. She continued arranging the seaweed. "Honey, can you hear me?" I called in a louder voice. Still, no response. Shaking my head sadly I recalled the two times in my life that I was temporarily deaf.

The first time was in 1974 in Ketchikan. Now, April in Ketchikan holds promise. The days are getting longer and warmer. It is a time of renewal, and of discovery. Two city employees made a discovery while engaged in spring-cleaning. They discovered a couple hundred rusty cans of ether from a WWII field hospital in the dark recesses of a city warehouse. Soon, a representative can found its way onto my desk.

I held the small can and examined it from all angles. I shook it next to my ear and there was a sloshing sound. "Ether" proclaimed the label. Also, "Extremely Flammable," and "Danger of Explosion." The explosion part worried me but also suggested a way out.

Cyril "Boom Boom" Cederborg had recently been hired as the Trooper EOD expert. I don't know exactly what "EOD" stands for except the first word is explosives. I made the connection and called Anchorage to speak with Boom Boom. He was excited and said he would respond to Ketchikan toot sweet.

April 24 arrived in Ketchikan and so did Boom Boom, closely monitored by Trooper Roy Holland. I took them to where the ether was located. Cederborg slavered over the cans of ether. He fondled them. He cradled them. He cherished them. He could hardly wait to blow them up. Roy Holland failed in his duty to contain the devil.

We found a gravel pit about three miles from Ketchikan. Boom Boom built a pyramid out of the cans with several blasting caps molded into some silly putty stuff in the center. We backed way off. Boom Boom uttered the understatement of the last century when he said, "This is going to be a bit loud." Those were the last words I heard for about an hour.

Cedarborg twisted a knob on the top of what looked like a Prince Albert tobacco can. That was followed by the loudest noise I ever heard. Debris rained down all around us while a small mushroom cloud of dust rose into the sky. KPD and AST got worried calls from Gravina, Pennock Island, Hole in the Wall, and Clover Pass. There was nothing left of the blasting caps, the ether, or the containers. They were gone, vaporized along with an astonishing amount of rock.

My second episode of temporary deafness was in the fall of 1979 in Anchorage. As Sergeants are wont to do, I was sitting around slurping coffee and thinking of ways to torment my hard-working Troopers. My reverie was broken when a gentleman presented himself at the door. He thrust into my hands a boxful of items he had discovered while cleaning a rental unit, and beat his retreat.

I recognized the drug paraphernalia and logged those items into evidence. The two grenade simulators were beyond my experience. I recognized them as some kind of military explosive, but beyond that, I was in the dark. I showed them to a couple of Troopers and one of them - Dennis Morrow, I think - said he recognized them from his stint in the military. "Sort of like a giant firecracker," he said.

He lied. I learned a great truth that October night. No matter how old they are, no matter how responsible their position is supposed to be, men are really just large boys.

"Giant firecracker." Those words echoed throughout the tin shack on Tudor Road. As swing shift ended and graveyard began, the men of the two shifts began an irresistible chant, "Giant firecracker, giant firecracker."

The IQ of a mob is determined by taking the lowest IQ there and dividing by the number of individuals present. Since there were no geniuses in attendance, the chant burned its way into our collective hummingbird mind and then into our collective alligator will. Soon the only question was who was going to pull the cord that ignited the pyrotechnic. Trooper Mike Jones was elected by proclamation.

Several dozen mercury vapor lights controlled by light sensing switches lit the equipment yard and parking area shared by the Troopers and Department of Highways. The lights came on when it got dark and went off when the sun rose. Along with the ten or so Troopers, those lights stood watch as Trooper Jones pulled the igniter cord and tossed the giant firecracker into the center of the parking area.

Jones raced back to where the rest of us were peeking around the corner of the tin shack that housed C Detachment. We all stood there watching and waiting. Nothing happened. Uh, oh. We were looking at one another with a rising realization that we could not go out and check on why nothing had happened when there was a blinding flash of light followed by the second loudest noise I ever heard.

The lights that had been watching this spectacle assumed the flash of light was the sun coming up and immediately turned themselves off. So there we were in the dark blinded by the flash of light and deafened by the blast. It was several minutes before the lights started blinking on, one by one, and we realized with relief that we had not blown anything up. We retreated into the building where the phones were all ringing. "No, we didn't hear anything." "Everything is okay over here." "Could you please speak a little louder, I'm having a bit of trouble hearing you."

Recalling the feeling of isolation I felt at those two times when a curtain of silence fell around me, I snapped back to the present with much concern for my wife. With a bit of panic and real worry I yelled, "Hey, Debra, can you hear me?" She straightened up from her gardening and pretending to be irritated at me she lightheartedly said through her clenched teeth,

"For the third time. Yes, I hear you. Now, either come out here and help me or shut up and leave me alone."

July 2002

Someday, I'll be an Alaskan Tew!

Sergeant George B. Cole, Retired

There is something Alaskan about deciding that a better life can be had off yonder. Away up north, where there's room to swing your arms and if you have a little accident, well there's a real good chance you won't hit anyone.

And so Pa and Ma Kettle decided to load up a second-hand truck with all their belongings and head north to Alaska. They piled five tons of stuff on a deuce-and-a-half and headed up the Alcan with bald tires and the unflagging spirit of true pioneers.

It was March 29, 1977 and time to turn in the monthly reports. The Tok Trooper Post was then in H Detachment and under the supervision of Sergeant Bob Cockrell in Glennallen. In overall command of the detachment was Lieutenant Harcourt Tew. I called Glennallen and made arrangements to meet near Duffy's Roadhouse to deliver Tok's monthly reports. A few minutes later, Glennallen Dispatch called back and said that Lieutenant Tew would be making the meet. Even the boss likes to get out on the road once in a while, especially on a glorious day full of the promise of spring.

To meet the Big Guy, I put on a pair of real Trooper pants instead of my normal blue jeans, made sure I wasn't wearing the tie with the soup stains, borrowed a clean car, and headed south on the Tok Cutoff. The road was pretty decent; a little ice here and there, but basically clear and dry. It was a pretty uneventful trip. Not much traffic. Gave me a chance to reflect on stuff. The kind of stuff that a post Trooper runs into.

It was clear sailing to Seven Mile Hill. The old Eagle Trail cuts off towards Tanacross at the base. Man, I scored a bunch of grouse on that trail. One time when I knew Bobby Glidden was an hour behind me, I breasted a bird and posed the carcass in the crook of a bush where I knew he would see it. Years later he admitted he blasted it 2 or 11 times before he walked up and saw how badly he had been duped.

I glanced at the turnoff to Clearwater Camp where that retired California police officer passed on and his widow sent me such a gracious letter. They finally took that long-dreamed about trip to Alaska. Spent a day or two at the Clearwater Camp and then he woke up dead. Seemed sad to me but his wife was so glad he got a chance to see the Greatland.

I felt a bit of a shudder entering the curve where Larry Folger ran head on into that family from Anchorage. My first fatal accident and it was called in as a vehicle parked on the highway. I almost didn't even respond to it. All alone at 2 a.m., with four dead, two injured, and no radio contact.

I kind of grinned to myself when I drove past the Mad Trapper's cabin. He broke himself out of the Tok holding facility in order to feed his dog. Scared the hell out of Kathy Morgan. A few years later I inventoried his belongings after his death. What a collection of magazines he had. And they weren't National Geographic. He had metal shutters on his windows and the only door had a secret trip wire to release the pin that held it closed.

Mineral Lake flashed by. A bunch of nice memories about grayling and pike and warm summer afternoons fishing with my sons, and sunsets when it all of a sudden got COLD!

Then it was Edie Smith's place. An Eskimo lady that I first met when she was cooking at Scotty Creek Lodge. She spent all summer gathering 55-gallon barrels full of gravel and black sand and then spent all winter in her cabin, panning for gold. She sold her old 30-30 to a friend of mine who gave it to me when he moved out of Alaska. I still have it.

The turn-off to Mentasta Village. Then the hill where that girl was killed when the motorcycle she was a passenger on went off the road. Mentasta Lodge and Goldie What's-her-name. Then Slana where no one spent much time, especially the road crews. Boy those frost heaves were something else.

Finally by Duffy's where old Mrs. Duffy used to call up whenever anyone suspicious was headed our way. She had been a part of my DEW line, along with Ralph and Ann Late at Dot Lake Lodge, Matt and Grace Grahek at Border City Trading Post, Ray and Malory Scoby at 40-Mile Roadhouse, and Jim Scoles at Scotty Creek Lodge. Between them, nothing moved without being noticed.

Now, I'm nosing into Glennallen's territory. Should have met Lieutenant Tew by now. Oh, well it is a nice day for a drive. Finally, the radio crackles— "1 H 40, this is 1 H 1. I'll meet you at Mile 45." Ha! The old man has been driving slowly.

Ma and Pa are making pretty good time. Why, they even got up to 30 m.p.h. once on a straight stretch where there wasn't too much snow and ice on the shoulder. Most of the time they play it safe by sticking their bald tires to the middle of the road. That is the case as they round a curve at Mile 45 and meet Lieutenant Tew. The good Lieutenant has no choice but to hit the ditch. He does a nice job and there is no damage as he finds a soft snow bank into which to gently set his car.

That is pretty much the scene as I arrived. Ma and Pa Kettle are chatting with Lieutenant Tew while the kids and dogs scamper about. I can barely choke back my chortles as I remark, "Looks like your car is stuck, Lieutenant."

"My car?" he inquired. "My car is sitting right there," pointing at the car I drove up in. "Your car is in the ditch, and after I am done with these people I might help you dig it out."

Shovels in hand, Pa and I contemplate what we learned as we got 'my' car unstuck. Pa considered the merits of driving on the right side of the roadway as he worked off his traffic citation and I pondered yet another lesson in leadership.

November 2003

Lucky

Sergeant George B. Cole, Retired

I was sitting in my outbuilding library reading a psychology magazine when I had a minor epiphany. After cleaning up, I realized I had just discovered the answer to an old puzzle and in so doing relieved myself (pun intended) of a small guilt.

The article was talking about something called muscle memory and neural pathways. I don't pretend to understand more than about 13.027% of what was written, but two things seemed to make sense. If you do an action often enough your brain can build up an enhanced neural pathway and the muscles involved seem to develop a sort of memory of their own that makes the action almost automatic.

Now, if I understand it, an enhanced neural pathway is sort of like a limited access freeway and once a thought is sent down it that thought sort of takes off on its own and doesn't require a whole lot of herding after that. That explains why I can get a song refrain going on in my head that seems to have a life of its own. Or, I can start counting to time something and without any conscious effort or actual recollection of the process I realize I am still counting, and while I meant to stop at 100 it is now 3 a.m. and I have reached 457,633 and still going strong.

Anyway, it seems like if you do something often enough you can give sort of a mental instruction to your body and it will carry it off without much further attention. Sort of a walking and chewing gum thing. Once I get the gum going, I can then take off walking, most of the time.

So one fine spring morning in 1973, I was patrolling north of Fairbanks on the newly constructed Goldstream Valley Road. There wasn't another living thing moving on this crisp morning except for a spotted dog of indeterminate parentage. He was sitting at the top of his driveway watching me drive down the roadway towards him. From here on I will call him 'Lucky.'

I was watching Lucky watch me, and I became certain from his body language that he was going to throw himself down the steep slope of his driveway and chase the patrol car. I was determined to teach him a lesson.

In those days, the speaker for the siren was mounted behind the grill and in front of the radiator. The siren was controlled by two knobs, one selected which warning signal would be active (Hi-Lo, Wail, Yelp, etc.), and the other was the on/off switch. Reaching over and turning on the siren was one of my neural pathway/muscle memory actions.

As I approached Lucky's drive I began to slow down. My plan was to be almost stopped when he hit the end of his drive, and I was going to give a quick on and off with the Yelp. It was going to be great! He would be right by the siren speaker, and the monster car would bark loudly right in his ear, scaring the needles off his spruce tree, and teaching him not to chase cars.

My five years as a Trooper had given me the skills needed to gauge our respective closing speeds and as Lucky hit the bottom of his drive I was there too, nearly at a standstill. I gave my right thumb and forefinger the signal to hit the Yelp.

Neither Lucky nor I had noticed the patch of ice at the bottom of his driveway. Several things happened in quick succession. His plan to execute a nifty 90-degree left turn and chase the car was ruined when his legs flew out from under him, and he found himself on his back, sliding wildly out of control towards the monster. My thumb and forefinger executed the first phase of a quick on and off of the Yelp. I saw Lucky slip and mashed the brake pedal.

Several things did not happen in quick succession. My thumb and forefinger did not execute the second phase of turning off the Yelp. Lucky did not execute any kind of a turn and slid directly under the front bumper of the patrol car. I did not run over him.

Fortunately, I was so close to being stopped that touching the brakes brought the car to a stop. Unfortunately, Lucky's two right legs got caught between the bumper and frame of the car. Fortunately, he was not really injured. Unfortunately, the monster was screaming at him at 110 decibels while apparently trying to eat him. Fortunately, my thumb and forefinger remembered how to shut off the siren. Unfortunately, Lucky could find no traction of any kind and could not get loose. Fortunately, I was able to free him.

Up his driveway he scooted. His head was so low and his tail was tucked so far under his legs that he looked like a furry clamshell, opening and closing and growing smaller until he disappeared around the back of his house.

Two really good things resulted from the Goldstream Caper. The first was that no one was up and saw it. As far as I know, I skated. The second good thing revealed itself a couple of days later when I again made an early morning pass down Goldstream Valley Road. As I approached Lucky's house, I saw him, and he saw me. He stayed seated by his house and watched me drive by with nary even the slightest twitch to chase my car.

I always felt a little guilty about turning on the siren as Lucky slipped under my bumper but now I know why it happened. Once I fired off the siren neuron, it was automatic. My mind became occupied with seeing Lucky slip and the stopping of the car. Neural pathways and muscle memory took over the now unattended task of turning on the siren. They were to blame, not me.

Neural pathways and muscle memory! Who'd a thunk? I'm going to dig some more magazines out of the recycle bin at the Petersburg Post Office for my library and see what else I can learn.

February 2005

The Case of the Big Head

Sergeant George B. Cole, Retired

In April, 1968 I was 22 years old. On the 27th of that month I drove my newly assigned patrol car to Tok. It was mine! A 1967 Plymouth 383 with only 34,782 miles on it. It had aircraft landing lights as high beams and one of the first 'Silent Patrolman' windows between the front and rear seats. I loved that car.

I reported to Trooper Bob Cockrell who was the Officer in Charge of the two-man Tok Post. He was going to show me the ropes about being a post trooper. I already knew and admired him from my first days in Fairbanks where he was one of my training officers. In Tok he did the best he could with such a young pup, but a family emergency caused him to quit about a month later and move back to Ohio, leaving me alone.

I began to take myself quite seriously. I was responsible for over 15,000 square miles of Alaska, nearly 400 miles of highway, eight communities, and numerous small enclaves. People called me for help at all hours of the day and night. I caught myself a case of the big head.

In September of that year I was scheduled to take a vacation and visit my parents in California. I was reluctant to go, feeling that if I did, the forces of evil would swallow up Tok, Eagle, Mentasta, Tanacross, Tetlin, Chicken, Dot Lake, and Northway. But, it was take it or lose it, so I took it.

I came back from vacation two days early. As I drove into Tok, I was surprised to see that all the buildings were still standing. The roadside was not littered with dead automobiles. There were no crazed people running around shooting wildly into the air. It seemed quiet, normal.

My first stop was at the Tok Post Office where I picked up my mail from Postmistress Millie Terwilliger. I importantly announced to her that I was back from vacation. She replied, "Oh, have you been gone?" I slunk out with a sudden case of the small head.

I went home and called Fairbanks to tell my supervisor, Sergeant Hal Hume, that I was back in Tok. He got on the phone and told me there was something important he needed to talk to me about, but not over the phone. He told me to drive into Fairbanks the next day to meet with him. My head began to grow once again.

The next morning I got up and left Tok about 6 a.m., and drove straight through, arriving at 1616 Cushman Street a little after 9 a.m. I went to Sergeant Hume's office. "Good, you're here," he said upon seeing me. "Grab a cup of coffee and come in."

I went to the coffee pot, borrowed a cup and poured it full. Upon returning to Sergeant Hume's office I saw Trooper John Rawson coming down the hallway towards me. He had a bunch of papers and folders under his arm. Rawson had recently transferred from Point Barrow to the University of Alaska. Even though it was just down the road, the UAF Post was considered an outpost, so Sergeant Hume was also his supervisor.

He looked like he was headed for Sergeant Hume's office so I nodded at him and waited for him to enter. I thought there must be something going on that involved the university and they might want my participation. Maybe an undercover assignment was in the offing. We both entered the office. Sergeant Hume waved me to a seat and beckoned Trooper Rawson to his desk.

The Sergeant leaned back in his chair and lit his pipe. (This was in the days before tobacco smoke was dangerous.) Soon the atmosphere was redolent with the aroma of expensive tobacco, the acrid smell of police coffee, and intoxicating police talk.

Trooper Rawson spread his diagrams and notes out on the Sergeant's desk. He spoke at length about evacuation plans, riot suppression tactics, and mutual assistance pacts. Sergeant Hume asked questions. Rawson answered the questions, clarified the answers and expanded on the clarifications.

After about an hour, I went back to the coffee pot and filled my cup. Upon returning to the good Sergeant's office, I reclaimed my chair and listened to them elaborate upon the expanded clarifications. I began to know more about emergency possibilities at the University of Alaska than I knew about anything else. There seemed to be no end to the contingencies that needed to be explored in minute detail. I was totally bored.

I excused myself to get another cup and headed for the coffee pot. With a fresh mug I wandered back to the squad room and chatted with some of the guys. Then I rambled up to dispatch and chatted with some of the dispatchers. Finally, I worked my way back to Sergeant Hume's office. He and Trooper Rawson were still swimming deep in the murky waters of possible university disasters.

I rinsed out my cup, went out to my patrol car, and drove back to Tok. The next day I called in to inform Sergeant Hume that I was back on duty. Neither he nor I mentioned my visit to his office the day before. I don't think he really remembered that I had been there or that I had left.

Over the last 36 years, I have spent many hours wondering what was so important that I needed to come off leave a day early and drive over 400 miles to talk about. I really don't want to know because I have thoroughly enjoyed those speculations, and I don't want them to stop. Besides, it keeps me from getting the big head. Like Millie said, "Oh, have you been gone?"

May 2006

Welcome to Bristol Bay 1963

Lieutenant John Elmore, Retired

Being a Bush Trooper in the '60s was a rewarding and special experience. The incidents related here were not unique, but everyday occurrences for all of us.

It was the spring of 1963. We were looking forward to new assignments away from Anchorage to really get involved in modern day police work. Turk Mayfield was calling us in one at a time to assign new duty stations. I was really looking forward to a post on the highway system.

My turn came. Lieutenant Mayfield had a smile on his face when he asked how I would like a transfer to Dillingham. I replied in a negative manner, expressing my preference for a highway post. I had been temporarily assigned to Bristol Bay the previous commercial fishing season. I knew there weren't any highways to patrol and that the surplus Fish and Game jeep I would be driving wouldn't top out at 35 m.p.h. on its best day. I had dealt mostly with drinking related problems, breaking up athletic contests between angry drunks.

The Lieutenant informed me that Dillingham was the only post that was left unfilled. He suggested I think it over and let him know. He was quite happy with the job I was doing in the Anchorage patrol unit, and I was welcome to remain there for another year or two. He knew I wanted a post assignment. The following day I informed the Lieutenant that I would love a transfer to Dillingham.

Shortly thereafter, my family and I were enjoying a Reeve Aleutian DC-3 charter to Dillingham surrounded by our worldly possessions. The weather was terrible — gusty winds and heavy rain. We circled the Dillingham airport several times looking for an opening. The pilot finally said he would make one more try. Then, we would have to go back to Anchorage while we still had enough fuel. We were not to be denied. On the next attempt, we bumped down on the dark gravel runway and pulled up to the Northern Consolidated terminal. In spite of the weather, it looked like most of the people in town were there to help us unload.

Our boxes were whisked away and disappeared into the dark. I thought no way will we ever see all of them again. I was told that there was a fight at the Green Front Café that needed attention. After lodging the participants in my guest quarters under the F&G office, I arrived home to find everyone settling in, and absolutely everything that disappeared at the airport piled in our living room. Our dog had survived his first fight with a husky that wanted to establish a chain of command in the neighborhood.

Thus started a three-year tour of duty that I will always remember fondly. I can't relate all the fun I had in three years in these few lines, but here are a few incidents that come to mind.

One of the first items to attend to was meeting my Magistrate in King Salmon. Bob Wright had his office in a room off his automotive repair shop, complete with chickens roosting on his file cabinet. I introduced myself and informed Bob that I wasn't out here to waste his time or mine with any marginal cases. When I brought a defendant before him, he would be guilty, and I would be able to prove it.

Several weeks later I made my first case involving selling prescription drugs in one of the villages. After taking care of the preliminaries, Magistrate Bob asked the defendants how they pled. They both responded "not guilty," a term my Magistrate wasn't familiar with. Bob looked up with a start and said, "Trooper Elmore wouldn't have brought you in here if you weren't guilty. I find you guilty," and sentenced them to the maximum penalty. No trial— end of case. Later, in private, we sorted out the proper etiquette.

One routine patrol involved me being dropped off by a friend in a float plane on the tide flats at South Naknek just before dark, with the tide out. I needed to make an unannounced check on the local bar, which had been the source of several complaints. After floundering through the knee-deep mud, I thanked the cook of a high and dry tender for throwing me a couple of planks to aid my progress to solid ground.

When I arrived at the bar, it was really jumping; wall-to-wall drunks. I wound up with eight guests of the state, handcuffed in pairs since I only carried four pair of cuffs. We stumbled our way back to the high and dry tender, as I didn't have anywhere to hold my guests on that side of the river. The skipper allowed us on board with a promise to take us across the river at high tide. Eight more guilty people for the magistrate to deal with.

I found the Air Police at the King Salmon Air Base helpful at times. They would let me borrow handcuffs on a hand receipt as long as I left them enough for an emergency. We didn't feel that violated the spirit of the Posse Comitatus Act. Sometimes, four pairs of handcuffs were not enough.

After a month or so at Dillingham, I was told that every time I left town, parking my vehicle at the airport, the town came alive with drunks and rowdies. Shortly, I had urgent business in Naknek. I had to leave my patrol vehicle at the airport. Just before dark, I found my way to a local air taxi operator's home in Naknek. He consented to fly me back to Dillingham, arriving with just enough daylight to land on the small airstrip behind my house. I stopped at home to let the boss know I was back and to have a cup of tea, then started on foot patrol to see some of the rowdy drunks, reported to be out while I was away. There was a commotion on the porch of my next door neighbor's house. It was a drunk trying to gain entrance while the Mrs. of the house was trying to keep the door closed.

The rowdy decided to accompany me to the state guest quarters, which was a couple blocks away. By the time we got there, I had convinced a couple more rowdies to accompany us. As I made them comfortable for the night, I thought, "Boy this is going to be a busy night." Heading out on further foot patrol, I found the town was very quiet. Someone passed the word that the Trooper was back. People in the Bush were very helpful.

I'll close with the time the Fire Marshal visited us and condemned my guest quarters under the F&G building. The U.S. Marshals had used the same facility prior to statehood and left a sign over the door that stated all prisoners not back by 9 p.m. will be locked out. I advised my lieutenant that I would no longer be able to arrest and hold prisoners because my facility had been condemned. Later that day I received a call from the Anchorage office informing me that after further evaluation, it was determined that my facility was up to standards and was okay to use.

June 2000

John Elmore entered law enforcement with the U.S. Air Force in 1956, serving at Elmendorf Air Force Base until 1959 when he began work as a boat operator for the Alaska Department of Fish and Game. In 1960, John began service with the Seward Police Department and moved on to the Alaska State Police in Anchorage in February 1962, and in the spring of 1963 he transferred to Dillingham. John served with the State Police in Anchorage, Dillingham, Juneau, Kotzebue, and Nome, and left the department in 1977. John served as Chief of Police in Nome in 1978 and then started a sporting goods store in Nome and initiated a fishing lodge in Council, Alaska. John and his wife Fran, the first female Alaska State Trooper, reside in Anchorage during the winter and spend their summers in Council, Alaska.

Jailers Were a Necessity

Lieutenant John Elmore, Retired

Locally hired jailers were an asset to Bush troopers in the 1960s. They provided useful service, information, and support, but they sometimes added to life's little adventures.

Every town has its local tough guys who make life miserable for those who don't see eye to eye with them. Some of these fellows are that way because they don't have both oars in the water at the same time, some just because they like to be that way. During the early 1960s, Dillingham had its share. One of those who had a problem coordinating his oars was John Mulkiet. A book could be written about his exploits, and the book might include a footnote about the time John and I had a little discussion.

I had only been stationed in Dillingham a short time before we became acquainted. My Mrs. had made me a new shirt, which I was wearing when a local stopped me Downtown and reported that Johnny had just kicked in his door and taken his radio.

John lived in an old house in a dark part of town. I told myself that since it was dark out, no one would see if I came out on the short end of my conversation with Johnny. He answered the door with a 'what the hell do you want?" After I explained the purpose of my visit, Johnny accepted my invitation to spend the evening in the holding cell in the basement of the Fish and Game Building. The cell had two-by-fours for bars, a couple of bunks, and a honey bucket. The forced-air furnace for the building was located next to the cell.

My jailer Harry and I made sure John was settled in for the night, and I went home, where my wife became upset because my new shirt had been torn in the conversation with Johnny at his house.

The following morning I arrived at the Fish and Game Building to find Harry standing in the parking lot. I asked him why he wasn't downstairs keeping an eye on his prisoner. Harry answered: "John broke out last night." When asked why he hadn't called me, he replied: "He's still in the basement." Curious, I entered the basement to find the two-by-four door laying in the hall, no longer attached to anything. Johnny was asleep on his bunk.

When I woke him up, he said: "I didn't try to escape." He said he was sleeping when the furnace kicked on with a whoosh, waking him with a start. In his surprise he headed for the hallway, taking the door with him. When he realized what had happened, he went back to bed. He had no idea where Harry was, hadn't seen him all night and didn't realize the jailer had left when the door came off its hinges. I credited Harry for a full night's work and redesigned the lockup.

A few years later I was assigned to the Kotzebue Post. It was my practice, when lodging a guest of the state on a liquor violation, to mark the bottle with the date, a case number, etc., and a mark to show the level of the contents. I would then stow it away in a drawer in the magistrate's desk.

One day I arrived before the magistrate and was typing up a complaint. I opened the desk drawer where I had placed the evidence the night before and found some additional information had been marked on the bottle's label. My jailer Walter had written a note saying that he would replace the contents up to my mark on payday and signed his name.

After a lecture, Walter left with the understanding that he would never work for me again. But a couple of nights later I found I needed a jailer and couldn't convince anyone that they needed the work. I stopped at Walter's house and asked if he had learned his lesson. He assured me that he had. Sometimes we have to bend with the wind.

Local jailers were a valuable source of information. They usually knew everyone, how they were inter-related, and what they had done in the past. They also acted as interpreters when needed. Many of the younger defendants claimed that they didn't understand English very well, but they actually understood it quite well. What they didn't understand was the criminal justice system. They felt they were better off claiming that they didn't understand English, though several times I overheard them talking to each other when they didn't realize anyone was around to hear them.

I was consistently amazed how a jailer could translate a defendant's rights or a lengthy complaint into a few phrases. And when asked how the defendant pled to a charge, somehow the words "not guilty" were never uttered. I sometimes suspected that the jailers thought the word "guilty" was synonymous with job security.

May 2001

Welcome to Bristol Bay 2000

Trooper Geoff Engleman, Retired

After reading John Elmore's account of his 1960s era Bush Trooper experiences in Dillingham, I'm left with the thought, "we've come a long way baby."

My voluntary assignment to Dillingham began March 15, 1999. Since beginning my Trooper career in 1976, I've known a number of Troopers who served within the Bristol Bay area. Tom Preshaw, Warren Tanner, Chuck Feller, and Roy Minatra all served in King Salmon. Others who served in Bristol Bay communities include Dave Drvenkar, Steve Dunnigan, Mike Gomez, Archie Barber, Dick Burton, John Clare, and of course John Elmore.

Just before transferring from Fairbanks I ran into Trooper Sergeant Tom Preshaw, who gave me reason to reconsider my up-coming venture to the Bristol Bay area. Tom calmly remarked (as only Tom can), "while in King Salmon, I had more fights in South Naknek bars than anyplace I've been stationed." This statement from a 6'3" 240 lb. giant led me to the map to determine where this notorious place was, and I made a mental note to avoid bars in South Naknek.

Bristol Bay today is no longer the wild place it was in the previous decade. Bristol Bay, particularly Dillingham, is served by two modern grocery stores, both of which carry a variety of produce as well as clothing and hardware. They also have a fair selection of furniture, hardware and a sporting goods store that also sells boats, snow machines, and ATVs.

The economy, although reliant on the commercial fishing industry, is also a major tourist destination, and with a few exceptions, the days of honey buckets are over. With cable TV, paved streets, internet service, taxicabs and a modern hospital, we have two local bars, two liquor stores, and most importantly, we have a 16-bed correctional facility and court with a Superior Court

Judge and Magistrate. Far different than what was available in 1962. Unfortunately, John's Magistrate friend is no longer on the bench.

Compared to the transfer of the 1960's era, our move was fairly easy. Our household goods were packed by a moving company in Fairbanks, actually North Pole, at minus 35 degrees Fahrenheit, which made our departure somewhat easier when we arrived at Dillingham, where the temperature was a balmy 30 degrees. Our household goods were shipped professionally aboard a Northern Air Cargo jet, and the family and I arrived at Dillingham on a Peninsula Air Metroliner, one of four daily flights from Anchorage.

When John Elmore was assigned to Dillingham, the era of snow-machine travel had not yet arrived. Nowadays, during the winter, the Dillingham post revolves around snowmachine travel. Of the villages within a 60-mile radius of Dillingham, many of the residents use snowmachines for travel, hunting and general transportation. This results in many search and rescues due to travel in poor weather, equipment failure, running out of gas, or just being lost.

Dillingham post has two snowmachines available for travel to these communities. Unlike many village residents, we only use them when snow is on the ground. Wash and wear uniforms are a significant change from my early entry into the Troopers in the '70s and, of course, what John Elmore experienced in the '6Os. In those days, the wool uniform with tie was standard, and today's wash'n'wears make it much more comfortable and easier to deal with outpost responsibilities.

The Division of Fish and Wildlife Protection has aircraft at several posts, including a Super Cub at Dillingham, Lake Iliamna and a Cessna 185 at King Salmon. Fish and Wildlife Troopers and their planes are a great assist during search and rescue incidents. The Fish and Wildlife Boston Whaler assigned to Dillingham also helps in Trooper travel to Nushagak Bay villages. We also have a standing invitation with the local Native corporation to utilize their river patrol boats to ride along during summer patrols.

Earlier this year I had a chance to speak with John Clare, a Trooper alumnus at Dillingham in 1965/66. John experienced the condemnation of the Jail and had to scrounge plywood and other supplies to create a jail cell in the Fire Hall hose room. Although not taught at the DPS Academy, the ability to permanently borrow unused items (scrounging) from other agencies has always been a necessary Trooper skill.

The Fire Hall is still in use today and since John Clare's time, has been used as the city Police Station, but presently is the Fire Hall and local bingo parlor. John said he was fortunate in conducting business in South Naknek after a large anchor was positioned outside the South Naknek bar. The anchor was a handy place to handcuff prisoners.

Pronunciation of local villages and places is always a challenge, and from time to time we are asked why we are not fluent in the Yup'ik Eskimo language. I often recall a conversation I had with Dave Drvenkar before I left Fairbanks. Dave said that on arrival in Dillingham, he wanted to make his presence known so he quickly identified the most notorious and rowdy village in the area. On arrival at the village, the majority of the villagers were in the Community Hall and Dave barged in, interrupting the meeting in progress.

When asked by an elder in Yup'ik "who are you?" Dave replied in Yup'ik saying, "I'm the one who takes you away." Dave indicated this was the only thing he ever learned in Yup'ik but apparently it went over okay because as I've talked to local residents, I've been asked many times how Dave Drvenkar is doing, and after my reply they comment back, "tough man, fine Trooper."

Travel within the Bristol Bay area is still a challenge. Even though there is a significant amount of aircraft support, Bristol Bay weather can be and usually is extreme and unpredictable. A favorite local saying is "wait five minutes and the weather will change." Unfortunately, it's not always for the better. Today we have hour by hour weather reports available through a local phone call or if one has the internet, through various online services. This technology has given us a little edge on Elmore and company's experiences in the 60s.

I've been asked whether my assignment in Dillingham is all that I had imagined it would be. In many respects, there were no surprises, but as always, the presence and support of the boss of our family has made the assignment easier. Times have not changed in that numerous uncompensated services that one's spouse makes during this type of assignment can never be fully appreciated.

On my departure from Dillingham, I do not expect to be fluent in the Yup'ik Eskimo language, but I am making headway thanks to KDLG Public Radio's daily call-in line. I have been paying close attention and can just about sing Happy Birthday to You in Yup'ik. For those of you who have served here, the names and locations would no doubt bring back fond memories (or not so fond memories) of their time in Bristol Bay. For those who have not had the experience, I highly recommend the assignment.

June 2000

Geoffrey Engleman attended the 27th Alaska State Trooper Academy held August-November 1976. His original assignments were in Anchorage Judicial Services and then Anchorage Patrol. He was then transferred to Northway Post, where Constable James Gallen introduced him to village-style law enforcement.

January 1980 found him assigned to Fairbanks Patrol and while there he moved to Nome for five weeks of temporary duty, holding down the fort there with F/SGT Larry Mix while the Nome Troopers and many other bush Troopers attended the first Village Public Safety Officer training session. After eight long years in Fairbanks, he was promoted to Sergeant and transferred to Palmer Post.

In 1990, he moved to Glennallen Post in time to oversee the office move from the Fish and Game building to the combined Courthouse and Trooper office in the Ahtna building, which also contained suitable quarters for holding prisoners. In September 1991, he returned to Fairbanks, and became a shift Sergeant in the Patrol Section. In March 1999 his final posting was to Dillingham as the Area Supervisor for Troopers in Dillingham, King Salmon, and Cold Bay.

October 2000 he entered retirement and moved his wife Brenda and children Brendan and Sinead back to their home in North Pole. Eleven years have passed since that day and he is continuing to enjoy retirement. He says his service to Alaska will always be one of the highlights of his life: As he read the confirmation of appointment letter dated August 9, 1976, in which Commissioner Richard Burton requested him to report to Captain Gilmour, Academy Commander in Sitka, he can still feel the thrill of accomplishment and excitement that the letter generated as he held it in his hand that day.

His Academy roommates and friends to this day: Ray Gary, Mike Gomez and Bill Gause are testament to the caliber of recruits during those years when Alaska became a wealthy state and recognized the need for more and better quality Public Safety.

Marshals Use Ploy to Make Kodiak Arrest

Chief Deputy US Marshal James "Jim" Chenoweth, Retired

Jim Chenoweth's unpublished manuscript, *Down Darkness Wide,* is an account of his law enforcement experiences in territorial Alaska from 1951 to statehood. The following excerpt from his manuscript is printed with his permission.

"We only have two things going for us," Deputy Marshal Eddie Dolan called in from Kodiak. "No one's been shot so far and no hostages are involved. All the rest is bad news."

Silently, I had to agree.

"I'll get back to you, Eddie. Meanwhile, find out as much as you can about this guy. Anything you can learn might be useful."

It was November 13, 1956. Eddie was in the town of Kodiak, on Kodiak Island, which is about 100 miles long and only 15 miles wide, lying along the western edge of the Gulf of Alaska. Located in the northeastern corner of the island, the town of Kodiak is the oldest surviving non-native settlement in Alaska. (Construction began there about the time George Washington entered his fourth year as president.) Currently we had no deputy stationed in Kodiak. Eddie had been sent from Anchorage to take care of official matters that had piled up.

Kodiak Island is rimmed along its coast with many small fishing villages. One of those sited just beyond Dangerous Cape on the island's southeastern flank is Old Harbor. And in Old Harbor, a mentally disturbed villager had just panicked the entire town.

Off the air, I thought about what Eddie had told me.

Robert Burrell was the schoolteacher in the village. Yesterday, his brother, Kenneth, returned there, having just been released after a sanity hearing in Anchorage. Kenneth then threatened Robert and Robert's wife, inflicted some bodily harm on their children, and promised to kill her: "You'd be better off dead!"

She fled by small plane to Kodiak with the children. Unable to reason with his brother, Kenneth followed her. Based on their statements, the U.S. Commissioner issued a warrant for Kenneth's arrest. That's where Eddie came into the picture. Details are what Eddie needed. Apparently, Kenneth had holed up in the school house, which was on a slight rise overlooking the village. Kenneth was a violent man and armed with the rifle that Robert kept in the schoolhouse. Kodiak police told Eddie that during their arrest of Kenneth a month earlier, he had badly beaten two officers. Even after being handcuffed, he had bent the cuffs so badly that they were no long usable.

Eddie checked with Kodiak Airways. They told him that after Robert had fled from Old Harbor, Kenneth scrambled out of the schoolhouse with his rifle whenever a small floatplane landed there, and then he'd duck into the thick undergrowth behind the school. Looking at charts of the area, Eddie knew we had a real problem. Kenneth had a clear field of fire as long as he was in the schoolhouse. Once he was in the densely wooded hillside rising behind it, flushing him out would be really tricky— and probably bloody!

I told Eddie what he already knew— the current situation was not promising. It would require too many men under hazardous conditions, to take Kenneth. (The only volunteer immediately available to him was Kodiak police officer "Mac" McKinley, who later became our Deputy Marshal in Kodiak). We simply had to find another answer to our problem.

"Listen, Eddie. Forget about any frontal assault. No one has been hurt so far and we want to keep it that way. I don't like trying to take him on his own ground, and he's not going anywhere. What we need to do is develop a situation that's more favorable to us and less favorable to him. He's not shooting at anyone so time is on our side. Talk to everyone who knows anything about him or has been in contact with him recently. See if we can't suck him out of his pattern. Maybe a girlfriend could help. Let me know what you come up with."

Then I waited.

The radio phone stayed silent for too long a time. Eddie finally came back to me again.

"It's all over, Chief. No one got hurt and there's nothing more to worry about. He's in the Kodiak jail, awaiting another sanity hearing."

"How the hell did you manage it, Eddie?"

"I found out he hadn't paid his federal income tax. That's the bait I used to reel him in."

It was true! Kenneth Burrell hadn't paid his federal income tax for the prior year and was arguing hotly with the Internal Revenue Service about it. The IRS thought he owed money, but Kenneth thought he was entitled to a refund. Learning this, Eddie persuaded the tax official in Kodiak to talk to Kenneth on the schoolhouse radio. The official suggested that Kenneth would get his money if he would be willing to fly to Kodiak to sign for it. Kenneth agreed but demanded that a local pilot, Vince Daly, fly in to Old Harbor to pick him up.

Daly told Eddie he'd do it but wanted someone to go with him in case Kenneth got violent on the plane. It had to be a local person who wasn't involved with police work; we couldn't afford to make Kenneth suspicious. "Tiny" Trokowsky (who was not really tiny) signed on. The two flew from Kodiak at 11 a.m. on November 15, arriving 30 minutes later at Old Harbor. Fifteen minutes after that, Daly calmly reported by radio that he was returning to Kodiak with "a passenger from Old Harbor." At 12:15 p.m., he landed in Kodiak Bay and taxied to the beach strip. Eddie Dolan and Officer McKinley were waiting.

(In the late 1980's, the Marshal's Service used a similar scam to lure fugitive criminals out of hiding by advertising the fact that the criminals had won certain financial prizes, which were waiting to be claimed. I was happy to learn that the same technique we had used 30 years earlier in Kodiak hadn't lost its charm.)

November 2001

Jim Chenoweth and his wife moved up to Alaska in 1951 after living in New York City for years. Then in 1952, the U.S. Marshal in Alaska at the time hired Jim as his Deputy. He came to Alaska with hopes of finding a job filled with personal values and a paycheck, which he found.

Upon statehood, Jim moved back east and was a criminal investigator for multiple government agencies. His time as an investigator was highlighted by investigations into the assassinations of John F. Kennedy and Dr. Martin Luther King Jr. Jim currently lives in New Hampshire and is a writer.

Carefree Jailer Ponies Up Outing for Prisoner

Senior Special Agent Robert "Bob" Olson

It was an eye-opening experience being the only Trooper in Tok from 1964 to 1968. In summer, all vehicular traffic entered and left Alaska through my area. I had little time for anything but work.

One summer Saturday night in 1966, I arrested an individual from the village of Tanacross for Drunk and Disorderly. I booked him into my quaint little jail and called my jailer, the late Bob Wadsworth, to report for duty. After he arrived and I could see all was well, I left the jail.

The next morning, I called Magistrate Alberta Clarke, telling her that I had a prisoner for arraignment and requesting a court time. She suggested 9:30 a.m. I drove over to the jail to check that everything was okay, but something was amiss; Wadsworth's pick-up was gone.

I hurried into the jail to find the place unlocked, the cell door open, and both my prisoner and jailer gone. Wadsworth owned a Texaco station. I drove there, but they were not there. Only two restaurants were open on a Sunday morning; I checked them both. Jailer and prisoner were not there and had not been there.

Bob Wadsworth was reliable, honest, and good at handling our prisoners— he knew most of them personally. He'd been Tok's jailer for a long time.

But this was something else.

I checked around town some more. Finding nothing, I went back to the jail, and there was Bob's pickup. I stepped inside the jail to find my jailer sitting calmly in front of the cell from which peered my prisoner.

Bob explained, "It was such a nice, warm, sunny morning," he said, "that we went over to a friend's house early, borrowed two horses, and went for a horseback ride. I thought we'd be back to the jail before you got here."

For a moment, I was speechless— then, I chewed him out. We barely made it to the arraignment on time, and the prisoner was released with a small fine and a big warning by Magistrate Clarke, who later choked with laughter when I told her about the morning's events.

I continued hiring Bob Wadsworth as my jailer, and to my knowledge, he never took any more prisoners horseback riding.

October 2002

Robert "Bob" Olson began his law enforcement career as a Deputy Sheriff in King County, Washington in 1956 and began duty with the Alaska State Police in 1963. He served in Fairbanks and Tok, leaving the Department in 1969 as a Corporal. He then served as United States Marshal for Alaska until 1976. In 1978, Bob was hired as a Senior Special Agent for the FAA. He served in this capacity in Anchorage, Phoenix, and Las Vegas, retiring in 1991. He was manager of the Kelso/Longview Regional Airport from 1993 to 2005. Bob spent 35 years in the Criminal Justice field and was a Life Member of FOAST and the Alaska Peace Officers Association. He passed away on June 30, 2007.

The Standard

First Sergeant Mike Metrokin, Retired

Shortly after my first posting to Sitka in 1973, my detachment supervisor, Sergeant Roger Iverson, visited the post for inspection. I think he mostly wanted to see what he had been sent from Anchorage Patrol, and to do a little bonding. The sergeant spent a day and a night in Sitka, then as he was leaving, he pointed his finger at my chest and said, "Metrokin, don't make it hard for the next guy." He left for Juneau without elaborating.

The sergeant's words rewound in my head for several days, and I came to understand what he meant. First and foremost (naturally) it meant I was not to back down. It did not mean I was to be a total (insert your own word here) all the time either. I believe overall it meant I was to be fair and consistent in my duties.

I came to the Troopers with no prior police experience, so my understanding of *The Standard* came from observing those at the academy and those I later worked with. In the early days and throughout my career, I tried to meet the standard set by those who came before me. It was the principal motivator during my privileged time with the Alaska State Troopers.

Before Roger Iverson came to Sitka, I had never been given such direction, and I never heard the words put just that way again, though I used them a few times myself. Frankly, I cannot say I never stumbled along my path. I would like to think, however, that the next guy didn't have it harder when I moved on.

The Alaska State Troopers is a unique organization. Other agencies have their own function and enjoy their own successes, history, and heritage, but the level of individual involvement while setting a course is not the same. For those who continue to serve the Great State of Alaska as one of the chosen few, there will always be the next guy. Keep in mind that you can make it hard for him or her if you don't work to The Standard of those who came before you.

It's the most any individual can hope to attain.

December 2002

Mike Metrokin was born in Alaska and raised in Kodiak. He joined the Alaska State Troopers in 1971, attending the 19th Academy at Sitka. During his career he worked Anchorage Patrol, Sitka Post, Valdez Post, Cordova Post, Glennallen, and Fairbanks. Mike ended his career in Fairbanks as First Sergeant, supervising both rural and patrol units, retiring in 1990. He lives in Anacortes, Washington with his wife Bobbi. For a number of years Mike worked for the Seattle Municipal Court. And later worked for Holland America Line as a Security Officer touring the world.

The Oral Interview

First Sergeant Mike Metrokin, Retired

I made an application to join the Alaska State Troopers after I found out how much fun Glenn Godfrey was having as a Trooper assigned in Anchorage in 1970. I, like Glenn, was from Kodiak, and I was working with Glenn when he told me in confidence one day that he had joined the Troopers. I was in shock as Glenn was just offered a promotion at work. When he told me he was going to the Academy I had, up to that time, never ever wondered where Troopers came from — they came up behind you. Who knew?

I later relocated to Anchorage and was working as a Native Hire Trainee at the Carpenter Shop on Ft. Richardson. I would visit Glenn on his days off and only knew he was having a good time being a Trooper. That was good enough for me.

I was moved quickly through the screening and testing process. Finally, the Oral Interview. I arrived at the appointed time and place and sat across a formal table of three people, Captain Bill Nix, Sergeant Don Tetzloff (Fish and Wildlife Protection), and Mary Montgomery, Human Resources/Juneau. I admit to being very relaxed to the point that I was not overly concerned that I had a tooth missing from my partial, and it just happened to be at the front of my smile. You can imagine.

During that time there was not the concept of staged questions, staged so each person is asked the same question. I was asked if I would arrest my mother if I caught her drunk driving. No. I was asked if I was not selected to be a Trooper would I join the Anchorage Police Department since I lived in Anchorage. No. Why not? I don't want to be an Anchorage policeman; I want to be a Trooper. Would I join the Kodiak Police Department since I was from Kodiak? No — same reason. There were other questions but it came down to this.

Captain Nix said to me, "There is one thing I look for in all my Troopers. I don't care if they are handling a lost puppy dog or a race riot, there is one thing they have to have. – can you tell me what that is?"

I sat back and told him what it was. He got a grin on his face and the interview was over, and I later was hired to join the 19th Academy.

Now, you could have told Captain Nix almost anything and been half right. You could have said "sense of humor" and been half right. But there is only one answer. Can you tell me what it is?

Did you say common sense? I did. My scores prior to this interview were not that good. I believe to this day my answer to this one question was the reason I was allowed to become a Trooper.

I have told this story many times when talking to younger police officers and have asked – "can you tell me what that is?" No one has said – common sense. Those of us who have or now work in law enforcement in Alaska, where backup is not there or is far away, can agree with the experience that dictated Captain Nix to ask that question.

June 2011

Stakeout

Deputy Commissioner Harold "Syd" Sydnam, Retired

In 1963, Fairbanks, and then Anchorage, had a series of armed robberies by a fellow we dubbed "The Shotgun Robber." The MO indicated one principal; he liked to hit grocery stores at night, particularly at the conclusion of long weekends.

In those days, "voluntary overtime" meant that you pulled your full shift and associated paperwork and then took on some special detail — such as a stake-out. On the night of a date not specified in November 1963, but likely an Armistice Day (remember that term?) or Thanksgiving weekend, I pulled some more "VOT."

Adjacent to this larger grocery store in Spenard there was a vacant store space formerly occupied by a shoe store. Through the wall from its men's room was the grocery store's small office and safe. We had a state-of-the-art Wollensack reel-to-reel tape recorder in the men's room, with a microphone wire through the wall to the grocer's office.

VOT was spent attending the recorder/speaker and the plan was to zip out the front door of the vacant shop in time to catch the robber exiting the front, and only reasonable, door to the grocery— a lovely plan that never bore fruit. In boredom, on a scrap of paper bag, I wrote:

Stakeout

Here in a men's room
Through the night and day,
I await a bandit
To come my way.

With flashlight and shotgun
All loaded and cocked,
Entrance surrounded and
Exits all blocked.

Microphone well placed
And recorder going —
Just who the hell
Do we think we are snowing?

Likely the bandit is
Out in the night
Just looking for love
And not for a fight.

My buttocks are sore
And my hair grows gray.
Who was it that said that
Crime doesn't pay?

November 2003

Deputy Commissioner Harold J. Sydnam Jr. arrived in Alaska in 1952 after serving two tours of duty with the U.S. Marine Corp. His first tour was in China shortly after World War 2, and the second was during the Korean War where he earned a Bronze Star and other commendations. Syd, as he was known by all, started as a dispatcher with the Territorial Police in 1959 followed shortly by being commissioned as a Trooper and working his way up the ranks.

Syd had multiple assignments, ending his career as Deputy Commissioner of Public Safety in Juneau. He retired in 1983, bought a 39-foot sloop, and moved to Wrangell, Alaska, then to Blaine, BC; then Canberra, Australia; followed by White Rock, BC; and presently is retired in Bellingham, Washington.

Serial Murders in Southeastern

Tom Brennan

In mid-September, 1912, a United States marshal showed up at the Treadwell Mine in Douglas, near Juneau, with a court summons for workman James Christie. Christie left with the marshal while his co-workers and supervisor watched, some shaking their heads. Mine workers were a rowdy bunch and Christie's arrest was not surprising; he was young and single and could have gotten into trouble on a trip to town. But when his friends tried to find out what happened to him, they hit a wall; he was not in jail and not in Juneau. Christie had disappeared and federal authorities said no summonses had been issued for Christie and no marshal sent to the mine.

The miners complained to the Treadwell managers. Christie was an officer in the company-dominated labor union, so the mine executives suspected that his disappearance had been arranged by the competing Western Federation of Miners, a violence-prone group associated with the Industrial Workers of the World, also known as the Wobblies, a radical national labor bunch. If the union was involved, the mine managers wanted to know about it. At first they offered a five-hundred-dollar reward for information, hoping that someone in the Western Federation would go for the cash and turn in his associates. But they got no bites, so the company hired the Pinkerton Detective Agency to find out what was going on and what happened to their union ally, James Christie. Bringing the Pinkertons to Juneau was expensive but, if it was a labor problem, the stakes could be high. And the Pinkertons had long experience investigating and battling with organized labor. The company had used them earlier to infiltrate the Western Federation in Alaska.

Early in the investigation, the Pinkertons and territorial authorities identified Edward Krause of Petersburg as a suspect. Krause was known as an oddball and a rabid Socialist who ran for the Territorial Legislature in 1912 as a self-appointed candidate on the Socialist Party ticket. The mine managers suggested to their detectives that a radical socialist like Krause might have hired himself out as a killer to the more violent wing of the outside labor union.

The case grew more complicated when the Pinkertons learned that Krause was also the last person to be seen with a Juneau charter boat operator before the man went missing. Then, before they could close in, territorial officials learned that Krause was the man who posed as a marshal at the mine. They charged him with impersonating a federal officer and sent real marshals to arrest him. But the marshals bungled the arrest; Krause escaped and made his way to Ketchikan, where he boarded a passenger steamer for Seattle.

Then Krause's luck ran out. A traveling salesman on the steamer recognized him and knew about the five-hundred-dollar reward, which was still in force. He alerted the ship's captain and Seattle Police were waiting for Krause as the ship docked in Puget Sound. When police went through Krause's valise, they found documents linking him both to the two Juneau disappearances and to at least eight other men who had vanished.

Krause was returned to Juneau and the case received wide publicity on the West Coast. When his photograph was published with the stories about the missing men, several people recognized him and came forward. They said he was really Edward Slompke, a soldier who first came to Alaska in 1897 and served with the U.S. Army at Wrangell during the Klondike Gold Rush. In 1902, after being transferred to China, he stole a military payroll, forged released documents and deserted from his regiment. Slompke changed his name to Krause, drifted for three years and came back to Alaska in 1905.

With Krause's arrest, the mine managers stopped paying for the Pinkertons' investigation, but a group of the area's private businessmen stepped in and paid the detective agency bills for a time. The possibility that a serial killer might be reducing Alaska's already small population led Territorial Governor J. F. A. Strong to ask the federal Department of Justice for financial help. The department recruited the Pinkertons' top detective working on the case and placed him on its payroll.

After a year's investigation, the newly organized Federal Bureau of Investigation stepped in and used its expertise to track Krause's past activities beyond Alaska. They found a long list of disappeared men and a complicated pattern of forged property deals extending across the United States and into Canada. The FBI learned that Krause had been recruiting and murdering young men for years; after each killing he used forged documents to take possession of the dead men's property, building murder and forgery into a lucrative career.

The FBI also determined that Krause had helpers and became convinced he headed a murder gang based in Petersburg, Alaska. The gang members were suspected of additional murders beyond those already discovered. But the issue became confused by Krause's political allies in the radical labor movement, people who were convinced that the murder and forgery accusations were an attempt by capitalists to railroad their man. At the top of their list of capitalist suspects was the Treadwell Mining Company, their principal opponent in the area. To counter their activities, government undercover agents infiltrated labor groups looking for evidence that the union was trying to get trial witnesses to perjure themselves and to intimidate potential jurors.

None of the bodies of Krause's victims were ever found. In Alaska, searchers trekked across uplands and beaches looking for graves. Divers worked the bottom of Juneau's Gastineau Channel for months, but nothing turned up. Prosecutors began to wonder if they would be able to make a solid case against him, even though they were convinced he had killed at least ten men and perhaps more. They had many documents to work with, including a letter to the Customs Office bearing the forged signature of James 0. Plunkett, the missing charter boat operator last seen talking to Krause. The letter said the boat had burned near Wrangell, though it was later found hidden in a remote inlet on Kupreanof Island.

Because of the varying quality of the evidence, prosecutors decided to hold a series of proceedings, bring him to trial on some charges and hold the murder trials for later. In the earliest, starting in 1917, he was convicted of kidnapping, robbery, forgery, using the mails to defraud, and representing himself as a federal officer. Then began the first of four murder prosecutions, a trial for the murder of Plunkett. Selecting a jury proved difficult because of the extensive publicity. By the time the panel was seated, the entire Juneau jury pool was nearly exhausted. The jury was sequestered, the first time any Alaska jury had been isolated from the public and denied the right to go home each day. But the court feared Krause's still-loyal adherents might try to intimidate those sitting in judgment on the case.

A prominent labor lawyer from Seattle represented Krause. The attorney was sure the fact that Plunkett's body had never been found would create enough doubt in the jury's minds to get him off. But the jurors decided the overwhelming pile of circumstantial evidence was enough; they found him guilty of first-degree murder. Since Krause stood to be hung for the offense, prosecutors decided to hold off on pursuing the other murder charges. No matter how many convictions they won, they could only hang him once.

The Seattle lawyer took his case to the Court of Appeals in San Francisco, but Krause's conviction was upheld and he was scheduled to be hung at Juneau on April 17. Two days before his execution date, Krause sawed through the bars of his cell in the Juneau Federal Jail in the basement of the court building. The escape triggered the most extensive manhunt in Alaska history. Fishing fleets were asked to look for him and the network of watching eyes spread throughout his possible escape route from Southeast Alaska and Canada to Seattle. Mines were shut down in Juneau and Douglas, freeing up a thousand men to join a posse formed and sworn in by a territorial judge. The posse conducted a house-to-house search in Juneau and rounded up and jailed Krause's labor union friends, who were suspected of helping him escape. Governor Strong announced a thousand-dollar reward for Krause and many considered it a "dead or alive" offer.

A few days later, a homesteader shot Krause as he stepped out of a stolen skiff on an Admiralty Island beach. The bullet ended Krause's criminal career and the life of Alaska's first serial murderer. But the homesteader's enjoyment of his reward was marred; a year later he left Juneau after being hounded by Krause's Socialist and labor union friends, who still believed him innocent of the crimes, and others who suspected the homesteader was helping Krause escape when he decided to cash in instead and shot him for the money.

President Woodrow Wilson fired the U.S. marshal in Juneau and replaced him with James Tanner of Skagway, one of the Skagway citizens who in 1897 rounded up and jailed the Soapy Smith gang. U.S. Attorney James Smiser of Juneau, who headed the Krause prosecution, wrote the Justice Department a letter saying, "The true story of Krause's criminal enterprises and their extent will never be known. But if the story could ever be told, it would undoubtedly be one of the most startling in the annals of American crime history."

November 2005

Tom Brennan was an editor and columnist for the Anchorage Times and is currently a columnist for the Anchorage Daily Planet. He is a member of the Fraternal Order of Alaska State Troopers. He is the author of several books about Alaska, including *Moose Dropping and Other Crimes Against Nature, Murder at Forty Below, Cold Crime* and *The Snowflake Rebellion,* a novel about Alaska seceding from the union. *Cold Crime* and *Murder at Forty Below* are filled with stories of Alaska Trooper investigations. Tom's son Tobin is an officer with the Soldotna Police Department, and Tom continues to be a big supporter of FOAST.

A Legendary Conman

Tom Brennan

Alaska's most notorious early criminal came to the territory in 1897 shortly after ships arrived in Seattle and San Francisco carrying small groups of suddenly rich miners and what was described as "a ton of gold." The men had made their fortunes in a fabulous gold strike in the Klondike mining district of Canada; their discovery launched the Gold Rush and brought thousands of would-be prospectors to Skagway and Dyea in Alaska. The neophyte gold-seekers prepared to find their own fortunes by struggling through either White Pass via Skagway or the Chilkoot Trail via Dyea. Both routes led to Lindeman Lake, where the adventurers built boats to carry them down the looping Yukon River to the Klondike.

Jefferson R. Soapy" Smith was an ex-cowboy who became a flamboyant grifter and swindler. He was born in 1860 to a wealthy slave-owning family in Georgia. The Smith fortune was swept away with the end of the Civil War, and the family moved west to recover its losses. The boy spent a number of years in the saddle, tending cattle, moving them from one range to another, and driving the animals to market.

But young Jefferson soon tired of working hard for a living and yearned for an easier way to make a buck. He was fascinated by a shell game he saw played by a conman in Leadville, Colorado. This seemed a far easier and more lucrative life than punching cows. He became the swindler's avid student. Smith learned quickly and was a convincing talker, so his experienced partner introduced him to another scam in which they wrapped a few five-cent bars of soap with large-denomination bills, then recovered them in the original wrappers and salted the few money bars in a display of unopened ones.

The con-man offered them all for sale at five dollars each, telling his customers that many of the bars had been randomly wrapped in money, though the truth was that the pile of soap contained very few bills— and almost all were of small denominations. One of his accomplices would buy one, open the wrapper, and gleefully show everybody a hundred-dollar bill he had found inside. That brought customers scrambling to give Soapy and his cohorts their five-dollar bills.

The soap bars were but one of Smith's many scams, which grew to include fake railroad tickets, a gambling den, and much more. The city fathers of Denver eventually tired of the Smith gang and ran them out of town, but Jefferson's nickname from that time forward was "Soapy."

Jefferson Smith knew an opportunity when he saw one and his arrival in Seattle shortly before the ship of gold was just such an opportunity. He bought passage aboard the first available passenger vessel headed for Alaska. Four days later he landed at the once-quiet Southeastern Alaska town of Skagway, where hordes of would-be miners were preparing for the arduous Journey ahead. But Soapy would have none of that for himself; he had learned his lessons about hard work in his cowboy days and was far more interested in mining the miners for their money and contrived numerous schemes to do that.

Skagway was fast becoming a boom town with illicit bars, gambling dens, and a makeshift red-light district where hookers in red petticoats enticed young men who were far from home, lonely, and quite naive. Soapy set up a saloon called "Jeff's Place," enlisted a group of like-minded helpers, and began fleecing the growing flock of gold-seekers. His businesses included a telegraph service which he claimed could relay messages from the homesick miners to those they left behind. Soapy would pretend to send telegrams south and promptly showed the miners responses from their wives asking for money. When the passing travelers gave him cash, he would pretend to remit it in southbound wires. Actually, his telegraph line ran just a few hundred yards from his door before disappearing into the sea, where it abruptly ended. He pocketed the miners' money and sent them off with his best wishes and heartfelt thanks from their loved ones.

Smith also had a non-existent freight line and an army enlistment tent where men could sign up for the Spanish-American War. While stripped to undergo examination by the military recruiting doctor, the miners' valuables somehow disappeared. Soapy's cohorts met arriving ships and posed as freight agents, newspaper reporters, and clergymen and directed the more gullible toward his fraudulent businesses. Soapy and his men virtually controlled Skagway and ruled it roughly, giving the town a reputation as the most lawless place in Alaska and Soapy as the territory's first gangster. He appointed himself grand marshal of the Fourth of July parade, which featured a brass band, and talked about setting up a fund for Skagway's widows, though some claimed the women became widows courtesy of Smith gang violence.

Eventually Soapy defrauded a gold miner of his entire grubstake, almost three thousand dollars, and the miner took the loss badly. His howls got the attention of citizens who were growing tired of Soapy Smith and what he was doing to their community. A vigilante group formed and dubbed itself the Committee of One Hundred and One. Its leader was Frank Reid, a fifty-four-year-old engineer and surveyor.

Reid confronted Soapy and several of his confederates at the town wharf on the evening of July 8, 1898. A gunfight erupted, and Smith was shot through the heart; he died on the spot, succumbing at the age of thirty eight. Reid was mortally wounded and died in Bishop Rowe Hospital on July 20. A coroner's inquest determined that Reid was murdered by Soapy in an unprovoked attack, but since Smith was also dead and couldn't be tried the case was closed.

March 2007

After-Hours Club

Investigator William "Bill" Roche, Retired

In the early 1980s, the Municipality of Anchorage adopted an ordinance to close bars at 2:30 a.m. on weekdays and 3 a.m. on weekends instead of 5 am, as required by state law. Almost immediately, unlicensed late night/early morning drinking places appeared in Anchorage. ABC investigators, working with Anchorage police, were tasked with addressing the problem.

A series of investigations began late one night when we drove Investigator John Charbonneau to Anchorage International Airport. After we dropped him off, he entered the terminal carrying a small suitcase. He exited the terminal about 3:30 a.m., and got into a taxi cab. He told the driver that he just arrived in Anchorage and needed a drink. The cab driver took him to a house on Minnesota Boulevard, a few blocks south of 36th Avenue. It was a busy after-hours club run by Rose Casey.

Investigator Charbonneau was able to gain entry and purchase alcoholic beverages after being introduced to Casey by the cab driver. After Investigator Charbonneau returned to the after-hours club a sufficient number of times to establish probable cause, a search warrant was obtained.

It was executed after legal bar closing hours by the ABC enforcement team accompanied by Anchorage police. As we gained entry to the illegal business, Investigator Charbonneau quietly slipped out the back door. A moving company had been employed to assist us. In addition to seizing alcoholic beverages as evidence, we took every stick of furniture and appliance in the club. Those items would later be forfeited to the state under the provisions of the alcoholic beverage laws. Rose Casey was found guilty of sale of alcoholic beverages without a license, and given a substantial fine.

Several months later, we heard that Casey was running an after-hours club in a house on 36th Avenue near Chilkoot Charlie's. Late one night, Investigator Charbonneau knocked on the door of Casey's club. Rose Casey answered the door, recognized Charbonneau, and greeted him like a long-lost uncle. Several days later, Casey offered Charbonneau the job of doorman at her club. Charbonneau accepted and was there to open the door when we arrived with the search warrant. Casey was found guilty again of sale without a license. This time she was sentenced to 30 days in jail and placed on two years probation.

About six months later, I was driving on Spenard Road past a number of "massage parlors." I noticed that one had a sign in the yard inviting patrons to "have a cold beer with one of our beautiful girls." I decided that I could save myself a lot of work by explaining to the proprietor that offering alcohol for sale without a license was a much more serious crime than prostitution. So, I knocked on the door of the business. Rose Casey answered the door. She took one look at me and the color drained from her face. The first words out of her mouth were, "am I going to jail?" I told her that if she didn't change the sign, she might be. The next day, the sign was gone.

That's the last we ever heard of Rose Casey.

November 2005

William Roche served 38 years in law enforcement. At age 22, he was appointed a special agent in OSI. He spent 8 years in that job; mostly in Anchorage. After OSI, he worked as a commissioned law enforcement officer at Anchorage International Airport for 14 months. In 1979, he was hired as an investigator for the Alcoholic Beverage Control Board. Five years later, he was appointed the ABC Board's chief enforcement officer. He held that position for 22 years until he retired at age 60. A year later his wife, Judy, and he moved to Tennessee. They enjoy the warm weather, the country living, and the ability to travel around the Lower 48.

36,000 Cans of Beer

Investigator William "Bill" Roche, Retired

The commercial use of alcoholic beverages without a license is a criminal offense. In the 1970's, Universal Seafood, a processor in Dutch Harbor, was offering free beer to fishermen that delivered their catch to the Universal Seafood processing plant.

After verifying that information with Royal Nelson, the Police Chief in Unalaska, I went to the DA's office and talked to Assistant DA Peter Gruenstein about getting a search warrant for the beer. I got the warrant and was on the way to Dutch Harbor the following day. I arrived in the early afternoon and was met by a police officer that Chief Nelson had assigned to assist me. We served the search warrant at four in the afternoon.

We discovered 1,500 cases of beer weighing over 7,000 pounds stored in the loft of the Universal seafood warehouse. With the assistance of the Police, I rented a 40-foot trailer van and began loading. Since there were only two of us, that took all night. We finally finished at approximately 7:30 the following morning. The trailer van was sealed and stored in the parking lot of the Unalaska Police Department. No one at the Police Department was aware that the asphalt parking lot was built on top of an old World War II landfill.

Several days later the weight of the trailer van on the thin asphalt covering the land fill caused the wheels on one side of the van to break through the asphalt and the whole van fell over. The temperature inside the van was pretty high. When it fell over, nearly half the beer cans exploded, causing a river of beer to flow through the police department parking lot.

In the meantime, the attorney for Universal Seafood offered to forfeit the beer if the state would agree not to prosecute criminally. The cost of that investigation included the rental and repair cost of the trailer van and $1,500 for overtime that Royal Nelson billed the state for his officer's assistance.

November 2005

Alaska Highway Patrol - 1950

Trooper George Glenn Rodgers

When I joined the Alaska Highway Patrol in 1950, it was a quite different service than the Alaska State Troopers are today. Like the men and women of AST today, we were a dedicated bunch and as professional as we could be under the circumstances, but there were never more than 40 patrolmen for the entire Territory of Alaska. Our approach towards many problems was what you might call informal.

The ranks included World War II veterans from various services, trappers and fishermen, heavy equipment operators, former deputy marshals, and police officers from various police departments in other parts of the country.

All had spent time in the Bush and remote areas of the territory. One of them, Fabian Carey, came to Alaska after the war and trapped alone for four years in the Lake Minchumina area. (Fabian later became the father of Michael Carey, retired editor of the editorial pages at the Anchorage Daily News and host of the public television program Alaska Edition.)

Fabian and I and Dave Henley joined the Highway Patrol on the same day, August 10, 1950, and were assigned to the 4th Division based in Fairbanks. Our vetting for the job consisted of an interview by one of the patrol's commissioners and— since there was no such thing as an academy in those days— our training involved riding with one of the older patrolmen until he decided you were ready to deal with the public alone.

My training officer was Gene Morris, who had previously been a police officer in an Outside department. Our "fleet" of patrol cars was pretty limited. One was a red Ford Mercury nicknamed "the little red schoolhouse," and I learned the tools of the trade in it.

After the training period, we were assigned to shifts. Fabian and I drew the midnight to 8 a.m. shift and — since the Highway Patrol by then had more patrol cars — we each had our own. One night as we approached the halfway time of our shift, we decided to make another patrol run. Fabian headed south on the Alcan to cover the Eielson Air Force Base and the Dike area. I headed north to cover the Farmer's Loop and College areas.

When I finished the patrol and went back to the office, I decided to take a break and go across the street to the WigWam for a cup of coffee. As I sat at the counter drinking my coffee, the owner looked over my shoulder and began to laugh. Coming down South Cushman Avenue was Fabian's patrol car. On its roof was a dog sled and sticking out of each open window was the head of a barking sled dog. Sitting in the front seat and chatting amiably with Fabian was a bewhiskered elderly man, an old trapper Fabian had known from his own trapping days.

Fabian had come upon the man and his team crossing the Dike and offered him a ride into town. That was just the way we did things in those days. It was the Alaska spirit, to help each other when you could.

Because we had so few officers, I spent a full year working the midnight to 8 a.m. shift. During that time I handled a dozen fatalities including fire fatalities, drownings, suicides, killings and auto accidents. I've talked to men who spent 20 years in police work outside and never handled a single death in their entire career. But with just a few good men and a lot of territory to cover, the Highway Patrol of 1950 often did every conceivable kind of police work.

May 2006

George Glenn Rodgers died December 26, 2006 at his Chugiak, Alaska home. He was born December 25, 1923 in Superior, Wisconsin and was self-taught, earning a GED. Later he attended four different art schools, polishing his natural ability as an artist. He served in the U.S. Marine Corps during World War II and moved to Fairbanks in 1950 and lived there until 1962. While in Fairbanks he worked several years for the Territorial Police and also served as an art instructor at the University of Alaska Anchorage and the Alaska Fine Arts Academy. In 1973, he moved to New York to further his career as a graphic artist, returning to Chugiak, Alaska in 1977. George won numerous awards for his artwork in pastels, watercolors and oils. He became involved with the Golden Anniversary Committee and the Fraternal Order of the Alaska State Troopers and painted the four-era picture of the Alaska State Troopers organization. He was a member of the Veterans of Foreign Wars, Masons, and the Fond Du Lac Indian Tribe and a life member of the Fraternal Order of Alaska State Troopers.

Air Crash in the Mountains

Radio Dispatcher John Eberth, Retired

If you look in the almanac under "plane crashes," you'll see: Alaska Airlines 727 crashed in Juneau in 1971, September 4, killing all 111 people aboard.

Ava Harris and I were working as dispatchers that day, a weekend, and received the first call: the FAA tower believed the plane was lost crossing the mountains from Anchorage into Juneau. Ava and I were the only ones in the office and immediately notified the on-call command officer, Sergeant Roger Iverson, who within moments was streaming Code Three[2] to headquarters. Lieutenant Harry McLaughlin was notified. He was on his boat and immediately powered toward his dock.

The plane could not be located; no contact. Nobody had a clue what had happened. The sincere hope was that it was a fluke in the radio transmitting system; maybe the mountains had blocked the signal. Anything—but not a crash. We knew there were people from Juneau on board.

Sergeant Iverson drove straight to the helo pad in Juneau and went up in the helicopter to try and find a crash site, although it was hoped there was none.

One by one, the Juneau command reported to the building. Sergeant Heddell and then Lieutenant Sydnam began poring over large topographical maps trying to pinpoint a general area to search. Others gathered in the dispatch area to listen to the progress of Sergeant Iverson, who continued to radio back, to everyone's relief, that nothing could be found. It was getting dark.

Robin Lown, an ex-crew-chief from Vietnam and now a dispatcher, and much later to become commander of Juneau Detachment, took over radio control at shift change.

---

2 Emergency response using lights and siren

Command personnel clustered around the dispatch console, monitoring the events as they were radioed back from Sergeant Iverson — still, nothing could be found. Hope began to blossom. Nobody could believe that an Alaska Airlines pilot, noted for being the best pilots in the world, could have crashed.

It was getting dark. Sergeant Iverson radioed us that he would soon have to head back to Juneau. "Wait..." came his voice under heavy static, and for a second all of us in the room held our breath. "We're seeing something down on the mountainside, on the snow. It looks like maybe debris of some kind, but it's too small to be it." We all breathed a sigh of relief. Sergeant Iverson said they were going down to have a closer look just to be sure.

Much speculation began in a quiet whisper around the room about what might have happened to the flight. It had to be the weather, the radio— anything but a crash. Not in Juneau.

Then Sergeant Iverson announced to all of us that they had found the crash site up in the godforsaken glaciers and snow country of the mountains— and there was nothing left but small pieces. All of us were momentarily stunned. You could have heard a pin drop in that dispatch center, just for a second.

The Lieutenant took control and organized recovery effort through command in Anchorage. I can't remember the Lieutenant picking up the Civil Defense phone, normally used for earthquake advisories, but he got in touch with the NTSB. The NTSB told him to secure the scene and under no circumstances let anyone else near the crash site. Sergeant Iverson was then notified to bar everyone, even FAA personnel, from entering the crash scene. Captain Bill Nix was appointed on-scene commander, and organized troopers from Anchorage as well as other posts in Southeast, and was ordered to Juneau to participate in a strenuous search and recovery effort at altitude and under adverse mountain snow conditions. Many troopers who were involved in it have horrifying tales to tell about the recovery effort.

After the order was over, the NTSB official would say that AST had handled the situation superbly— better than any other agency he had worked with.

July 2008

John Eberth began his career as a Dispatcher in Juneau from 1970 to 1972. He then worked in Anchorage until 1980. John and his wife initially moved to Alaska following his military service. In 1982, John and his wife returned to Ohio, where he worked for the Toledo Police Department. John now enjoys cycling, an addiction he picked up from Trooper Kolivosky and Palmer AST.

Looking for Old Files?

Captain Steve Reynolds, Retired

When our Protection Division moved over from the Department of Fish and Game to the Department of Public Safety in April, 1972, I was transferred from McGrath into Anchorage to head up the newly-formed detachment there as sergeant.

Captain Hal Sydnam was the blue-shirt commander and was helpful in getting us set up comfortably at the office on 36th Avenue. I inherited the office equipment that had belonged to the F&G Protection Regional Office, which included five four-drawer metal file cabinets. I had plenty to do since my detachment spread all the way to Nome and Kotzebue, and I didn't take the time to look into those cabinets. They could wait. I kept personnel files of my officers in my desk drawer. It didn't appear I had a need for those large file cabinets and they took up a lot of room.

I pointed them out to Captain Sydnam one day and he suggested that I simply turn the cabinets around to face the wall to see if I really needed to look in them. If I needed to find something bad enough, he said, I could start turning them back around again. I did what Syd suggested, with some help, and as time wore on, I soon got requests from the likes of Lieutenant Tom Anderson, Sergeant Walt Gilmour, and Cpl. Don Lawrence for a file cabinet or two. The Department didn't have a lot of money in those days and most everyone was shy of equipment. In a short time, I gave all five of the cabinets away with only the stipulation that the contents, whatever they were, be put in cardboard boxes and stored in the warehouse, properly marked.

To this day, I don't know what was in those cabinets. If anyone is snooping around the old shed out behind the Department aircraft hangar, they might check those cardboard boxes out. There could be a treasure in there - an old wolverine's hide or a photo of Uncle Bill Egan, or something like that.

March 2009

Stephen Reynolds now lives near Montague, California with his wife, Judy. He began his law enforcement career with the U. S. Fish and Wildlife Service as a stream guard in 1957. In 1959, he joined the New Mexico Department of Game and Fish as a game warden, leaving there after 10 years and coming to Alaska to work as a protection officer with the Alaska Fish and Game Department in 1969. In 1972, when the Protection Division was transferred to the Department of Public Safety, he was promoted to Sergeant in charge of the Anchorage Detachment. Other assignments before and after included Nenana, McGrath, Bettles, Aniak, King Salmon, Soldotna, and Kodiak, where he was Captain in charge of both AST and Fish and Wildlife Protection for Kodiak Island, Bristol Bay, and the Aleutian Islands, in addition to the statewide Vessels Section. He is a graduate of the Alaska State Trooper Academy and the 136th Session of the FBI Academy. He is a writer, has had two books published, and writes a regular column for his local newspaper and one for the *International Game Warden* magazine.

The Polar Bear Chase

Captain Steve Reynolds, Retired

In early March, 1971, I went to Kotzebue in a Piper Super Cub to patrol the polar bear hunt, a learn-as-you-go experience. I had been a Fish and Wildlife officer in Alaska for a couple of years at the time and had not yet flown a state airplane to Kotzebue. It is more than 400 miles to the Northwest of where we lived at Anderson Village, along the Nenana River in interior Alaska.

Everything was white at that time of year. South of the Brooks Range there were at least trees and brush to show the contours of the land beneath and ahead of you. The Arctic coastal area was another story. As I topped the divide between the Koyukuk watershed and the Selawik River drainage, toward Kotzebue from Galena on the Yukon River, an immensity of white, treeless, flat country greeted me. I had to trust the Automatic Direction Finder to point the way to Kotzebue 150 miles beyond. The myriad of lakes and waterways on the chart, distinguishable by unique shapes in the summer, were blended into sameness and absent of any outlines in the winter.

Kotzebue and the narrow Baldwin Peninsula were surrounded by the frozen waters of Hotham Inlet and Kotzebue Sound during that time of year. The Chukchi Sea beyond is solid, lumpy, and windswept. I couldn't always tell where the land ended and the sea began.

At Kotzebue, there were more than 50 Super Cubs, which belonged to polar bear guides, toggled to the sea ice when I got there. The sewage from the town of 1500 or so people was dumped on that same ice throughout the winter to be carried away in the ice breakup of late spring. However, the danger of stepping in sewage was not my main concern. What concerned me was the danger of stumbling over a frozen pile from a bucket or breaking a gear from running into it with the airplane.

Residents also kept freshwater ice on the roofs of the houses to keep it away from the dogs. The ice was cut and hauled from the mouth of the Noatak River about 15 miles away then brought inside to thaw when needed.

Guides with clients hunted the Chukchi Sea from the Alaska coastline all the way to Russia. These were the final years of the free-for-all sanctioned killing of the big bears by allowing the use of airplanes.

A hunt went like this: The hunter flew commercially from his home in the Lower 48 to Kotzebue where he stayed in a hotel or lodge overnight. The next morning he flew in the rear seat of a Super Cub over the ice to look for bears, sometimes crossing open leads of water twenty miles in breadth. Another Super Cub accompanied them with an assistant guide as a passenger. When they spotted a bear of acceptable size, they dropped off the assistant and the hunter, and the two planes then drove the bear to them.

The hunter killed and skinned the bear. They then loaded the hide and skull onto the plane to return to Kotzebue. Jack Jonas or another known taxidermist usually met them at the tie-down to take the hide. The taxidermist often turned it over to one of the Eskimo women to wash, flesh, and prepare for shipping to Seattle or Denver for mounting.

The hunter celebrated his good fortune that night and likely returned to his home the following day. The hunt of a lifetime was over. The hunter configured his memories in whatever manner that made them seem something other than they were. The bear would be mounted appearing to be forever in a raging charge or an intimidating, open-mouthed stance, with all but the slobbers frozen in time.

A charging bear was one thing. A harried bear running from an airplane into an ambush was something different, and the story was not quite so heroic of the hunter, if told with all the facts included. Admittedly, there was an element of danger involved. The largest carnivore on the continent making a beeline for a hunter out on the ice could make him feel insignificant and hopeful that the assistant guide crouched next to him was dependable and adequately armed for the bear.

At the time it was illegal to kill brown or grizzly bears on the same day someone was airborne, but that restriction did not yet exist for polar bears. The fair chase method of taking the white bears without the use of an airplane was almost unheard of. Normally, that required the assistance of Eskimo hunters with dog teams or snowmachines. Very few guides were set up for that, and polar bear hunting as we knew it was almost over for the modern sportsman.

I patrolled the airplane hunts for the final three seasons before it ended. As for flying the sea ice and coastal Arctic in the winter, I was quite happy to leave it all to the raven and the snowy owl.

June 2010

A Rookie Investigates His First Major Crime

Sergeant Bob Robertson, Retired

In 1961 I was sent to the far end of the Alaska Peninsula to investigate a report of a suspicious death. A woman had died in the small, isolated community of Belkofski, and villagers reported she had apparently been raped and murdered.

I was a recruit Trooper still in my probation period and assigned to work a major crime in one of Alaska's remotest villages. I set off with visions of the Lone Ranger in my head, but soon found that getting there would not be a matter of riding into town on a horse.

The closest airport was at Cold Bay, and all flights there on the Reeve Aleutian Airways schedule board were listed as "weather permitting." The airport was an old World War II base, originally called Fort Randall, and its long, paved runway was used primarily as an emergency runway for Trans-Pacific air traffic and aircraft serving the Peninsula and the Aleutians. Its few trailers were occupied by airline flight crews and support personnel. From Cold Bay, I would have to charter a single-engine amphibious aircraft, which could land in the water at King Cove, and then hire a boat to get to Belkofski, which has a rocky shore unfriendly to light aircraft and large boats.

As the big Reeve turboprop approached Cold Bay, I could see the tundra was littered with 55-gallon drums, dumped there in wartime after the fuel in them was used. I was met by the Magistrate's husband, who was the airport's official greeter, and put up at the transit crew trailer. That evening my host drove me to an Air Force radar site a few miles out of town, a place where our military kept their eyes and ears on the Russians. I got an extremely limited tour of the facility, but we did manage to visit the most important— to us— part of the installation, the bar at the small enlisted/officer's club. The airmen were very congenial and made me an honorary Air Force officer. For part of the evening, I wore a military Captain's shirt and cap. The Captain had on my Smokey Bear hat and Trooper shirt, with badge.

My host's driving skills were limited even with a clear head. His primary use of the pickup seemed to be to drive out to the radar site once a week. On the unsteady return trip he told me he had nicknamed the pickup "Titanic," which didn't calm my fears.

Next day I found a Bush pilot who flew me to King Cove, landed on the water, and taxied to the beach. There I hired a boat from the maintenance crew at the cannery, which was closed for the season. The water was very rough, and the boat was unable to land at Belkofski, so the driver signaled for a small boat to come out from shore and get me. I didn't want to get stranded there, so I asked the fishing boat to wait.

The village consisted of 57 people, most of whom had probably never seen a State Trooper before. Many of the older people did not speak English, but I found a young woman who attended high school in Oregon, probably the Chemawa Indian School in Salem, and she became my translator.

I was shown the body of an elderly woman, with obvious signs of rape and strangulation. By the time I got there, she had been dead more than 10 days. I started the investigation by interrogating the men of the village, not a huge chore since there weren't too many. I asked each for his name and its spelling, but keeping accurate records proved impossible since Aleut is a spoken language, not written. So I spelled each one phonetically for the official record, probably badly enough to cause each of their ancestors to roll over in his grave.

It looked like I had the case solved with the first interview, since when I asked questions the man started sweating, his Adams apple bobbed up and down, his hands shook and he wouldn't look me in the eye. Sure signs of guilt, I thought. But my big break fell apart when I continued grilling other village men and they all had the same reaction.

They couldn't all be guilty, and I only had one set of handcuffs, though I briefly wondered whether the excess suspects might volunteer to keep their hands in their pockets while we made the convoluted trip to Anchorage. Then my interpreter explained that a bootlegger's boat had made a visit the night before and the men were just suffering from extreme hangovers— and probably guilt about getting drunk.

The Native people seemed to be exceedingly honest, so it was up to me to ask the right questions. I settled on just one: "Did you do it?" They all said no, but eventually a teenager named Ivan admitted he had been drunk and had a vague recollection of raping and strangling the old woman. I arrested him and asked for a small boat to take Ivan and me out to the still-waiting fishing boat.

The village had no electricity, no radio and no telephone, so there was no way to communicate with headquarters. Ivan was very friendly and docile, so getting him back to Anchorage seemed to be not a problem. When the villagers asked permission to conduct the proper Russian Orthodox ceremonies and bury the deceased, I told them to go ahead. The evidence of rape and strangulation was obvious and getting a 10-day-old body back to Anchorage via small boat, fishing boat, float plane, and airliner — with no real way to prepare it for shipment— was daunting, so I told them to go ahead.

Ivan and I were rowed out to the fishing boat, which headed back to King Cove. The weather had been bad and was getting worse. Enroute, the fishing vessel was half boat and half submarine. From the cannery I reached the amphibious aircraft pilot by radio, but he said the weather included wind, rain, cold, low clouds and fog - no-fly weather. The cannery crew put us up in an empty bunk room.

When we went to bed, it occurred to me that Ivan - having already killed one person - might not be as friendly as he seemed. So I handcuffed him to his bed and we both slept soundly. Next morning at breakfast I was introduced to what was apparently a typical cannery meal. They didn't give you a menu; they simply offered you everything that would be on one. Ham, bacon, sausage, hot cakes, waffles, donuts, biscuits, sweet rolls, toast, steak, eggs, omelets, potatoes, or if nothing there suited your fancy— the cook would whip up something else. Only question was how much and how many you wanted. It was that way every meal. Then at 10 a.m., 3 p.m., and 9 p.m., they had "mug up," which was a coffee break with cookies, cakes, pies, rolls and donuts.

The cannery crew worked off some of their calories, but my prisoner and I had nothing to do but eat and wait. We were socked in by weather for three days. I was gaining weight by the hour. Finally, the Bush pilot came for us and we flew back to Cold Bay and caught a Reeve flight back to Anchorage. Ivan was entering an entirely different world.

As we circled to land at Anchorage, Ivan looked out the window and was awestruck, practically speechless. He had never seen a village that large and had never seen a building bigger than the cannery at King Cove. A trooper and a patrol car met us at the airport to transport him to jail. I realized that the prisoner would be too late for supper at the jail, so we stopped downtown at a fast food restaurant. I asked him if he would like a hamburger and a milkshake. He gave me a blank stare; he had never heard of either one. He inhaled them and asked for more, but I was out of money, so we headed for the jail. He rolled down the patrol car window and marveled at what for him was a metropolis. We drove a few blocks out of our way to show him more buildings and took him to booking.

Next day Captain Turk Mayfield mildly chastised me for taking a murder suspect to dinner on the way to the lockup. Then he asked when the woman's autopsy was scheduled. I explained the problem of getting a 10-day-old corpse back to Anchorage from a remote village and the obvious signs of rape and strangulation. He asked me how we were going to prove she had not died a natural death without an autopsy. I told him the cause of death seemed obvious and Ivan was going to plead guilty, so there would not be a trial.

Ivan did plead out. I suspect that, since he was a juvenile, he only had to stay in custody until he turned 21. During our time together, we had talked a lot and become pretty close— for a cop and a killer. About four years later Ivan wrote me a letter. He remembered I had three daughters and wanted to write them letters. Though I liked him— he didn't seem all bad— I couldn't take a chance. I didn't answer him.

I still wonder about Ivan. I hope sometime, somewhere, somebody gives him all the milkshakes he can drink and all the hamburgers he can eat.

June 2009

Robert James "Bob" Robertson moved his wife and eight children from Spokane, Washington to Alaska in 1959 for a construction job. When that didn't work out he began work with the Alaska State Police as a dispatcher and later Trooper. He served in Anchorage, Eagle River, Kenai and Juneau and was promoted to Sergeant. In 1968 he returned to Spokane with his family and spent his remaining work years with the Division of Motor Vehicles in Washington. He's the author of "Tall Tales of an Alaska State Trooper" and a Life Time Member of FOAST. He passed away in March of 2013.

How Would You Like to be Transferred to Fort Yukon?

First Sergeant Gene Kallus, Retired

Settling in to a new assignment is always interesting, especially at 45 below.

After commissioning as an Alaska State Trooper in April 1972, my first duty station was the Fairbanks Detachment. The following January, when it was 40 below zero, I received a phone call from Captain Ralph Shaffer, the Detachment Commander.

It was a Sunday morning and my day off, so I was trying to sleep in. The Captain wanted me in his office in one hour. That brought me fully awake. As I showered I tried to think of anything I had done wrong, or maybe hadn't done. Nothing came to mind.

In those days, when a Trooper was called in by the Commander, that meant reporting on time in a clean uniform with spit-shined shoes. I arrived right on time and stood at attention in Captain Shaffer's office. He asked me to have a seat. This seemed like good news, since if he was going to chew me out, I surely would have had to remain at attention.

Then just as I was beginning to relax, he said, "How would you like to be transferred to Fort Yukon?" My butt slammed shut like a suitcase. "No sir, I would not like that," I said. Shaffer then rephrased his words to make it clear he was not really asking a question. I was to report to Fort Yukon on February 15, just 30 days from then.

I had 30 days to sell our double-wide trailer, vehicles, boat, and everything else we wouldn't need in the Athabascan village just north of the Arctic Circle.

Fish and Wildlife Protection Officer Jack Allen and Corporal Claude "Swack' Swackhammer flew us the 140 miles to Fort Yukon in the department's Cessna 180 with Tail Number N7066. (An airplane I would spend many hours flying after I received my pilot's license in Fort Yukon.)

It was 45 below zero when we landed and went to check out our new housing. The Trooper quarters were a 14-year-old 12x45 mobile home with an unheated lean-to attached.

When we opened the door, it was colder inside than outside. The furnace had gone off, apparently quite a while ago. Everything was frozen, including the propane, which had liquefied. That meant we couldn't even use the kitchen range to heat up the place.

Allen and Swackhammer got the old drip-oil furnace going and slowly the place began to heat up. We put a light bulb on an extension cord in the insulated box that housed the propane cylinder and the propane began to flow.

Things seemed to be going well until the warming air in the trailer thawed the water in the copper pipes. The pipes had split from the ice expansion and water began flooding the kitchen and living room floors. We ran around outside until we found the water shut-off valve and stopped the flooding.

When we arrived, we had put some canned goods in the kitchen cupboard. Carol took one out the next day and found they were all frozen. Then the next morning something went awry with the furnace and too much oil accumulated in the burn chamber: When it went off, a small explosion shook the trailer. I was sitting on the throne and was lifted at least two inches.

That was it. I called my new boss, Outpost Commander Sergeant Walt Zahn and told him we needed a few things and would be staying at the only hotel, the Sourdough Inn, until they arrived. The list included a new furnace, some one-inch Styrofoam to insulate the cupboards, and new indoor/outdoor carpeting to make the trailer habitable.

Zahn rounded up everything next day and had them loaded on a Wien Airlines F-27, a twin-engine turboprop. Swackhammer and Investigator Jim Hemphill flew in with the 180 the next day to help me install everything.

After two more days, everything was working well, and I was ready to begin patrol duties. The Fort Yukon Post covered a vast area ranging from the White Mountains north of Fairbanks to the Brooks Range, to Circle City to the East, and Stevens Village to the West. It included the villages of Beaver, Birch Creek Village, Venetie, Chalkyitsik, and Arctic Village.

March 2011

Technical Sergeant Gene Kallus retired from the Alaska State Troopers in October 1990. At the time of his retirement, he was the Outpost and Search and Rescue Commander for the C Detachment on the Kenai. He spent 10 years in drug and narcotics units, as well as homicide investigation and other facets of law enforcement. He was a department pilot and attended the first session of the Tactical Diving Unit. T/Sergeant Kallus served on the Alaska Peace Officers Executive Board and is a lifetime member. He currently resides in Soldotna with his wife Carol.

Call the Patrol

Clerk Flo Janning

Wherever Alaska highways go
Like a bell with a friendly toll,
This well-known phrase all travelers know
When in need, just call the Patrol.

When a tire goes flat and the jack won't work
And the car may start to roll,
Folks run to the nearest phone at hand
For what? Why, to call the Patrol.

While driving perhaps some matchless scene
Has captured your very soul,
And a dozen questions you'd like to ask,
For your answers, call the Patrol.

You see they have viewed it all before
From the pink of the early dawn,
Till the breathless sunset settles down
And the full Moon's looking on

As the finite human traveler
Finds an Inn by the road and stops,
In the night the glistening glaciers glow
Patrolling the mountaintops.

Nowhere but here in Alaska, could
A motorist on the loose
Round a mountain curve and view head on
With no warning at all, a Moose.

A common occurrence it is up here
When a car and a Moose collide,
Folks may call the beast a lot of things
But they call the Patrol besides.

Twenty-four hours of every day
Seven days of every week,
The trusty Patrol is on the job
Folks wonder when they sleep.

These watch dogs of the winding ways
Have an honor that all extol,
They are friendly all, when you need them call
The Alaska Highway Patrol.
60th Anniversary

The Territorial Police Gazette, the first departmental newsletter, began in 1955 and continued on a quarterly basis for approximately four years. Mrs. Flo Janning, who doubled as Anchorage Detachment Commander's Secretary, radio dispatcher and clerk from 1949 until her retirement in 1963 was a regular contributor. Mrs. Janning passed away in the late sixties.

The Escape

Trooper Joe Swain, Retired

Robert S. Wotring left St. Louis, Missouri in a hurry. He was wanted on charges of transportation of forged securities (15 counts). He traveled west to Seattle with a woman companion and somehow obtained a cabin cruiser in Seattle. He headed for Alaska via the Inside Passage figuring no one would be looking for him there.

I've forgotten who arrested him, but I think it was the U.S. Marshals with the assistance of the Royal Canadian Mounted Police. He was brought to Ketchikan where he was found guilty by a jury and sentenced by U. S. District Judge Raymond Kelly to 10 years in the Federal Penitentiary, McNeil Island. Wotring was being held in the Jail on the fifth floor (top) of the federal building when he escaped.

The escape was around 3:00 p.m. The weather was extremely stormy, even for Ketchikan, with high winds and unusually heavy rain. The U. S. Coast Guard, U. S. Marshals, Ketchikan Police Department and Alaska State Police began the search for the escapee.

I was paired with Officer Jack Webb of the Ketchikan Police Department. We began by searching Thomas Basin, the large boat moorage immediately adjacent to the Federal building. I'm sure there were at least 80 to 100 boats moored there. It was getting dark, but we checked locks and tried doors on all of the unoccupied boats. We also questioned persons on all of the occupied boats with no luck or information on the wanted subject.

We then began searching the rural roads and main highway. We went seven miles south of town and 11 miles north; we searched the pulp mill parking lot, Saxman Village, and Totem Park areas.

On our way back to town, we were notified that a Ketchikan Public Utility truck had been stolen. Remembering we had seen such a truck in the pulp mill lot, we headed back to the mill. In the meantime, the mill watchman, Art Kienel called to say he and foreman Ivan Biehl, and worker Michael Salamanchuck had flushed a man out of the mill who was probably the suspect. When we arrived and were talking to the men, Officer Webb spotted a man trying to hide behind a log barrier in the lot. With guns drawn, we approached the man, who surrendered.

Wotring stated he had found an unlocked door at the mill and knew there was a Japanese ship in port loading pulp. He planned to stow away on this vessel. He had simply escaped by walking down the stairway of the Federal building and walked out through the Post Office on the main floor, stealing a parka and canned meat on his way out.

I believe this was the only escape that ever occurred from the Federal Jail in Ketchikan.

60th Anniversary

In the fall of 1953, Joe Swain and a friend, B. W. (Bill) Finley, both patrolmen on the Vancouver, Washington Police Department, flew to Ketchikan to take the test for the Alaska Territorial Police (ATP). Swain received notice that he was accepted and reported to Anchorage in January 1954 to attend the first class of the ATP, which had a total of 9 officers.

He was stationed in Anchorage for two years, and in 1956, he volunteered for transfer to the Ketchikan Post, where he served for four years; a time he recalls as "the best period of my life," and Ketchikan was a great place to live. When William Egan was elected first Alaska governor and selected a head of the department, Swain was transferred "FBI" style to Fairbanks with no prior notification. Costs were high, he had to sell his home, and uproot his family.

The Crash of USCG Aircraft 2121

Trooper Bertram C. Kellogg

(The following is from a report on the crash of the Coast Guard aircraft 2121 in Lynn Canal on December 14, 1954. The original report was written by Bertram Kellogg, Officer in Charge, Territorial Police, Haines, Alaska. It has been edited for brevity. Editor.)

At 7:30 a.m., the writer came on duty at the Department of Territorial Police Station at Haines, Alaska. At 8:00 a.m., I was at the Haines City Jail and checked on the relief of the guard for committed mental patient Fredrick B. Harrington.

At approximately 9:30 a.m., I received information that the Coast Guard had dispatched an Albatross aircraft to Haines to remove the mental patient. Deputy Marshall Miller was on board the aircraft. They were scheduled to arrive in Haines at about 11:00 a.m.

At about 11:00 a.m., due to the very heavy weather in the area, I checked on the aircraft and noted the plane was approaching Haines. I left for the airport and flagged the plane off because the runway snow had not been cleared enough for a safe landing.

I went back to Haines and notified Coast Guard operations in Juneau to instruct the aircraft to wait for a green smoke bomb at the airport prior to landing, and I returned to the airport. A larger portion of the runway had been cleared, and I attempted to ignite the smoke bomb, which did not go off. One party from the Alaska Road Commission at Haines assisted me in marking off the runway for the pilot. I returned to Haines to get a green blanket because of the previous message transmitted to the aircraft.

When I returned to the airport, I was handed a message bomb dropped from the aircraft which read "Do not plan to land here. We can land on the water at Portage Cove. If you have a boat available to transfer patient from Haines to us write out "YES" in snow and depart for Haines," Signed U.S. Coast Guard.

I then left for Portage Cove to meet the plane. Upon arrival, I found the aircraft had made its initial pass over the area, had dropped a smoke bomb for wind indication, and was on final approach. The aircraft landed at a point between Haines and Port Chilkoot and, after numerous attempts to contact the plane, we were successful in establishing voice contact with the aircraft at Port Chilkoot dock. The pilot notified us he would launch a life raft and come to shore, which he did. The pilot arrived with U. S. Deputy Marshal Miller and two enlisted men. It was approximately 12:00 noon.

The raft was left at the side of the road, and we left for Haines. I called U.S Public Health Service Nurse Olive Walker and asked her to meet us at the Haines City Jail in about ten or fifteen minutes. Deputy Miller and I departed for the home of U. S. Commissioner Ross Hevel and picked up the commitment and other papers on Mr. Harrington. Deputy Miller and I then went to the Haines City Jail and were met by two guards, the aircraft commander and his party, the nurse and two men from the Tide-Bay Company. Nurse Walker administered a sedative to Mr. Harrington while he was still in his cell.

At approximately 12:25 p.m. I unlocked Mr. Harrington's cell and led him out to the City Council Chambers which adjoin the cells. We placed Mr. Harrington's jacket on him and persuaded him to enter the straitjacket, which he did. Mr. Harrington was then placed in a Stokes litter and leg cuffs were placed on him. He was then strapped into the litter by the litter straps. We placed Mr. Harrington in Patrol Car #32 and departed for the beach where we had left the life raft.

The raft was launched about 12:40 p.m. with five persons aboard. I noted the sedative given Mr. Harrington earlier had apparently started to take effect as he appeared to be just about asleep.

After the raft left the beach for the aircraft, which was lying at anchor, I went to the Port Chilkoot dock to watch the plane leave. From the dock, I saw the raft approach the aircraft and transfer the men aboard. The raft was deflated and hauled aboard. The door was secured and the anchor pulled in.

The aircraft's motors were started at about 12:55 p.m. and the aircraft proceeded to taxi around the Portage Cove area. At this time I observed a light covering of snow on the aircraft wings, body, and tail surfaces. The aircraft continued its taxi, and headed toward

Low Point across the head of Lynn Canal from Port Chilkoot. I watched the aircraft, but visibility was low at times due to snow squalls. The aircraft continued its course toward Low Point, and after getting out quite a ways, I noted and heard power being applied to the engines for takeoff. I saw the aircraft rise out of the water onto the "step" then, after a short run, the aircraft lifted from the water at a very steep angle. Being somewhat familiar with aircraft, the first thought I had was that the plane would stall out. It did. It fell off on the right wing which hit the water.

It is hard to say just how high the aircraft was at the time the right wing dropped, or how long the plane was in the air. It is my estimation it was in the air about five to ten seconds from liftoff until the right wing hit. This was at approximately 1:10 to 1:15 p.m.

I immediately turned the patrol car around and, using red light and siren, went to Haines for help. I first contacted the local Alaska Communications Systems office by telephone and requested they notify Coast Guard Operations at Juneau of the plane crash. Numerous persons were on the street, and I requested assistance from all parties in rounding up small boats. I informed them of the location of the crash, requesting two men to a boat and to proceed at once.

I was informed of some small boats available at Fort Chilkoot, and I immediately left to enlist aid of all parties in that area. One small boat was launched from the barge grid, but no oars or motor were available. I located another boat at the ferry ramp. I asked others who were entering the area to launch immediately. I dispatched other men to look for motors.

I was then informed that Mr. Jeff David of the Native village at Haines had a boat close to the water and was able to leave immediately. I went to the village and found Mr. David had already departed for the crash scene in his boat. I found another boat being readied by James Lindoff, Tom Hard, and one other party. I asked the third party to leave the boat so I could go to the scene and assist in direction of other boats which were being launched and getting underway.

While in the boat, I was keeping the aircraft under observation by field glasses. I noted it was lying on its back, and apparently sinking rather rapidly. The survivors were making their way toward the tail section. They were picked up in a matter of a minute or two by Mr. David who immediately turned and started toward shore. As Mr. David's boat passed, I identified Mr. Miller and two others from the aircraft. Mr. Miller appeared to be in fair shape, but the two others were bloody about the head.

Mr. David pointed out a person floating in the water close by the tail section. We came alongside the party in the water, later identified as Mr. C. E. Habecker. As we approached, I reached out and caught him by the top of his uninflated life jacket and tried to hold his head above water. He was unconscious. We were unable to bring him aboard because of heavy seas and our small boat of about 12 feet in length.

We waited alongside Mr. Habecker until another boat with Chief of Police Battrick of the City of Haines and Mr. Fred Beacock of Haines came alongside and assisted us in loading him into our boat. We then started for shore. I requested Mr. Battrick take command of the boats entering the area and to direct search operations for other survivors. As we were making our way away from the aircraft, it sank out of sight.

After getting Mr. Habecker aboard, I immediately tried to administer artificial respiration as seas and conditions permitted. But practically all efforts were in vain because of ice conditions in the boat, heavy seas, and the danger of going overboard. We fought heavy seas all the way, and the motor quit on several occasions.

It is my estimation the total elapsed time from the crash until the first rescue boat was at the scene was about 15 to 18 minutes. I was later told a total of seven boats were used in rescue operations.

Mr. David's boat was already in when we arrived back at the beach at about 2:00 p.m. I was momentarily out of commission due to mental and physical exhaustion. After getting helped up the beach and placed into a vehicle, I was able, in a very short while, to pull together and continue to assist.

I was informed Mr. Miller was in good shape in a nearby home. I went to the house and found Mr. Miller by the stove trying to get warm. We placed him on a couch, started treatment for shock, and called Miss Walker, who instructed us to administer 1 ampoule of morphine.

At approximately 4:00 p.m., I was notified that Dr. O.J. Fortun was arriving from Skagway via speed boat. I went to the beach area to stand by and provide transportation. When I got to the beach area, I noted Miss Walker had checked on Mr. Miller and found he was in good shape.

I was informed that the USCG Cutter Citrus was standing by and wanted assistance in locating the scene of the crash. I had several people who had taken a bearing while at the scene prior to the sinking of the aircraft stand by to relay the information once a phone patch had been established with the Citrus.

When Dr. Fortun arrived at the Health Center, he examined Mr. Habecker and pronounced him dead at approximately 5:15 p.m. From the time Mr. Habecker was brought to the Health Center, artificial respiration along with the use of an inhalator had been applied. Mr. Miller was transported to the Health Center at about 7:00 p.m. by the writer.

A complete verbal report was given to Sergeant Eugene B. Morris of this department by telephone at approximately 9:00 p.m. Commander Hancock and Lieutenant Butler were kept at the Health Center until the arrival of the USCG Cutter Storis. They were then transferred to the Storis at approximately 3:00 a.m.

I secured the station at 0600, 15 December 1954, and went to bed.

Signed, Bertram C. Kellogg #75
60th Anniversary

Bertram C. Kellogg was one of the Highway Patrolmen who also became a member of the Territorial Police force when it was formed in 1953. He died January 21, 1993, in Sacramento, California.

Kellogg came to Alaska with his parents in the early 1940s during the construction boom that preceded Pearl Harbor. The Kellogg family operated a service station on 4th Avenue in Anchorage where Bert helped out driving the wrecker. It may have been his experience hauling in wrecks from the Glenn Highway that got him interested in police work. He joined the Highway Patrol in 1949.

Bert died of heart failure and cancer. He is survived by his two sons and two daughters. Bert's body was returned to Alaska and interred at Angelus Memorial Park on Klatt Road on June 21, 1993.

Alaska State Police 1959 - 1967: A Time of Transition

D.S. "Skip" Braden

The State of Alaska was only a few years old. The transition from a Territory to a State was underway. Bush cops like Joe Rychetnik were still around. Federal Wardens and Marshals were either transitioning to the State or figuring where they were going to go next.

Alaska Department of Fish and Game (ADF&G) managed to end up with some airplanes and a boat or two after Statehood. Most of these were appropriated from the United States Fish and Wildlife Service (USFWS). Accordingly, ADF&G were called on to perform a variety of tasks, with convenience rather than protocol taking precedent.

It was not for some time that an integrated approach to law enforcement in Alaska was undertaken. Even at that, it was not without growing pains. In the interim, the personalities of the personnel of the two agencies did more to cement enduring relationships than most anything else. It was a time of transition.

Fairbanks AK, Winter 1962

It did and still does get cold! Temperatures will commonly run at 50 to 60 degrees below zero for several weeks. Welcome to Alaska. My wife and I landed in Fairbanks after leaving the U.S. Weather Bureau in Cold Bay. I headed back to school to finish my second degree (Civil Engineering).

Modern lube oils were not around yet so we took the car battery in the house at night, and used a heat lamp under the oil pan so we could start the engine. I finally ran out of money going back to school, and Bud Weberg of the ADF&G was looking for a pilot and a Protection Officer. I had a pilot's license and was hired for the

Fairbanks office. Nick Fields and Bill Burns had transferred from the Territorial group and were also in the office that Protection shared with the Game Division staff.

Uniforms did not exist, so we wore whatever would keep us warm. I remember a patrol flown in a DeHavilland Beaver the following spring that took us to Circle Hot Springs, where we stayed for a day or two and got to go swimming in the outdoor pool at -40 F. I was wearing a Navy leather flight jacket and was the envy of the group.

Bud Weberg and Fred Wolstad, along with Sid Morgan, talked to me about taking over the Yakutat District, which I agreed to do. I went first and my wife followed. The Federal Aviation Administration (FAA) was very generous and allowed us the use of a surplus warehouse to live in and work out of. I scrambled around, and with the help of the FAA's lead mechanic made up accommodations consisting of an oil-burning range that we scrounged, along with a picnic table and some surplus steel shelving. Our bed was a convertible sofa that the FAA had declared surplus, and we topped the household furnishings with a kitchen sink and an oil drum from the local dump.

The sink was set up on a 2 X 4 frame and drained directly under the building. The oil drum was split in half lengthwise, and the ends were welded back together to form a beautiful bathtub when painted white. A split rubber hose covered the raw edges for the finishing touch. Running water was arranged by acquisition of two water pails, which I dutifully carried across the road to the FAA shop daily, where I dumped the honey bucket and filled the water bucket. I do not remember if I color-coded them or not.

I was privileged to meet and work with a number of fascinating people while stationed in Yakutat. Pete Crosby, the Magistrate from Juneau, would stop by for a day or so at a time and bunk in with us. Crosby always had lots of interesting stories about the old days and was gracious enough to share them. State Trooper John Monagle, Jr. from Juneau, would stay with us while on patrol, and we would spend much time discussing local affairs. Sometimes visiting troops would borrow the State vehicle, or I would fly them around for an "orientation flight." For some reason this seemed to happen with increasing frequency during moose hunting season.

The old FWS weir cabin on the Situk River became a very popular place both during the seasonal salmon run as well as during moose season. The U.S. Coast Guard was most helpful with maintenance and supply items from Seattle (Annette Island). Having that cabin on my property list was a definite asset in running the district. It seemed like we all scratched each other's backs. I have to admit that I never was short on a place to stay when I went to Juneau.

Trooper Hal Hume would stop in for a tour through the village and a long series of talks about law enforcement in general. He borrowed my pickup one time to make a highway patrol through the village. As I recall, he pulled over the local owner of the gas station and was going to cite him for no tags when he noticed I had not gotten around to putting the new ones on the State vehicle.

All I remember of this was that he returned to my warehouse and inquired where the plates might be, and then he went and put them on the truck. I thought that was real nice of him to do that for me since we were making "Home Brew" at the time. I also recall that it cost me a few bottles. Naturally you could not drink that stuff without having some Situk River smoked silver salmon to accompany it. His wife did set a good table in Douglas however.

Doug Blanchard and I – Doug was the ADF&G agent at Petersburg and had been the U.S. Customs agent on the Stikine – developed some innovative enforcement concepts for commercial fisheries problems in Southeastern Alaska. One was to use Troopers to parachute behind the beach line at night and run a surveillance operation during the day until we had information to make an apprehension. I had several Troopers lined up, but Headquarters said 'no.' Apparently it would have been too efficient and made some political waves they did not want to deal with. We did use boats and stakeouts to accomplish a similar operation in Southeastern. It was very successful.

At that time, a good "round haul" was worth more than any bank robbery, and the fishing hauls occurred with greater frequency. We finally got Jack Asher, the First District D.A., to push legislation that would allow for the confiscation of gear and the vessel. That gave us some teeth. Both Bud Weberg and Fred Wolstad played a positive role in this.

There was also a U.S. Coast Guard Cutter stationed in Juneau, but that is another story. The Admiral of the District at the time of that caper later made Commandant, as did his Executive Officer. I had occasion to see them at several functions later, and invariably the story would come up. Fred Robards (USFW agent), Sid Morgan, and I ran an informant on that one.

The year of 1963 was memorable for several reasons. First, Bud Weberg decided that I, along with Joe Brantley and one other ADF&G enforcement type, would attend the State Police Academy. We were all pilots, and I was what was called a Conservation Officer. Basically, this meant I was supposed to work for the biological side of the house as well as the enforcement side, a concept that came "Out of Africa." I might add that it did not work that well in this country.

Basically, there was too much internal dissension over turf. The Academy per se did not yet exist but rather used the Army National Guard Armory in Anchorage for classrooms and put us up at the Barrett Inn in Spenard. Sgt Jim Goodfellow (Sergeant Badfellow to us cadets) lectured us on a number of subjects, in conjunction with Sgt Jerry Williams of Kodiak fame.

Not much before this, he and Mac McKinley had taken on the Japanese fishing fleet in Shelikof Strait and turned the U.S. State Department around in its thinking about where the Alaskan boundary was. I seem to recall that the Governor's Office was somewhat interested in the entertainment bill that Mack ran up while the fleet's Skipper and his Officers were awaiting trial. It seems that his ADF&G Field Purchase Order book was used liberally.

As I recall, the first exposure at the Academy was for a four-week period in residency, followed by a short break, and then two weeks of more intensive study. Trooper Ed Eckhoff was my roommate. The final exercise was a raid on an old building out at Anchorage International Airport where I got to shoot tear gas at/into a building full of Army Guard volunteers who were supposed to be the "Bad Guys." I don't know who got the worst of that deal. They had gas masks, and I had no padding for my shoulder.

The second memorable thing about 1964 was a boat trip. For some unexplained reason the Department decided I should make an offshore patrol up the coast from Juneau to Seward. We used an appropriated Fish and Wildlife Service patrol boat.

I cannot recall the name, but it was built for duty in the Aleutians and skippered by Howard Marks. The trip started out by going to pick up the motor vessel Shad, (skippered by Harry Curran) which had just come out of overhaul in Sitka. We were going to accompany her to her homeport in Cordova.

The weather was nice, and everything was going fine until we got abeam of Yakutat on Good Friday. There were flat and calm seas when we felt a shudder run through the 65-foot patrol boat. "Moe," the skipper, ran back from the wheelhouse and asked me to get on the radio and see if I could find out anything.

Well, I did find out a few things. First thing I heard on 2182kc was the Commander of the U.S. Pacific Fleet ordering all Navy vessels on the West Coast to put to sea immediately and secure for a tidal wave. Yes! The hackles on the back of my neck did stand up. Then we heard Kodiak had been hit hard, and that the Coast Guard Cutter Sedge, berthed in Cordova, had been left high and dry when she lost some 30 feet of water out from under her.

The skipper was asking Kodiak Fleet Central to advise him. The response was that he was the skipper, and the decision was his. We turned Harry Curran loose over the Cordova flats to check on his family.

The Department directed us to Seward to see if we could assist. What a mess. Coming around the entrance to Seward, we saw the commercial dock floating out into the Gulf of Alaska. Railroad locomotives were lying on their side, and martial law was being declared.

We made a trip into Ailik Bay looking for seal hunters and spent the night anchored up in a small cove looking at where the water inside the fjord had sloshed 200 feet up the hillside. We never did find any hunters. I do not know how anything could survive that.

I flew out of Seward on a military flight and went to Yakutat, where I picked up the State plane and flew on to Cordova and picked up an ADF&G enforcement agent, Gene Tautfest, and flew him over Valdez where he had lived at one time. Not a pretty sight. I went on to McGrath.

Leroy Bohuslov, was the ADF&G enforcement agent at McGrath. He was killed in a rather tragic accident while flying a mission at Farewell, Alaska, leaving his wife at the facilities in McGrath. She had no place to go, and the State was dragging its feet on deciding what, if any, compensation she should receive.

I was transferred to the McGrath District and had to move into the quarters there. It really bothered me the way things were going, so I arranged to make a long patrol that lasted for a week or so, which gave her time to get organized. It turned out later that she did get State compensation but only through the administrations of, I believe, Warren Taylor, a rather prominent Fairbanks attorney at the time. McGrath was/is a large District, and I had a fair amount of interaction with the Troopers at Bethel, such as Harky Tew and John Clare. I would bunk them at our place on their way through or fly patrols for them. Patrols included Nunivak Island as well as flying support for the musk ox transplant.

At that time, the ADF&G planes were about all the State had except for the National Guard. Accordingly, we got involved in a number of search and rescue missions all over the State.

I remember well one trip during the summer of 1965, when I got a radio message that some military personnel at Galena were missing and presumed drowned in the Yukon River. I flew to Galena and then flew all night looking for anything along the river. Unfortunately, there was nothing seen, and I returned to McGrath arriving just about sunrise. I will never forget how smooth the air was that summer night.

Another search and rescue trip from McGrath found the Leslie family from Nome. They had become lost on a flight to Anchorage and run out of fuel, finally putting the plane down on a ridgetop outside of Flat, Alaska. We had been searching for a couple of days when I stumbled over them and was able to land. I called back on the aircraft radio to have McGrath fly some cans of avgas down to us, which they did, and we flew them and their plane back to McGrath. They were both extremely happy to have been located and able to fly out. Typically, they will ask what they can do for you. The good feeling you get from having been able to help them is a big reward in itself.

Turmoil within the ranks was rearing its head with increasing discussions between the ADF&G biologists and the enforcement staff. Because of my background as a geologist, I was offered a job with the State Division of Lands in Anchorage at a pay increase, and I took the job. That move led to the Prudhoe Bay oil field and many other adventures.

On reflection, I had a wonderful time and would not trade the memories for anything. I was privileged to visit the Academy at Sitka this last summer and feel that it is a fitting tribute to those who came before and those who pass through it.

60th Anniversary

Skip Braden and his wife Audrey drove the Alcan and arrived

in Anchorage in June of 1961 when he started a new job with the State Highway Department as a field geologist. This led to a stint with the U.S. Weather Bureau in Cordova and Cold Bay. Afterward he and his wife ended up in Fairbanks, where he applied for a job with the ADFG as a pilot/Protection Officer. He was assigned to Yakutat as the District Officer.

While there he was selected to attend the State Police Training Academy which was being held in Spenard at a local motel and used the National Guard facility. From there he was assigned to head the McGrath District where he worked until leaving to take a job with the Department of Natural Resources. After working on the Prudhoe Bay oil sale, he was recruited by BP Alaska where he served as the Environmental Coordinator advising the corporate office on environmental matters dealing with Prudhoe Bay development and the TAPS line.

He later moved to Washington, DC, where he worked for the Director of the Minerals Management Service until his retirement in 1995. He and his wife live in Winchester, VA, where they periodically travel to Africa and Europe, as well as around the lower 48 states. Their children reside in Boston, Mass and Richmond, Va.

Alaska State Troopers 1967 - Current: Kenai Post: The Oil Boom Years

Trooper Barry Pegram, Retired

In the late fifties, oil was discovered on the Kenai Peninsula, and activity of all sorts was booming. The oil fields and refineries brought in people from all over the world who were seeking high paying opportunities. There were numerous legitimate job seekers, but as with any boom, it also brought in its hustlers, drug pushers, con men, people wanted by other jurisdictions and some just plain bad men.

At that time policing for the area was the sole responsibility of the Alaska State Troopers. There were no city police departments, so we were it. The Trooper Detachment at the time of this story consisted of four Troopers directed by Sergeant Ray Rush. The assigned Troopers were Don Lawrence, John Guzialek, and myself, Barry Pegram.

Partially because of the physical activity this area required, the assigned officers were larger than the average Trooper. That is, all except for Trooper Guzialek. Both Sergeant Rush and Lawrence were over six feet tall and north of two hundred pounds. I was six-feet-four inches and weighed approximately two hundred and sixty pounds. Trooper Guzialek, on the other hand, was the model for the impressive new uniforms we received when we evolved from the State Police to the State Troopers and is the same uniform worn to this day. Guz really looked sharp in this new uniform as he was the ideal size for a model. Guz was five-feet ten-inches tall, weighed about one hundred and sixty pounds and could make a K-Mart suit look like an Armani.

The booming times brought booming problems. Our little two-cell holding facility was usually filled with those arrested for assorted drunk, disorderly, and assault crimes. In this atmosphere, simply telling an individual he was "under arrest" was quite often insufficient. Certain miscreants didn't believe they had been arrested until it had been "demonstrated."

Dalton Mosby* was one of these characters. Mosby was an itinerant oil-field worker, hardened by many years of rugged work. Mosby stood six-feet five-inches tall and weighed two hundred and fifty pounds.

During one of his drunken adventures, Mosby had the misfortune of meeting Trooper Don Lawrence in an official capacity. Throughout his life, patience was not known as one of Lawrence's virtues. Neither did he suffer fools who dared to resist his efforts in affecting an arrest. As Lawrence was making the arrest, Mosby made a gross tactical error by swinging at Lawrence. Lawrence completed the arrest by promptly striking Mosby a sharp blow with his nightstick, propelling the subject into a solemn state of coolness.

Two months later, about 3:00 AM on a Sunday morning, I was in our little two-cell station doing the paperwork on a disorderly drunk I had just arrested when I heard a noise coming from the parking lot. I ran outside and observed our friend Mosby and a female. Mosby had his hands in a strangling position around her neck and was dragging the woman from her car to his truck. I intervened with words and mace but no results. Mosby attempted to assault me as he had Trooper Lawrence.

With no backup possible, my adrenalin must have been flowing at peak levels as I swung with all two hundred and sixty pounds, catching him flush in the face. Mosby immediately lapsed into another solemn state of coolness where he remained for several minutes. Meanwhile, I placed him in a cell and commenced the paperwork. Becoming concerned because of the silence emanating from the cell, I investigated just as Mosby was regaining consciousness and standing up. Upon seeing me, Mosby said, "Good God man, what did you hit me with?"

I apologized for having to hit him, but explained his actions left me no alternative. Mosby looked at me with one eye swollen shut, dried blood on his face and said, "That's alright, I had it coming. You whupped me fair and square. You're okay by me."

That was Mosby's criteria for a lawful arrest; being "whupped fair and square."

After arraignment the next day, Mosby was returned to our station to be processed out. Trooper Guzialek was there to complete the process. After Mosby's encounter with Trooper Lawrence and myself, he calculated that all Troopers on the Peninsula must be our size.

Mosby leered at all one hundred and sixty pounds of Guzialek and said, "How did you end up down here with them bears. Next time I get arrested I want you to arrest me. I think I can whup you." Although this proposed event never took place, I've no doubts as to who would have prevailed. Smaller in size, Guz made up for size with heart. This made him a giant.

With Sergeant Ray Rush as our Detachment Commander, we made a formidable team. I learned a lot about leadership and life from Ray Rush those many years ago. Those experiences contributed immensely to whatever degree of success I may have attained in later years.

As I look back on my life, those were rough times but they were also the best of times. I thank Ray Rush for his guidance, training, patience, and for being a friend in my life at a time one was so needed.

Sadly, my friends Don Lawrence and John Guzialek have passed on.

I miss them.

*(*Name changed to protect the guilty)*

60th Anniversary

Barry Pegram began his career in law enforcement in 1961 in the U.S. Air Force serving four years in the Air Police and Combat Defense Force in SAC. He joined the Alaska State Troopers in 1967 serving in Anchorage, Kenai and Palmer. He was promoted to Corporal in 1968 and served as Detachment Commander of the Matanuska Detachment. In April of 1972 he accepted a position as Chief of Police in Kenai. Several years later he left to operate Burger King franchises in Alabama where he is now retired.

One Lucky Break... Is All It Takes...

Trooper Chuck Lamica, Retired

Reprinted from Public Safety News 1992

While Anthony Garcia drove the knife repeatedly into his struggling victim, his girlfriend, Cindy Galvin, held a shotgun and watched. After his victim died in a pool of blood, Garcia calmly took a beer from the man's refrigerator and drank it before stealing the video cassette recorder. For 28 year-old Anthony Garcia, this was no big deal.

In the preceding two weeks, Garcia had been released from prison in Colorado, bludgeoned to death a former cellmate, and moved to Alaska. Garcia's murder of Juneau resident Jerry Arima was so random the investigators in the case still don't know if the motive was robbery or just sheer bloodlust.

Jerry Arima was a 35 year-old accountant for the U.S. Forest Service. His co-workers described him as quiet, shy and well-liked. Arima lived alone in a three-bedroom suburban home in Juneau's Mendenhall Valley. Jerry was the type of man who never missed a day of work and always showed up early.

That's why his co-workers became worried when he failed to come to work on the morning of July 17, 1989. They sent a friend to Jerry's house to check on him. At approximately 9:00 a.m. that morning, the friend found Jerry Arima's body lying in the living room floor near the front door.

Teamwork

Although the murder occurred within the city limits of Juneau, Juneau's Police Department and Alaska's Department of Public Safety worked it together. Two of the first officers on the scene were

Juneau Police Investigator Walt Boman and Trooper Investigator Roy Holland.

They found Jerry Arima had evidently answered a knock on his door and then was viciously murdered with a knife. Arima had 22 stab wounds, mostly on his chest, neck and lower face. Clues at the scene indicated a violent struggle between Arima and his murderer. Stereo speakers were tipped over, blood spatters were on the floor and walls, and Arima's bathrobe was torn to shreds.

Evidence

Juneau Police Investigator Steve Kalwara, one of the first investigators at the scene, noticed the murderer had stolen Arima's video cassette recorder. Then Investigator Boman found the remains of a Kool cigarette burned into the rug. Jerry Arima did not smoke. A bloody handprint was found on the living room wall near the front door.

Because of the seriousness of the crime and the large quantity of obvious evidence at the scene, the Juneau Police Department requested members of the Statewide Scientific Crime Detection Laboratory assist in processing the scene. Criminalist Jim Wolfe and Latent Print Examiner Dan Fullerton subsequently spent several days assisting with the scene investigation.

As a result, two important pieces of evidence were obtained. One was the bloody handprint found on the living room wall. In order to preserve this print, a large section of the wall was completely removed and sent to the Crime Lab for analysis. Dan Fullerton was able to determine there were identifiable palm ridges within the print, but they could not be matched to any possible suspects.

The other important evidence found at the scene was completely invisible to the naked eye— footprints left by the suspect. During the struggle, Jerry Arima lost a great deal of blood. The suspect had stepped in some of this blood and had later walked around the house. Unfortunately, the blood on his shoes was not thick enough to leave visible prints.

Revealing

Jim Wolfe used a chemical reagent known as Luminol to develop any microscopic blood patterns that might have been present. Luminol is a chemical which is sprayed upon a surface and reacts with any blood that might be present. When the sprayed surface is removed from any source of light, the Luminol which has contacted blood can easily be seen because it glows in the dark. Without the Luminol process, these footprints would never have been found.

When Jim Wolfe darkened Arima's house and sprayed it with Luminol, he found the suspect had left a trail of bloody footprints. The shoe prints that were subsequently photographed showed an unusual V-shaped notch in the heel. During this time investigators found a packing box which they felt belonged to the stolen VCR. This box not only told the investigators the missing VCR was a Panasonic, it also provided them with a serial number. This information was entered into the Alaska Public Safety Information System computer. The entire scene investigation took about a week.

On July 20th, the Juneau Police Department invited any interested law enforcement officers to attend a briefing concerning the murder. Trooper F/Sergeant Robin Lown was one of the persons who attended the briefing. Although it was unknown at the time, Lown's attendance at this briefing would later solve the murder.

Less than 24 hours after the briefing, at about 4:45 a.m. on July 21, F/Sgt Lown was contacted at home by a dispatcher who advised him that Trooper Don Otis and Trooper Cindy Pollitt were responding to what was reported as an assault with a knife. F/Sergeant Lown decided to respond to the incident.

F/Sergeant Lown found a drinking party involving minors had been in progress. One of the young women at the scene told Lown a man named Tony had tried to choke her earlier that night. (The reported knife assault proved to be unfounded). While attempting to locate persons involved, Lown started to walk toward the front door of the house where the party had taken place.

At this point, a young man, who later was found to be Anthony Garcia's cousin and who owned the house, began yelling at Lown. This man told F/Sergeant Lown if he was going inside the house he had better "be prepared to kill."

The man made a number of comments which indicated to Lown a threatening or dangerous situation might be present in the house. Lown thought the man was yelling so loud that he might be intentionally trying to warn someone in the house. Lown decided to have Trooper Otis go with him to the house so they could cover each other.

Lown found the front door of the house to be ajar. After entering the house, he found a female inside who told him no one else was there, and he could look around the house if he wanted. While searching the house for other people, F/Sergeant Lown saw a Panasonic VCR lying on top of a dresser. A pack of Kool cigarettes was next to the VCR. Without moving the VCR, Lown was able to read the serial number.

Hit

Since he remembered a VCR had been stolen from the home of Jerry Arima, F/Sgt Lown checked the VCR through the APSIN computer. The VCR was found to be the one taken from the murder scene. That was the turning point. Juneau Police Officer Steve Kalwara said, "We had absolutely no idea who killed Jerry Arima. If Robin Lown had not found that VCR, this case might still be unsolved."

During the course of this investigation, several people were arrested. One of these was Anthony Garcia. He was charged with Assault in the Fourth Degree and Contributing to the Delinquency of a Minor. This arrest opened up the opportunity that made it possible to solve the murder.

Lucky Break

As a result of this lucky break, a search warrant was obtained for the house in which Garcia had been living with his cousin. Troopers, Juneau Police investigators, and members of the Crime Lab all participated in the subsequent search.

During this time, a young woman, later identified as 33 year-old Cindy Galvin, showed up at the house. Galvin was using a false name and pretended to know nothing about the happenings of the previous night. Later interviews with Galvin revealed she was Anthony Garcia's girlfriend, and she had travelled with him from Colorado to Alaska where they had taken up residence with Garcia's cousin.

During the course of this residence search, Police Investigator Boman found several used gauze bandages and dressings. The peculiar blood markings on the bandages led Boman to believe that someone had received a severe human bite.

Desperate Bite

Anthony Garcia, who was still in jail on the misdemeanor charges, had such a wound on his left bicep. Subsequent examination of Garcia's clothing revealed he had been bitten by someone who was very desperate. Garcia had been wearing a heavy denim jacket, a long sleeved shirt, and long sleeved underwear, all of which had been bitten through with enough force to remove flesh from his bicep.

After obtaining another search warrant, Investigator Boman made a plaster cast of the bite marks on Garcia's arm. Jerry Arima's body had already been flown to his family in Idaho and was about to be buried when a forensic dentist was allowed to obtain casts of his teeth. Soon, the evidence began to fall into place.

Garcia's palm prints were found to match the bloody hand print found in Arima's house. His shoes were found to have a large V-shaped notch cut in the heel. It was learned Garcia had been released from a Colorado prison less than two weeks before Arima's murder. At the time of his release, he was allowed to keep his prison issued shoes. Shoes issued to prisoners in Colorado are routinely cut with a large V-shaped notch to make it easier to track escapees.

Plaster casts of Garcia's bite wound and Arima's teeth were sent to a forensic dentist in Seattle. Dr. Gary Bell reported, because of the amount of clothing which had been bitten through, he could not be completely sure Arima's teeth had caused the bite on Garcia's arm. He could, however, say Arima's dentition was consistent with Garcia's bite wound.

Although Garcia decided to remain silent, his girlfriend, Cindy Galvin, did talk with investigators. From her they learned they had murdered a man in Colorado a few days after Garcia's release from prison. This man was a former cellmate of Garcia's. Galvin had reportedly lured him into a room where Garcia then bludgeoned him to death with a hammer.

Anthony Garcia was later convicted in Alaska of First Degree Murder. He subsequently was transferred to Colorado where he pled out to Second Degree Murder in order to avoid a death penalty.

Cindy Galvin was convicted of Second Degree Murder for her participation in the killing of Jerry Arima. She is currently pending trial in Colorado for kidnapping and assaulting another woman before coming to Alaska. She has not yet been charged with aiding in the murder of Garcia's former cellmate.

Timing

As it turned out, the timing in the case was critical. At the time of their arrests, Garcia and Galvin were preparing to leave Alaska. They would have been out of the state in just a couple more days.

60th Anniversary

Lieutenant Charles Lamica joined the Department of Public Safety in 1981. Following the Academy, he was assigned to Fairbanks patrol, the General Investigation Unit, Judicial Service, and Burglary Suppression. He was a member of the Special Emergency Reaction Team, an advisor for the Student Troopers, and participated in search and rescue missions. He also completed several tours at Prudhoe Bay and Coldfoot posts.

In 1988, he transferred to Yakutat where he worked patrol and search and rescue cases. In 1991, he transferred to Juneau, where he served as the Detachment Search and Rescue Coordinator, Village Public Safety Officer oversight Trooper, and adult leader for the Juneau Civil Air Patrol Cadet Program.

Lamica was promoted to Corporal in 1996 and transferred to the Public Safety Academy where he taught first aid, emergency driving, search and rescue, wilderness survival, traffic stops, and verbal communications.

In 2001, he was promoted to lieutenant and took over the job of EOC Supervisor and Statewide Search and Rescue coordinator in Anchorage.

After Shave

Trooper Lew Rieth

One of my favorite stories happened during the first few days that I was a Trooper. I was stationed in Juneau, and the Trooper office in those days was on the fifth floor of the Capitol Building downtown. It had a high-ceiling setting right out of the 1940 police movies.

At the time (1969) there was a commercial on TV advertising a man's aftershave called "High Karate." In the commercials, a man wearing the aftershave just walked into a room and strange things happened. Damsels in distress were rescued, train wrecks prevented, etc.

Beside the door in the squad room was a sink, above it a board that held all the keys. The Detachment Commander, Capt. Richard Burton, who in later years became Commissioner, walked into the office one day and as the door closed behind him, it slammed. The board holding the keys split in two, dropping the bottom half and a bunch of keys into the sink, making a loud racket.

The Captain turned, looked at the mess, and calmly remarked, "I'm wearing my High Karate," and continued on to his office.

60th Anniversary

Lew Rieth passed away January 6, 2006 in Aurora, Colorado after a short battle with cancer. He was born January 7, 1945 in Schenectady, New York. He joined the U.S. Air Force in 1964, and after his discharge, he joined the Anchorage Fire Department. He began his career with the Alaska State Troopers in 1969, serving in Juneau, Ketchikan, Craig, Soldotna, Moose Pass and Dillingham.

In 1986, Lew and his wife Rene, retired and spent the next 20 years traveling the United States in their RV. During the last four years, they lived in Lander, Wyoming, where they made many friends. Lew is survived by his wife of 40 years, Rene, daughters Christine, Cathy and Sherry, and their extended families.

The Naked Cabbie

Trooper, Lew Rieth

I was stationed at Moose Pass from July 1974 thru September 1981. The section of the Seward Highway from the Seward Wye to Seward was a generally quiet section of road compared to north of the Wye to Portage and west to the Lower Skilak Cutoff, the boundaries of my area. The only time the Moose Pass section was busy was during the annual Seward Silver Salmon Derby in August.

One of my early Salmon Derbies, I was on duty late and was returning to Moose Pass about 1:30 A.M. I was more than ready to call it a day. A mile or so south of town I came up behind a northbound, older, large sedan that was merrily weaving about the highway. My first thought was a drunk. This would mean arresting the driver, impounding the car, and going back to Seward where the Breathalyzer and jail were.

I turned on my red lights and the vehicle immediately straightened up its path, pulled to the right and stopped. I was, at this point, hopeful that all I had was a sleepy driver.

I walked up to the car, shined my flashlight onto the driver, and found a 400+ pound man in his 50s, naked. He was looking at me with what I can only recall as a silly grin. I asked him what he thought he was doing. His reply, "It's just one of my little quirks."

I asked for his license and registration. He started to reach over to the passenger side floor for his wallet. (His size made this no easy task). I told him to proceed slowly so I could see his hands at all times. He finally reached his pants and got out his wallet. He produced a driver's license.

He offered to look for his registration, but I told him not to bother. I told him to get dressed and then step out of his car. Just how he managed that, I am not sure. I went back to the patrol car and radioed Seward PD. (In those days we didn't have communication with anyone other than Seward PD or my house). They ran a "wants" check for me, and no one wanted the naked man. The car was his and - it turned out - his mother's.

Through some feat of magic, he managed to get dressed and step out of his car. I started on a field investigation card. When I asked him where he lived, he replied "with my mommy." He said he worked as a cab driver in Anchorage. I got all his information and gave him a rather stern lecture about him keeping his "quirks" off "my" highway. I was somewhat sterner than I would normally be. I felt that he wouldn't call the Colonel on Monday morning and say "I was driving thru Moose Pass naked and the Trooper yelled at me." He didn't.

I followed him north of town a ways and then went home to bed. A couple weeks later I was at Trooper Mike Radish's house in Cooper Landing for an important conference (coffee) and ran across two Criminal Investigation Bureau investigators that were in the area on equally important business (fishing). I don't recall just who they were. Anyway, shoptalk came around to a problem they were having in the Anchorage area with a taxi driver that was exposing himself to very young children. The kids were too young to give much of a description other than "he's fat."

I told the investigators that I knew who this probably was. I got my notebook and gave them the information, along with his "mommy's" address. Word that got back to me was that he was the offender and was prosecuted.

60th Anniversary

Shoot-Don't Shoot

First Sergeant Drew Rotermund, Retired

I was a member of Recruit Class 17 during the summer of 1970 at the old Academy building on the Sheldon Jackson College campus in Sitka. Lieutenant Penman, Sergeant Monagle, Sergeant MacConnaughey, and Corporal Korhonen were the staff at that time.

I was first exposed to something called "Shoot-Don't Shoot" during that summer of training. One by one, each recruit was taken from a class in progress into an adjoining room. We were handed a belt with holster and a training revolver and were told to face a movie screen.

The instructor worked a movie projector and showed three or four 30-second scenarios on the screen. We were to react as we deemed most appropriate, including drawing (or not drawing) the firearm, aiming and shooting (or not shooting). There was no ammunition, just the sound of the gun hammer falling on an empty chamber. After each scenario, our performance was critiqued for us. The entire exercise lasted no more than 10 to 15 minutes.

In 1976, after two-year tours each at Soldotna, Anchorage and Barrow, I returned to the new Academy in Sitka as a freshly promoted Corporal to join the staff as an instructor. Captain Gilmour was the Commander, Lieutenant Korhonen the Deputy Commander, and First Sergeant DeTemple the academic ramrod. I was given my instructional assignments and set about to make up my lesson plans and other classroom preparations.

At that time, the film library was in a room between the two classrooms. I was looking for a particular Emergency Medical Technician film when I came across the Motorola film "Shoot-Don't Shoot" (S-DS).

After-hours that day, I reviewed the S-DS film, recognized a couple of the scenarios from 1970, and began envisioning a training program expanding upon those 1970 experiences. I drew up a written proposal, submitted it and was soon given the 'go ahead' to develop my idea.

Thus began the S-DS program I taught to every Department of Public Safety recruit and Municipal Police Officer who came through the Academy for the next four years.

If you contact any of those trainees today who went through the Academy from late 1976 to 1980, and ask them if they remember S-DS and Sergeant Rotermund, you'll probably see their eyes open wider, their brow furrow, and get a response like, "Are you kidding? How could you possibly forget something like that!"

I taught the first S-DS in the studio on the ground floor of the Academy. Trainees would be taken out of class, one at a time, and I would issue them a belt with holster and firearm, identical to the ones they would be issued upon graduation. For ammunition, I used plastic casings with primer caps, and a hard plastic bullet. I had to display the film on a white bed sheet because the plastic bullets fired with sufficient force to pierce a standard movie screen. I had cut and spliced the more than 16 scenarios on the Motorola film down to about 10 scenarios and had a scoring sheet for each scenario.

The trainee's performance was critiqued for him/her after each scenario. They were scored by their actions or inactions, verbal commands or lack thereof, physical movements, weapons use/non-use, timeliness of any action, accuracy of any shot, and answers to any of my questions about why they did what they did, etc. The entire session took about 30 minutes per trainee.

That first class gave the S-DS sessions high praise and command staff seemed to approve, but there were major problems that made it doubtful it could be repeated in its present form. The biggest problem was caused by that 30-minute loss of other instructional time while the trainee was with me.

The command staff pretty much decided that while S-DS was worthwhile, it was simply too disruptive to the overall instructional curriculum. I could see it was going to die an infant unless I could figure out some other way of doing it. I'd put a lot of work into this prototype and believed in its worth. I just couldn't bear to see it cast aside before it had a chance to mature.

My solution was to volunteer to do S-DS on my own time, in the evenings after the day's scheduled training was over. Given approval, I set about to modify the program and eliminate some of the early problems.

I selected some new movie scenarios and got rid of some that had proven too controversial or confusing, thus negating their training value. I eliminated the plastic bullet, as it was too dangerous; it sometimes ricocheted around the room and it caused occasional arguments about its "strike" location on the screen, again negating the training value. I revised all score sheets to address previously unforeseen problems in scoring. I modified and expanded my critiques after each scenario.

The original 30-minute session with each trainee grew to 45 minutes and then to 60 minutes, as I expanded my critiques and other instructors asked me to incorporate material from their classes into S-DS. Eventually, my S-DS sessions with each trainee extended to 90 minutes, one-on-one, me and the trainee, all after hours in the evenings on my own time and on their own time.

I continued to teach and develop S-DS during my four years at the Academy. After that first year, it became mandatory training for all DPS and Municipal Police trainees, and it was always given high critiques at the end of each Academy by everyone who went through it. The sessions stressed the effectiveness of everyone's underarm anti-perspirants. They caused some trainees to leave the room after 90 minutes on very wobbly knees and pressured many bladders to need periodic release during that "time in Hell."

I taught S-DS to countless hundreds and hundreds and hundreds of police trainees. It continued to be taught by other instructors after I left the Academy staff. It also went to the field as refresher training where it was taught by the field First Sergeants to their personnel.

Today, S-DS is history. Technology killed it. Today's F.A.T.S. system (Firearms Training System) can do so much more and do it better than I and all the other First Sergeants could possibly do with our plastic bullets, spliced film segments, and paper score sheets.

I believe S-DS served a very worthwhile purpose and service during its short lifespan. We can never quantify that which does not occur, but I honestly believe some firearms incident, somewhere, sometime, was successfully resolved and possibly lives were saved by the training S-DS provided to all those Troopers and Municipal

Police Officers who received it. That was my goal when I developed the program, and I've always believed I accomplished that goal.

60th Anniversary

Drew Rotermund began his career by reporting to the old Academy building on the Sheldon Jackson College campus in Sitka in the summer of 1970. His first duty assignment was in Soldotna working for Corporal George Pollit. In 1972, he was transferred to Criminal Information Bureau in Anchorage. In 1974, he was assigned to the Barrow Post. He rose through the ranks to First Sergeant, and in 1980, he was moved to Fairbanks. He remained there for 11 years, running at times the Patrol, Outposts, and Operations Units. In 1991, he moved to Palmer, and in 1993, to AST Headquarters in Anchorage. He retired in April of 1994 at the rank of First Sergeant.

Drew now lives in Bayside, California, a small coastal community in the redwood country of northern California. He has a small ranch at the 3600 foot elevation in the coastal mountains about a two-hour drive inland, which keeps him busy.

The Day Cy Cederborg Almost Started WW III

First Sergeant Drew Rotermund, Retired

The Banner articles about Cy Cederborg reminded me of the time he came to Barrow when I was the Trooper stationed there in 1974-76.

Barrow was a pretty remote location in those days and any materials shipped there were kept there. Why ship them back when you might need them some day?

Among the items sent to Barrow were explosives used by scientists at the Naval Arctic Research Laboratory in their offshore ice studies, including dynamite, naval depth charges, and more. NARL and the big DEW Line Station in Barrow code-named POW-MAIN shared a common airport runway and could bring things like explosives in on government planes. Often they would just ship them up on the annual seagoing barge supply runs. Anything left over was simply stored in underground bunkers.

In early summer of 1975, we had a particularly strong storm with high winds and seas, and open water offshore. A week or two after the storm, I began to hear rumors about local people having old dynamite and other explosives. We also found some unusual items when making domestic disturbance arrests and drunk-in-public arrests.

Those possessing the questionable fireworks admitted that an old concrete bunker had been uncovered by the storm on the peninsula north of POW-Main. The age of the bunker was unknown, but it had obviously been forgotten by those running the two government facilities.

I took a walk out on the loose sand of the peninsula and, a half-mile north of the DEW-Line station, came across a half-buried bunker with evidence of foot traffic and a partially open door. Inside were pools of what looked like Jell-O, with more

Jell-O dripping from and running out of stacks of boxes. The boxes were labeled dynamite and the Jell-O was obviously nitroglycerin. I was young and stupid in those days, but I was smart enough to know this was way beyond my capabilities. I went back to town and called the information in to Fairbanks, then made arrangements with Barrow PD for security on the bunker.

The next day I got word from the Department of Public Safety that an explosives expert named Cy Cederborg would be coming. I'd never heard the name but said I would gladly meet him at the airport as soon as he could get there.

A day later, Cy stepped off the Wien flight accompanied by a couple of Army guys. We got their luggage, and I took them to my house and filled them in. They decided to get on the matter right away.

Cy and the two Army guys opened their luggage and pulled out boxes of blasting caps, rolls of detonating cord and some specialty tools. (Airport security in those days used the honor system on what you could bring in your luggage).

We headed for the bunker, and the three explosives experts were very impressed with the bunker's contents. They decided it was too much to destroy in place, so they found a natural depression in the sand and decided we would have to carry the boxes by hand. We decided to deal with the dynamite and let other military people deal with their ordnance in the bunker.

If I had known then what I do now, I would have been a half -mile away from that stuff, but being young and stupid, I helped as best I could. I kept asking Cy if that was enough and he insisted we could put more on top of the growing pile. Finally, he decided the pile was high enough, and they switched to installing blasting caps and det-cord.

I had no experience with explosives whatever. Not expecting anything really major, I had not advised NARL or the DEW-Line station that we would be exploding dynamite. Barrow PD knew what we were doing because they had been helping with security, but even they weren't expecting anything sensational.

And, naturally, it was an overcast and cloudy day. When that pile went off, I began to understand what an atomic explosion might be like. My God!!!!

It took about an hour for us to gather our gear and walk back to the vehicles. When I got there, all hell had broken loose. Among the angry people were the directors of NARL and POW-Main. Apparently, when the blast went off, the shock wave had bounced off the low cloud cover and come back to earth, completely knocking POW-Main and all its sensitive equipment and radars offline.

In those pre-satellite Cold War days, the DEW-Line was a critical component of American security and the possibility of Russia launching an attack on the United States from across the North Pole was a worrisome scenario.

POW-Main had gone into DEF-CON status and word had flashed across the entire DEW-Line system and all the way south to Colorado Mountain that a possible attack was in progress. POW-Main had quickly figured out what happened, that it was just me, Cy, and two Army guys, so they stopped all alerts and responses.

For about 10 minutes, Cy and I were the most unpopular people in the area. It took me many months to repair my damaged image with NARL and POW-Main — and I don't think I ever completely succeeded. The incident dogged me until I left Barrow in 1976. When Cy left Barrow the next day, he left me with a couple of boxes of blasting caps and unused rolls of detonating cord. After all, you never know when you'll need that stuff.

That's my memory of Cy. Rest In Peace, ol' timer!

September 2010

SHORT CASES

Your Editor recently visited Skagway and had coffee with longtime retired Trooper John Broderson. John, age 85, along with wife Barb, formerly Barb Dubell, have lived in Skagway for many years. John started service with the Alaska Territorial Police in 1959 and later transferred to Fish and Game Protection with the Dept. of Fish and Game. He was stationed in Fairbanks, Bristol Bay, and Sitka and retired in 1979. After retirement he lived in Wrangell, has attended a number of reunions at Chehalis, and is a lifetime member of FOAST.

John reminisced about his first month on the job in 1959. Shortly after going on duty, Sergeant Walt Sinn, his supervisor, received a call that a mentally ill person was causing trouble at Fox, a small community north of Fairbanks. Walt and John proceeded to Fox and picked up the mental case. In those days that was a problem. The Federal Jail would not accept a mental case unless he was charged with a crime and the local hospital wasn't equipped to handle these types of cases. This was prior to the sophisticated medicine of today.

Walt noticed the individual had a cross around his neck. The light bulb went on and they decided to deliver their charge to the Catholic priest. On their arrival at the rectory, the sister called for the priest. As the priest arrived he looked through the window, saw who the person was, and very succinctly said to Walt Sinn: "You SOB."

September 2011

....

During Bob Olsen's term as United States Marshal for the District of Alaska, when at the same time he was State President of the Alaska Peace Officers Association, he was occasionally interviewed by the media on various law enforcement issues pending in the criminal justice system. One evening Bob arrived home, and his ten-year-old daughter, Dana, asked if she could go outdoors and play with her little girlfriend until dinner. Bob indicated, "Yes honey, but the six o'clock news will soon be on and I will be on television. Wouldn't you like to wait and see me on TV?"

Assuming she would reply in the affirmative, Bob was quickly brought back to earth when she replied, "I see you all the time, Daddy," and out the door she went.

February 1998

Remembering back in the day...

Lieutenant Howard Luther, Retired

I remember working with Ray Rush and Dean Bivins. The three of us earned nicknames given to us by the local Magistrate. Ray's came from an accumulation of accidents in his first year or so; the Magistrate called him: "Go Slow." Dean Bivins was barely old enough to come into the department and he looked it; his nickname was "Ivory Snow." Since I was a flier, I was nicknamed "Trooper Altitude."

One day Ray and I were driving to an important call. Suddenly there was a big bull moose in the middle of the highway. Luckily Ray swerved and put on his brakes, barely missing it. He backed up a bit and hit the horn. The moose did not move. He hit the horn again and the moose's hackles went up. "What are you going to do now, Ray?" I asked. "I'm gonna honk one more time and if he doesn't move I'm gonna drop him." Guess the big old moose heard 'Go Slow's' threat because he finally moved out of the way. So Ray avoided being renamed 'Drop Em Rush.'

I remember Hal Sydnam was working a homicide case one time. A woman had been killed at the Copper Kettle and her pick-up truck came up missing. Ray found it stuck in the middle of the Mat Su River. I was called in to help with the investigation so Ray, Syd and I all went to the river to try to get the truck unstuck. Syd was in a really nice suit and Ray was wearing a freshly pressed uniform. Syd and Ray looked at me. I was in Levi's and tennis shoes so they tied a rope to me, and I walked out in the waist deep water to connect the winch cable to the truck. They said they wanted me to wear the rope so they could locate my body... without getting wet.

September 2011

Arresting a Fugitive in Canada - Big Mistake

Agent Dick St. John, Retired

I identified a fugitive as being employed by a company doing repair work on the Haines Highway. Sergeant Bob Hollofield, AST, kindly offered me a ride up the highway to effect the arrest. We got all the way to the border without seeing the construction crew. I could, however, see about 100 yards past the Canadian customs building. Bob wisely said we couldn't cross the border. I, the big braggadocio FBI agent, thought I recalled from FBI training that I could go 25 miles into Canada or Mexico after a fugitive. Boy was I wrong!

So I went the rest of the way on foot. After identifying myself at Canadian customs, they permitted me to continue to the construction site. After some persuasion to get the fugitive to descend from a crane, I arrested him and marched him back across the border.

There were a few eyebrows raised at the time but nothing to compare to when I reported his arrest to my headquarters. I was ordered to Anchorage on the next plane and spent the next three days reviewing every conceivable rule, regulation, operational procedure, etc. Knowing Mr. Hoover would be very upset, I carefully composed my letter of explanation. Luckily I found a loophole which headed off disciplinary action. The next revision of rules and regulations plugged the loophole. I had learned my lesson.

December 2008

"Hooker"

Trooper John Broderson, Retired

The year was 1967 or 68. I was a trooper stationed in Fairbanks and in court arraigning a hooker for soliciting for prostitution. The only people in the courtroom were Judge Mary Alice Miller, the court clerk, the defendant, and me.

Mary Alice advised the defendant of the charge and set bail at $300. The girl did not have the $300. Mary Alice didn't want to be too hard on the girl so she released her on O/R (own recognizance) and gave her until 2 p.m. to get the money. After the defendant left the courtroom, Mary Alice said, "I shudder to think what she's going to do to raise the money." I said, "If she's any kind of a hooker it won't take her until 2 o'clock."

At this time, the clerk said, "Oh, oh. I forgot to shut off the tape recorder." I'm glad that this never went for appeal. Her lawyer would have the time of his life with that one.

December 2008

Fred Wanted to Charge for Taking Charge

Colonel Tom Anderson, Retired

A recent obituary listing for Fred Stickman brought back to mind an incident involving Fred Stickman, Sr., a well-known resident of the Central Yukon River area during the early 6Os. Fred Stickman, Sr. was a Native of Nulato, spending most of his time in the local Yukon River villages and Fairbanks. His claim to fame was that he was a very vocal letter writer to the Fairbanks Daily News Miner, expounding on a multitude of subjects.

Fred also had a habit of writing NSF checks and on a Yukon River patrol in the summer of 1962, I served a warrant on Fred at Nulato for passing bad checks in Fairbanks. With Fred in tow, I proceeded by mail plane to Koyukuk and picked up two more locals on "failed to appear" charges. With three prisoners in custody, I continued on the mail run to Galena, standing by for the Wien Alaska C47 scheduled for Fairbanks.

Shortly after arriving at the Galena Airport, I received a frantic call from the village of Galena that a subject was holding a local resident at knifepoint and they needed a trooper immediately. I checked with the local Air Force station for Security Police assistance to guard my prisoners, but no one was available. At that moment it came to me that Fred Stickman was the logical person to take charge.

Fred had an imposing physical presence and was several years older than the other two prisoners, so I said to Fred, "We've got a problem, Fred. I need you to take charge of these two prisoners." Fred immediately responded, puffing out his chest and herding the prisoners over into a corner, and I proceeded to the village to apprehend the subject with the knife. This subject turned out to be a violent mental case, and I took him into custody and returned to the Airport at the same time the Wien Airlines plane arrived from Fairbanks.

My hands were full with the mental case. I advised Fred to handle the other two prisoners and we arrived at Fairbanks International Airport and were met by several Troopers who took the four prisoners to the Fairbanks federal jail.

That evening I received a call from Fred from the federal jail requesting reimbursement for prisoner escort. I contacted my supervisor, Sergeant John Bradshaw, who in his own indomitable way, said no we would not reimburse Fred. I conveyed the news back to Fred, who was extremely upset.

A week later, the Fairbanks Daily News-Miner published a letter from Fred Stickman, Sr. The letter described how he transported two dangerous prisoners from Galena to Fairbanks and the State of Alaska refused to pay him for prisoner escort duty. He went on to relay how this was a miscarriage of justice and unfair, but never once mentioned that he also was a prisoner.

April 1998

An Eye-Opener Before Work

Lieutenant Gerald O. "Jerry" Williams, Retired

Frank Metcalf as Territorial Highway Engineer was not only the head of the Alaska Highway Patrol, but also served as an ex-officio member of the Territorial Board of Liquor Control. There wasn't much regulation of the liquor industry prior to Statehood. Very few laws were passed that limited the industry in any way, and the Legislature wasn't likely to do anything to limit their unrestricted operations as long as the liquor business was, next to the Salmon Lobby, the largest source of political contributions.

Cities could regulate liquor dispensaries within city limits, and most did by establishing reasonable closing hours. Outside cities, the bars operated on a 24-hour basis, and many of the wildest were congregated along Gambell Street in Anchorage and Cushman Street in Fairbanks, the demarcation line marking city limits. During one of the meetings of the Liquor Board in 1952, the almost unheard of suggestion was made that reasonable closing hours should be imposed on a Territory-wide basis, from 5 a.m. to 8 a.m. as a starter.

Metcalf, an old-time Alaskan who as a civilian engineer during

WWII had supervised construction of airfields on the Aleutian Chain, voiced an immediate objection to the other members of the board. "Personally, I'm against any closing hours because anybody ought to be able to get himself a little eye-opener in the morning before going to work." In spite of Metcalf's opposition, the proposal was adopted.

September 1997

The Subpoena

Lieutenant Gerald O. "Jerry" Williams, Retired

Old-timers familiar with courtroom scenes in Southeastern Alaska will recall that until the 1950s the most common means of travel between the far-flung communities was by boat, and the LIZBET from Juneau frequently carried passengers and cargo to Haines and Skagway. The Deputy Marshals also utilized this means of transportation on their rounds and when taking prisoners back and forth.

In 1950, in the midst of a criminal trial in Territorial Judge George Folta's Juneau courtroom, a question was raised as to whether or not a Native woman witness from Haines had been properly subpoenaed. She was an important participant in a criminal case who seemed to be waffling on her testimony, and the District Attorney was anxious to examine her as a "Hostile Witness." Whether he could do so was dependent on whether she had appeared voluntarily or under court-issued subpoena.

Judge Folta, in an effort to clarify the issue, turned towards the witness in the box and asked if she had been served with a subpoena by the Deputy Marshal, requiring her appearance as a witness. Looking up at the judge, the girl replied, "Oh, yes. The Marshal subpoenaed me three times... once in his room at the hotel at Haines, and twice on the boat coming here."

May 1997

That's Him!

Lieutenant Gerald O. "Jerry" Williams, Retired

Ed Merck was a Fairbanks bar operator who fancied himself as having a lot of "political pull" since he contributed regularly to the Democratic Party. He also felt he was immune from arrest, and whenever a Territorial Police Officer accosted him, Merck had to be wrestled all the way to the Federal Jail. Once, Emery Chapple creased his forehead with a gun barrel when Merck tried to forcibly interfere with Chapple's collecting evidence at Merck's Cushman Street bar.

It was the "roaring '50s" when Alaska was in the midst of a construction boom because of the Cold War. During the summer months in particular, the bars and strip joints were crowded with construction workers and soldiers looking for action or a fight.

Ted Stevens was the U.S. Attorney for the 4th Judicial District, and one of his assistants, just out of law school, was a short, slight young man who sought to obtain a better understanding of the Fairbanks underworld by accompanying the crime squad on its weekend rounds. He was told to stay in the background when arrests were being made, but proved helpful to the officers in preparing search warrant affidavits.

The crime squad in Fairbanks was roughly comparable to the vice squad, which operated contemporaneously in Anchorage. Both were made up of representatives from the U.S. Marshal's office, Territorial Police, City Police and military law enforcement services.

Merck, true to form, tried to interfere with the officers making an arrest one night, and ended up in the Federal slammer with a few bruises that were not serious, but managed to bleed copious amounts. Merck worked assiduously to keep scabs from forming, distributed blood over his white shirt, and even refused to wash the blood off his face while waiting in a cell for morning arraignment. It was a Saturday and due to the illness of the U.S. Commissioner, mild-mannered Territorial Judge James Forbes was conducting the morning's business.

Merck appeared before the judge covered with the carefully nursed bloodstains on his face and clothing, and called attention to his condition in a loud voice. "Look what they did to me; they beat me up and used excessive force."

Forbes looked down and asked, "Who are you talking about, who did this to you?" Merck saw an opportunity to create a little more mischief and glanced around the courtroom filled with jailers, a few city police officers in uniform and the usual flotsam and jetsam of a weekend arraignment calendar. Only one face seated at a table seemed vaguely familiar to Merck, who leveled his finger and shouted, "He did." Jay Rabinowitz was unerringly identified as the culprit responsible for administering the brutal beating.

February 1997

(Editor's Note: Jay Rabinowitz was then Assistant to the U.S. Attorney and later became Chief Justice of the Alaska Supreme Court.)

ALASKA

- State Motto-North to the Future
- Became 49th state on January 3, 1959
- Largest US state with 6640 miles of coast line
- 571 thousand square miles
- Measuring north to south 1400 miles long
- From east to west 2700 miles wide
- Highest point in North America, Mt McKinley at 20,320’
- Coldest recorded temperature minus 80 degrees in 1971